T0235245

Lecture Notes in Computer Science　　10466

Commenced Publication in 1973
Founding and Former Series Editors:
Gerhard Goos, Juris Hartmanis, and Jan van Leeuwen

Editorial Board

More information about this series at http://www.springer.com/series/7407

Kamel Barkaoui · Hanifa Boucheneb
Ali Mili · Sofiène Tahar (Eds.)

Verification and Evaluation of Computer and Communication Systems

11th International Conference, VECoS 2017
Montreal, QC, Canada, August 24–25, 2017
Proceedings

 Springer

Editors
Kamel Barkaoui (iD)
CNAM-CEDRIC
Paris Cedex 03
France

Ali Mili
New Jersey Institute of Technology
Newark, NJ
USA

Hanifa Boucheneb (iD)
École Polytechnique de Montréal
Montreal, QC
Canada

Sofiène Tahar
Concordia University
Montreal, QC
Canada

ISSN 0302-9743   ISSN 1611-3349   (electronic)
Lecture Notes in Computer Science
ISBN 978-3-319-66175-9   ISBN 978-3-319-66176-6   (eBook)
DOI 10.1007/978-3-319-66176-6

Library of Congress Control Number: 2017950042

LNCS Sublibrary: SL1 – Theoretical Computer Science and General Issues

Printed on acid-free paper

This Springer imprint is published by Springer Nature
The registered company is Springer International Publishing AG
The registered company address is: Gewerbestrasse 11, 6330 Cham, Switzerland

Preface

These proceedings contain the papers presented at the 11th International Conference on Verification and Evaluation of Computer and Communication Systems (VECoS 2017), held at Concordia University, Montreal, Canada, during August 24–25, 2017.

The aim of the VECoS conference is to bring together researchers and practitioners in the areas of verification, control, performance, and dependability evaluation in order to discuss the state of the art and challenges in modern computer and communication systems in which functional and extra-functional properties are strongly interrelated. Thus, the main motivation for VECoS is to encourage cross-fertilization between various formal verification and evaluation approaches, methods, and techniques, and especially those developed for concurrent and distributed hardware/software systems.

The Program Committee of VECoS 2017 includes researchers from 20 countries. We received 35 full submissions from 15 countries and each paper was evaluated by at least three reviewers. After a thorough and lively discussion phase, the committee decided to accept 13 papers (which represents an acceptance rate of 37,14%).

The conference program also includes three invited talks. The invited speakers for VECoS 2017 are: Mourad Debbabi from Concordia University, Montreal, Quebec, Canada; Michel Dagenais from Polytechnique Montreal, Quebec, Canada; and Zhiwu Li from Xidian University, China.

We are grateful to all members of the Program and Organizing Committees, to all referees for their cooperation and to Springer for their professional support during the production phase of the proceedings.

Finally, we would like to thank the sponsoring institutions without whom VECoS 2017 could not have been a reality. We are also thankful to all authors of submitted papers and to all participants of the conference. Their interest in this conference and contributions to the discipline are greatly appreciated.

August 2017

Kamel Barkaoui
Hanifa Boucheneb
Ali Mili
Sofiène Tahar

Organization

VECoS 2017 was organized by Concordia University in Montreal, Quebec, Canada with the support of Polytechnique Montreal, New Jersey Institute of Technology, Le Cnam, and Formal Methods Europe.

VECoS was created by a Euro-Med network of researchers in computer science in the form of an annual workshop series. The first workshop, VECoS 2007, took place in Algiers (Algeria), VECoS 2008 took place in Leeds (UK), VECoS 2009 in Rabat (Morocco), VECoS 2010 in Paris (France), VECoS 2011 in Tunis (Tunisia), VECoS 2012 in Paris (France), VECoS 2013 in Florence (Italy), VECoS 2014 in Bejaia (Algeria), VECoS 2015 in Bucharest (Romania), VECoS 2016 in Tunis (Tunisia).

Steering Committee

Djamil Aissani   LAMOS, Université de Bejaia
Hassane Alla   GIPSA Lab INPG Grenoble
Kamel Barkaoui   CEDRIC CNAM Paris
Hanifa Boucheneb   Veriform, Polytechnique Montreal
Francesco Flammini   Ansaldo STS, Milano
Belgacem Ben Hedia   LIST CEA Saclay
Mohamed Kaaniche   LAAS CNRS, Toulouse
Bruno Monsuez   ENSTA UIIS, Paris
Nihal Pekergin   LACL Université Paris Est Créteil
Tayssir Touili   LIPN, CNRS Université Paris Nord

Executive Committee

Conference Co-chairs

Sofiène Tahar   Concordia University, Montreal, QC, Canada
Ali Mili   New Jersey Institute of Technology, Newark, NJ, USA

Program Co-chairs

Kamel Barkaoui   CNAM, Paris, France
Hanifa Boucheneb   Polytechnique Montreal, QC, Canada

Organizing Chair

Otmane Ait Mohamed   Concordia University, Montreal, QC, Canada

Publicity Co-chairs

Belgacem Ben Hedia   CEA-LIST, Saclay, France
Vladimir-Alexandru Paun   ENSTA ParisTech, Palaiseau, France

Referees

T. Abdellatif	M. Van Eekelen	O. Korbaa
D. Aissani	M. Escheikh	L. Kristensen
H. Alla	A. Fantechi	Z. Li
Y. Ait Ameur	A. Felty	D. Liu
M.F.i Atig	F. Flammini	M. Maouche
E. Badouel	M. Frappier	A. Melo
K. Barkaoui	F. Gadducci	A. Mili
F. Belala	B. Van Gastel	B. Monsuez
I. Ben-Hafaiedh	A. Geniet	M. Mosbah
B. Ben-Hedia	M. Ghazel	A. Nouri
S. Bensalem	S. Haddad	M. Ouederni
A. Benzina	B. Heidergott	M. Oussalah
S. Bliudze	M. Ioulalen	V.A. Paun
P. Bonhomme	M. Jaber	R. Rebiha
F. Boniol	R. Janicki	A. Rezine
T. Bouabana-Tebibel	A. Jaoua	R. Robbana
A. Bouabdallah	C. Jerad	S. Tahar
H. Boucheneb	M. Jmaiel	F. Thabet
S. Bouzefrane	J. Julvez	T. Touili
F. Brandner	M. Kaaniche	F. Toumani
F. Chu	L. Kahloul	R. Villemaire
G. Ciobanu	R. Khedri	K. Wolf

Additional Reviewers

B. Aman	P. Saivasan
I. Ghorbel	L. Sfaxi
S. Ghoul	R. Sirdey
M. Jan	M. Soualhia
H. Khemissa	E. Tuosto
B. Liu	N. Wu
H. Sahli	

Sponsoring Institutions

Concordia University, QC, Canada
Polytechnique Montreal, QC, Canada
New Jersey Institute of Technology, NJ, USA
Le Cnam, France
Formal Methods Europe
RESMIQ, Canada
CEA-LIST, France

Keynote Speakers

Live Run-Time Verification of Parallel Heterogeneous Real-Time Systems

Mourad Debbabi

CSL - CIISE, Concordia University, 1455, de Maisonneuve Blvd.
West, EV 14.185, Montreal, QC H3G 1M8, Canada
debbabi@ciise.concordia.ca

Abstract. By massively deploying information and pervasive communication technologies, the smart grid has become smarter by providing a plethora of previously unsupported services (e.g., smart control, two-way communication, bidirectional flow of energy, and real-time sensing) in addition to enhanced responsiveness and efficiency. However, the deployment of information and communication technologies introduces new attack surfaces and vulnerabilities. The exploitation of these vulnerabilities will result in dramatic security, privacy and, safety consequences. Recent incidents and studies demonstrate that power systems could be subjected to debilitating and disrupting attacks that might lead to severe social and economic consequences. In this talk, we will first present our ongoing research activities on smart grid security. Then, we will present some of our recent research contributions in terms of security metrics for the smart grid.

Measuring and Enhancing Smart Grid Security

Michel Dagenais

Ecole Polytechnique de Montreal, 2900 Boulevard Edouard-Montpetit,
Montréal, QC H3T 1J4, Pavillion Pierre Lassonde, bureau M-4015, Canada
michel.dagenais@polymtl.ca

Abstract. What are the most difficult systems to analyse (Parallel, Heterogeneous, Real-time, Virtualised...) and the most evasive problems to diagnose (races, interrupt latencies)? Our group has been working on tools for those difficult situations for over a decade. Many if not most systems are now indeed parallel and heterogeneous (from smart phones to cloud servers) and often involve virtualisation or real-time constraints. Therefore, difficult problems, which only manifest themselves in live systems, in production under full load, are a common occurrence. While structured design methodologies and static validation can avoid many problems, errors remain possible, often in hardware or third-party software which do not satisfy the design constraints. The right tools are needed to tackle those problems.

During this talk, the design and implementation of various tracing and debugging tools, many developed in our group in collaboration with several industrial partners, will be discussed. Representative examples of real industrial problems will be presented, along with the diagnosis process using the tools described.

Deadlock Analysis and Control of Resource Allocation Systems: Structural and Reachability Graph Approaches

Zhiwu Li

Systems Control and Automation Group, School of Electro-Mechanical Engineering, Xidian University, No. 2 South TaiBai Road, Xi'an 710071, China
zhwli@xidian.edu.cn

Abstract. This talk exposes the recent advances of deadlock problems in resource allocation systems using Petri nets. The pertinent methodologies are categorized by structural analysis and reachability graph analysis techniques. The former, without enumerating the reachable states of a system, utilize structural objects to derive a liveness-enforcing supervisor, while its structure can be compact. The latter can usually lead to an optimal supervisor with a minimal control structure subject to a full state enumeration and solution to integer linear programming problems. Open issues in this area are outlined.

Contents

Formal Probabilistic Analysis of a Virtual Fixture Control Algorithm for a Surgical Robot

Muhammad Saad Ayub$^{(\boxtimes)}$ and Osman Hasan

School of Electrical Engineering and Computer Science (SEECS),
National University of Sciences and Technology (NUST), Islamabad, Pakistan
{saad.ayub,osman.hasan}@seecs.nust.edu.pk

Abstract. With the ever-growing interest in the usage of minimally-invasive surgery, surgical robots are also being extensively used in the operation theaters. Given the safety-critical nature of these surgeries, ensuring the accuracy and safety of the control algorithms of these surgical robots is an absolute requirement. However, traditionally these algorithms have been analyzed using simulations and testing methods, which provide in-complete and approximate analysis results due to their inherent sampling-based nature. We propose to use probabilistic model checking, which is a formal verification method for quantitative analysis of systems, to verify the control algorithms of surgical robots. The paper provides a formal analysis of a virtual fixture control algorithm, implemented in a neuro-surgical robot, using the PRISM model checker. We have been able to verify some probabilistic properties about the out-of-boundary problem for the given algorithm and found some new insights, which were not gained in a previous attempt of using formal methods in the same context. For validation, we have also done some experiments by running the considered algorithm on the Al-Zahrawi surgical robot.

Keywords: Probabilistic model checking · PRISM · Surgical robotics

1 Introduction

Minimal-invasive surgery (MIS) [16] is a surgical procedure in which a laparoscope (a thin lighted tube), along with a high resolution camera, and other surgical instruments are inserted into the human body through small incisions rather than a relatively larger incision commonly used in the traditional open surgeries. The internal operating field is then visualized on a video monitor connected to the scope. MIS has become quite popular these days as it facilitates quick patient recovery and has less chances of post-operative infections. However, these added benefits come at the cost of highly precise movements required by the surgeons in the confined space provided. Robotic arms and hands have a high degree of dexterity and thus are playing a promising role in facilitating surgeons for operating in very tight spaces in the body that would otherwise only be accessible through open (long incision) surgery. Operations relevant to microanatomy and neuro-endoscopy are specifically performed through robotic-assisted MIS because of the static nature of human skull. Moreover, treating the

K. Barkaoui et al. (Eds.): VECoS 2017, LNCS 10466, pp. 1–16, 2017.
DOI: 10.1007/978-3-319-66176-6_1

brain tumor via small hole surgery and precise robotic arms also reduces the risk of damaging the brain tissue overlying the tumor.

Despite the extreme precision of surgical robots, these man-made machines have their own inherent inaccuracies. There is always a risk that these robotic arms may go out of control and damage other organs instead of working in the surgical area. This problem is termed as the *out-of-boundary problem*. As these robots are operated by humans via a software interface, so the substantial loss of force feedback (haptics) and a lack of adaptability are the most common risk factors that lead to the *out-of-boundary problem* [12]. These issues may lead to life threatening situations [10]. The conventional approach to test the out-of-boundary problem is by manually operating the robot. The more the user operates the robot, the more are the chances of finding errors but this method is very time consuming and it also does not ensure a reliable system behavior for all possible scenarios. The other most commonly used analysis method for finding the out-of-bound errors is computer simulation [24], where a computer-based model of the robot is tested systematically but this method is very expensive in terms of computational resources and memory, due to the continuous and randomized nature of the problem. Moreover, it is also not possible to simulate each and every case for success and failure and thus most of the times an incomplete analysis is done by leaving a significant number of test cases.

Formal verification methods [8], i.e., computer-based methods for mathematical analysis for systems, have been used to overcome the above-mentioned inaccuracy limitations for many hardware and software systems. Model checking [8] is based on state-space exploration methods and is one of the most widely used formal methods. The system under verification is mathematically modeled as state-transition system. This model is then used within a computer to automatically verify that it meets rigorous specifications of intended behavior [8].

We propose to conduct the formal analysis of control algorithms used in surgical robots using probabilistic model checking. The proposed framework allows us to capture the uncertainties of the real-world scenarios using Markovian models and verify probabilistic properties within the sound environment of a probabilistic model checker. The quantitative information provided by these probabilistic properties can play a vital role in designing safer and more performance efficient surgical robots. In particular, the paper provides the formal probabilistic verification of a control algorithm for the neuro-mate robot that is used to perform skull surgeries [24]. We verified the deadlock freedom, reachability, out-of-boundary and collision freeness properties. Moreover, we validated our results by conducting real experiments on the Al-Zahrawi robot [9].

2   Related Work

Given the safety-critical nature of robotic applications, formal verification methods have been widely used to conduct their analysis. For example, Mikaël [17] used probabilistic model checking to verify the flexibility property of swarm robots in a collective foraging scenario. Kim et al. [11] developed the discrete control software of the Samsung's home robot (SHR) using Esterel and used the XEVE model checker to verify the stopping behavior of SHR. Webster et al. [23] verified the autonomous decision making system of a personal home robot using the SPIN model checker. Scherer et al. [22] built a method for the verification of robotic control software based on the Java path finder. They verified the safety and liveness properties for a line following robot. Model checking has also been used to verify the motion planning algorithms of various robots. Lahijanian et al. [14] verified the probability of the robot reaching its destination via a safe path. Similarly, Fainekos et al. [4] addressed the problem of generating continuous trajectories for mobile robots while satisfying formulas in temporal logic using the NuSMV model checker. Saberi et al. [21] used the mCRL2 language [6] to create a formal model for a multi-robot system by creating different communicating processes and the Modal u-calculus [5] to formally specify *deadlock freedom*, *collision-freeness* and the *reachability* properties. Li [15] used the HOL4 theorem prover to verify the collision freeness property for collision-free motion planning algorithm (CFMC) of a dual-arm robot.

In the context of surgical robotics, Bresolin et al. [3] used hybrid automata [1] to formalize an autonomous surgical robot and analyzed the surgical task of "puncturing", i.e., the method of piercing a biological tissue with the help of a needle. Similarly, a formal modeling and verification approach for the virtual fixture control algorithm for a surgical robot has been reported in [12]. The authors used a hybrid logic, i.e., differential dynamic logic and quantified differential dynamic logic to model the system and verify it using the KeymaeraD [19] theorem prover. They showed that the algorithm is unsafe and modified it to satisfy safe operation. This work modeled and analyzed the real-time dynamics of the system quite well but ignored the randomized aspects, such as the input from the surgeon (force exerted and direction of motion). The main focus of the current paper is to overcome this gap and provide quantitative information about the formally verified properties of control algorithm of surgical robots.

3   Preliminaries

This section gives a general overview of probabilistic model checking and the virtual fixture based control algorithm that is formally verified in the paper.

3.1   Probabilistic Model Checking and PRISM

Probabilistic Model Checking [18] is used for the formal analysis of systems that exhibit random behavior and thus can be represented as Markov chains [13]. The probabilistic behavior of systems can be captured via discrete-time Markov chains (DTMCs), continuous-time Markov chains (CTMCs), Markov decision processes (MDPs) and probabilistic timed automata (PTAs) [18]. Once the Markovian model of the system under verification is finalized, then the probabilistic properties of the system are formally specified. The commonly used specification language for probabilistic model checking is Probabilistic Linear

Temporal Logic (PLTL). The model and property of the system, expressed in the language of the probabilistic model checker, is then given to the model checker. The tool explores the model exhaustively to check all possible executions and the probabilistic queries are solved through numerical methods [18].

PRISM [13] is a widely used probabilistic model checker that supports DTMCs, CTMCs, MDPs and PTAs. It allows describing the probabilistic behavior of the given system using the reactive modules formalism [2]. PRISM incorporates state-of-the-art symbolic data structures and algorithms, based on Binary Decision Diagrams (BDDs) and Multi-Terminal Binary Decision Diagrams (MTBDDs), and its discrete-event based simulation engine provides support for statistical model checking. The components of the given distributed system are modeled as modules, which can either be synchronous or asynchronous in nature. Each module mainly consists of variables and commands. The variables describe the possible states that the module can be in and the commands describe its behaviour, i.e., the way in which the state changes over time. Variables in PRISM can be declared both globally and locally. PRISM supports (finite ranges of) integer or Boolean as data-types. Moreover, multiple instances of modules can also be instantiated. Verification properties are expressed in PRISM using the probabilistic computation tree logic (PCTL). Once a property is formulated, then the PRISM tool automatically verifies that the property conforms to the model or not. The verification results can also be logged and plotted [13].

3.2   Virtual Fixture Control Algorithm for Surgical Robots

Surgeries are usually conducted in a specific zone, which is identified for the surgical robot using a virtual boundary, usually known as the *virtual fixture* [20]. With the aid of these virtual fixtures, the robot manipulator is guided to move within the specified region [24]. A surgeon describes the operating volume by a series of planes oriented and positioned in space. These planar boundaries are divided into three zones [12,24]: *Safe zone* is safe for the movement of robot. *Forbidden zone* is out-of-bound for the robot. *Slow zone* is the region between the safe and the forbidden zones where the movement is somewhat restricted.

The control algorithm exhibits different behaviors in the above-mentioned zones. In the safe zone, the controller allows the robot to move freely. In the slow zone, as the boundary of the forbidden zone approaches, the controller increases the resistance for movement while alarming the surgeon that she is getting closer to the boundary and also prevents the robot from crossing it [12]. The equation governing the control circuit in this region is as follows

$$\overline{p}\prime = K(\overline{p})G(\overline{f})\overline{f} \tag{1}$$

where overbars indicate vectors and the prime ($\prime$) indicates a derivative with respect to time. p is the position and $p\prime$ is the velocity of the tip of the surgical tool attached to the robot. f is the force applied by the surgeon on the robot manipulator. G is the scaling factor, which controls the precision of the tool tip. The value of G should be high when the surgeon desires to have flexibility to move rapidly and should be low when fine movements are required. K is the gain term, which is used to impose motion constraints on the tool. It is taken as an identify matrix in the safe zone and zero in the forbidden zone, respectively. Whereas in the slow zone, K is chosen such that the velocity is scaled down by a factor proportional to the distance of tool from the forbidden zone. The behavior of K can be abstracted as the following equation:

$$K = \frac{d}{D} \qquad (2)$$

where d is the distance of the tool from the forbidden zone boundary at any instant and D is the width of the slow zone region. The Eq. 1 works fine in preventing the tool from crossing the safety boundary but once the tool is in the slow zone, it attenuates motion in all the directions. Therefore the equation was modified so that once the tool enters the slow zone, the control algorithm restricts the movement of the tool in the direction of the forbidden region and allows free movement in the direction opposite to the forbidden region. This behavior is implemented using the following equation where $n1$ is unit normal to the boundary.

$$\overline{p}\prime = \overline{p}\prime - (1 - \frac{d}{D})(\overline{p}\prime.n1)n1 \qquad (3)$$

The purpose of this paper is to verify probabilistic properties related to the above equation using probabilistic model checking.

4 Formalization of the Virtual Fixture Algorithm Using the PRISM Language

The first step in modeling the given virtual fixture algorithm, explained in Sect. 3.2, is the translation of Eqs. (1) and (3). After some arithmetic simplification and decomposing the force and velocity into the Cartesian plane, we obtain the following equations:

$$px = G(\frac{dx}{Dx})fx, \quad py = G(\frac{dy}{Dy})fy, \quad pz = G(\frac{dz}{Dz})fz \qquad (4)$$

The second step is to develop a model for the control algorithm. We have chosen to model the given algorithm as a DTMC. The virtual fixtures are defined using the Cartesian plane, where the origin is taken as the center point of the safe zone as the surgeon is quite likely to start from the center. Considering the Cartesian coordinates, the boundaries for each plane may lie on the positive axis or the negative axis. Thus for each plane, we defined four boundaries, i.e., two for the safe zone and the other two for the forbidden zone. The movement of the tool in the virtual fixture is modeled using a grid of blocks, which represent 1 unit of movement. The distance of the tool from the boundary and the boundaries of the safe and the forbidden zones are thus determined by the number of blocks on the grid as illustrated in Fig. 1 for a 45×45 grid.

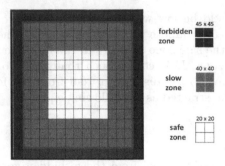

Fig. 1. Virtual fixture zones

The scaling factor G in Eq. 4 is responsible for translating the force applied by the surgeon to the velocity of the tool. It depends on the virtual fixture area and the force applied by the surgeon. If the area of operation is small then the scaling factor is kept small so that a sudden force applied by the surgeon is not completely translated into tool velocity. The scaling factor changes with the amount of force or movement applied by the surgeon on the control stick. As the maximum force applied is limited by the movement of the control stick due to mechanical constraints, the scaling factor is responsible generating variable velocities for movement of the operating tool. In our model, the scaling factor is taken as a constant since the area of the robot is fixed and the force applied by the surgeon is non-deterministic and not limited by mechanical constraints. The model consists of three main components: the force module that is responsible for generating the force applied by the surgeon and the velocity translation module that converts the force applied by the surgeon into the tool velocity. It is also responsible for introducing the damping factor in the velocity. The position update block changes the current position of the tool based on the velocity and previous position and also checks the boundaries of operation. The modules are implemented as Finite State Machines (FSM) with augmented probabilities. The environment is modelled by defining the bounds of all the zones as shown in Fig. 1. Data Sharing among various modules of the Control Algorithm is done via variables created in each module.

4.1   Force Module

The force module captures the behavior of the interaction of the surgeon with the system, which includes the behavior of the force applied by the surgeon's hand on the controlling tool. The force applied is further divided into three components based on the Cartesian coordinates, i.e., f_x, f_y, f_z. The force applied by the surgeon is non-deterministic with probabilistic bounds, such that the probability of the force applied by the surgeon in the direction of force applied previously is higher than the force applied in the opposite direction. Based on surgical statistics [7], we used a probability of 0.75 for the tool to retain the previous direction of movement and a probability of 0.25 for a change. The force f = * represent non-determinism in the case when the force is zero initially.

1: $[](f = 0) \rightarrow 1/n : f = *$;
2: $[](f > 0) \rightarrow 0.75 : f >= 0 + 0.25 : f < 0$;
3: $[](f < 0) \rightarrow 0.25 : f > 0 + 0.75 : f <= 0$;

4.2 Velocity Module

The velocity module determines the instantaneous velocity of the tool using the force exerted by the surgeon and the position of the tool. The velocity is also divided into three components, i.e., v_x, v_y, v_z. The control algorithm under verification is basically modeled in this module. If the position of tool is within the safe zone represented by **sl** and **sh** as the safe zone upper and lower limits in a single axis, then the force applied is directly translated to velocity. If the position of the tool is in the slow zone defined by **bl** and **bh** as the upper and lower limits for a single axis and the force is applied in the direction of the boundary, then the translated velocity is attenuated based on the scale factor K. If the tool crosses the boundary of the slow zone then the velocity is completely nullified restricting further movement in the forbidden zone.

1: $[](p > sl \ \& \ p <= sh) \rightarrow (v' = gain * f)$;
2: $[](p <= sl \ \& \ p > bl) \ \& \ f <= 0 \rightarrow (v' = (dl/Dl) * gain * f))$;
3: $[](p > sh \ \& \ p < bh) \ \& \ f >= 0 \rightarrow (v' = (dh/Dxh) * gain * f))$;
4: $[](p <= sl \ \& \ p > bl) \ \& \ f > 0 \rightarrow (v' = gain * f)$;
5: $[](p > sh \ \& \ p < bh) \ \& \ f < 0 \rightarrow (v' = gain * f)$;
6: $[](p <= bl \ \& \ f >= 0) \rightarrow (v' = gain * f)$;
7: $[](p <= bl \ \& \ f < 0) \rightarrow (v' = 0)$;
8: $[](p >= bh \ \& \ f > 0) \rightarrow (v' = 0)$;
9: $[](p >= bh \ \& \ f <= 0) \rightarrow (v' = gain * f)$;

4.3 Position Module

The position module determines the number of blocks on the grid that the tool will move depending on the calculated velocity. It is also divided into three components, i.e., p_x, p_y, p_z. If the position of the tool is within the limits specified by the grid size defined by **n**, then the tool is allowed to move based on the velocity. However, if it is at an edge of the grid then its movement is restricted towards the end of grid but it is allowed to move in the opposite direction freely.

1: $[](p + v < n \ \& \ v > 0) \rightarrow (p' = P + v)$;
2: $[](px + v > -n \ \& \ v < 0) \rightarrow (p' = P + v)$;
3: $[](v = 0)|(p + v >= n)|(p + v <= (-n)) \rightarrow (p' = P)$;

4.4 Multiple Surgical Tools

Most of the surgical procedures involve multiple robotic arms that are independently controlled. In order to formally model this scenario, we replicate the
above-mentioned modules for force, velocity and position and allow them to run
concurrently. The tool boundary limits are considered to be the same for both
tools in our model. The modules are initialized such that both tools operate
simultaneously and independently; a choice that makes collision a possibility as
well. We enhanced the control algorithm with collision avoidance capabilities by
treating the location of one tool as a forbidden zone boundary for the other and
vice versa. This will ensure that when a tool is moving towards the other tool its
velocity will be attenuated to avoid collision between the two tools. The attenuation will increase as the tool gets nearer to the other tool. Thus, in essence,
the main modeling concept is basically to treat the previously considered static
forbidden boundaries as dynamic ones using a module `obstacle`, which creates
boundary points from the other tool's position.

1: $[]ox < n$ & $ox > -n \rightarrow (ox' = ax1)$ & $(oy' = ayl)$;

These boundary points are then used in the `velocity` module as additional
boundaries for the model. The `velocity` module then restricts the movement of
the tool if they are moving towards the other tool by a factor M, which is the
ratio of distance between both tools and the maximum distance between both
tools. The maximum distance is computed depending on the width of the slow
zone and the distance between both tools is computed in each iteration. This
will ensure that the tools are less likely to collide with each other.

$$M = \frac{d_{obs}}{D_{obs}} \qquad (5)$$

Where d_{obs} is the distance between both tools with a maximum value of D_{obs}.

5 Virtual Fixture Control Algorithm

In this section, the formal model of control algorithm, described in the previous section, is verified using property specifications introduced in the proposed
methodology. We verified these properties using PRISM 4.1.2 on Windows 7
64-bit operating system running on an Intel Core2 Quad Q9100 processor at
2.66 GHz with 4.0 GB of RAM. The grid size is taken as 45×45, the range of
the width of the slow zone is taken to be 0 to 20 and the maximum value of the
force is taken to be 6.

5.1 Deadlock Freedom

We verified the deadlock freedom of our virtual fixture control algorithm by
using the built in deadlock property of the PRISM model checker. This property
checks if for some states the transition from the present to future state will result
in a deadlock. Our algorithm was found to be deadlock free.

5.2   Reachability

This property ensures that the surgical robot will move to the position desired by the surgeon in a finite number of steps. The presence of two robotic arms in the virtual fixture makes the verification of the property quite important. The fact that the control algorithm, under consideration, attenuates the movement of tool, makes the verification of the reachability property very important as it may happen that the algorithm does not allow the tool to reach some areas, especially the ones that are very close to the boundaries where the attenuation is the maximum. The reachability property can be verified by checking that the tool moves from its current position and reaches the required destination in a finite number of steps if the required force is applied to it. We verified this property by associating a reward with every step of the algorithm, i.e., a reward of 1 is added to the existing reward value at every step of the algorithm. The reachability property, based on the reward accumulated along a particular path, can now be expressed as:

```
R=? [px=0 & fx>0 -> F px=(width zone limit/2)-1]
```

This property states that if the tool position is 0 and a force is applied in the positive direction, then the tool will eventually reach the boundary of the forbidden zone in a bounded number of steps or rewards. The property is not verified probabilistically as the result will not clearly depict if the tool reaches the boundary in minimal number of steps or not, while using the reward based approach we can ensure the tool will reach the boundary in a limited number of steps. The property is verified for the x-plane while observing the impact of varying the width of the slow zone. Checking this property returns the reward or number of steps that the algorithm would take to get to the edge of the forbidden zone. The properties for the y and z-planes are given as follows

```
R=? [py=0 & fy>0 -> F py=(width zone limit/2)-1]
R=? [pz=0 & fz>0 -> F pz=(width zone limit/2)-1]
```

These properties are verified for different widths of slow zones and the resultant rewards for the x-plane, while keeping the value of the maximum force constant. Figure 2 shows that the rewards calculated are always a finite number and their value increases with the increase in the width of the slow zone. This is because as the width increases, the distance from origin to the edges of the virtual fixture increases and the steps to reach them also increase. This is because at each step towards the boundary of the forbidden zone, the attenuation in the velocity increases and the tool moves slowly towards the boundary, therefore, more steps are required to cater for this attenuation. These verification results show that the algorithm under verification satisfies the reachability property.

The properties are also verified by varying the scaling factor and Fig. 2 shows the resultant rewards. It is observed that increasing the scaling factor increases the velocity of the tool and thus the reward value decreases. This happened because as the velocity increases the tool moves more distance in a single iteration and thus requires less number of steps to reach the destination.

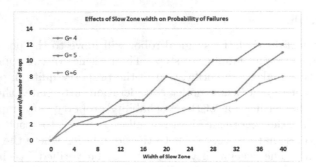

Fig. 2. Impact of changing the width of slow zone on the reachability rewards vs width of slow zone property

5.3   Out-of-Boundary

As described previously, the main focus of this paper is the formal probabilistic analysis of the out-of-boundary problem. The most important aspect of any surgical robot is to stay within the operable area at all times. If it is allowed to move out of the operable area it may damage sensitive organs, which may lead to the loss of human life in worst-case scenarios. The given algorithm is therefore checked in the proposed methodology for boundary crossovers and their probability. In the context of our modeling, the problem can be stated as follows: At any given time during the operation, if the surgeon starts in the safe zone then the tool should not cross the boundary of forbidden zone. This property can be formally expressed in terms of the boundary limits defined for our virtual fixtures. We can simply check that the position of the tool is within these limits in every state, i.e.,

```
forall (px< bxh & px>bxl)
```

where px is the position of tool in the x-plane, bxh is the higher boundary limit and bxl is the lower boundary limit of the slow zone. The same condition should be checked for the y-plane and z-plane.

```
forall (py< byh & py>byl), forall (pz< bzh & pz>bzl)
```

The main issue with these properties is that they will either be True or False. In the case of failure, we would not know the probability of failure, which is a desirable performance characteristic as well. This limitation can be overcome by verifying the probability of failure of this property:

```
P=? (px>0 & px>sxh & fx>0 => F px>bxh)
```

Where P is the probability of failure, sxh is the boundary of the safe zone and fx is the force applied by the surgeon. This property checks the probability

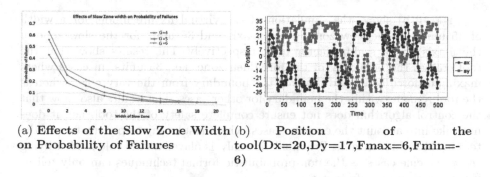

(a) **Effects of the Slow Zone Width** (b)   **Position**   of   **the**
on Probability of Failures   **tool(Dx=20,Dy=17,Fmax=6,Fmin=-6)**

Fig. 3. Results of verification of out-of-boundary properties

of crossing the boundary of the forbidden zone if the tool is in the slow zone and accelerating towards the forbidden zone. The same property can be checked for the y-plane and z-plane as follows:

P=?(py>0 & py>syh & fy>0 =>F py>byh),P=?(pz>0 & pz>szh & fz>0 =>F pz>bzh)

These properties are for a boundary in the positive plane for each axis. The corresponding properties for the negative planes are as follows:

P=?(px<0 & px<sxl & fx<0 =>F px<bxl),P=?(py<0 & py<syl & fy<0 =>F py<byl)
            P=?(pz<0 & pzl<szl & fz<0 =>F pz<bzl)

The size of the virtual fixture and its boundaries have a great impact upon the verification time and computational requirements. Therefore, in order to avoid the state-space explosion problem, the maximum size of the virtual fixture has to be bounded and the boundaries for the safe and forbidden zones have to be varied accordingly.

Figure 3(a) shows the resultant probabilities computed after the verification of the above-mentioned properties at different slow zone widths and Scaling factor. It is seen that when the width of slow zone is increased, the probability of the surgical tool crossing the boundary decreases (Fig. 3(a)). The probabilities change by varying the scaling factor. However, after a certain width of the slow zone, the probabilities become constant. This happens because as the width of the slow zone increases the chances of the surgical tool to enter the forbidden region, due to a sudden change of the velocity in the direction of the forbidden region, decreases. But no matter how much the width is increased, if the tool is at the very edge of the forbidden region and sudden changes of velocity occur in the direction of the boundary, then the tool would always cross it. Therefore, the probability does not reach zero. This is validated by simulating the extreme cases using PRISM. These probabilities are also found to be dependent on the force applied by the surgeon. This shows that the algorithm will not restrict the surgical tool from crossing the boundary if the surgeon exhibits sudden changes near the boundary of the forbidden region. The control algorithm needs to be updated to cater for these cases.

Figure 3(b) shows the simulation of the virtual fixture model for a width of 35 units for the slow zone in the x-axis and 35 units for the slow zone in the y-axis and a scaling factor of 6, respectively. The results show that the tool crosses the boundary of the forbidden zone, i.e., 35 units, in cases where maximum force is applied towards the boundary from the very edge, whereas the tool remains within the boundary for other cases. The results also show that the control algorithm does not ensure complete safety of the tool, i.e., it does not take into account the extreme cases, which results in the penetration of the tool in the forbidden zone. Probabilistic analysis played a vital role in identifying these extreme cases as the non-probabilistic formal techniques can only tell us if the algorithm is safe or not.

5.4   Collision Freeness

In a laparoscopic surgical operation, more than one tool are inserted inside the patient. The corresponding control algorithm is supposed to ensure that these tools do not collide with each other inside the patient. Instead of formally verifying the collision freeness property for the robotic arms, we verify the probability associated with the event when the tools collide with one another. In particular, this will compute the probability that the tools share a same grid point. This property can be defined in the context of our model by ensuring that, at any given time during the operation, the tools should not share the same position in any zone. The property can be stated by considering the position of one tool as a boundary point for other tools. For two tools, the property can be specified as

```
forall (px1!=px2)
```

where $px1$ and $px2$ are the positions of the first and second tool in the x-, respectively. The same properties are verified for the y and z-planes.

```
forall (py1!=py2), forall (pz1!=pz2)
```

These properties result in either True or False and do not give us information about frequency of failures. In order to find quantitative information in this regard, we compute the probability of failure associated with these properties

```
P=?(px1>sxl & px1<sxh & px2>sxl & px2<sxh => F px1=!px2)
```

where P is the probability of failure, $px1$ is the position of first tool, $px2$ is the position of second tool and sxh and sxl are the upper and lower limits of virtual fixture, respectively. This property is also checked for the y and z-plane.

```
P=?(py1>syl & py1<syh & py2>syl & py2<syh => F py1=!py2)
P=?(pz1>szl & pz1<szh & pz2>szl & pz2<szh => F pz1=!pz2)
```

The size of the virtual fixture and the force applied have a great impact on the verification of this property. In order to avoid the state-space explosion problem, the size of the virtual fixture is fixed and the maximum force applied is varied

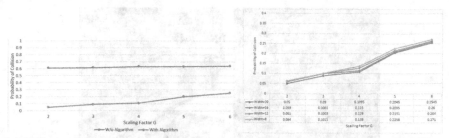

(a) **Effect of Force on Probability of Collision for Both Models**

(b) **Effect of Force on Probability of Collision for Different Widths of the Slow Zone**

Fig. 4. Results of verification of collision freeness properties

by changing the scaling factor. These properties are verified for both models, i.e., with and without obstacle avoidance algorithm, using different force limits keeping the width of virtual fixtures and the boundaries constant.

Figure 4(a) shows the probabilities associated with the above-mentioned properties when verified for the model with and without obstacle avoidance algorithm at different scaling factors. The probability of collision for the model without algorithm remains almost constant by varying the scaling factor as there is no restriction on collision and changing the scaling factor will not affect the collisions. On the other hand, for the case with the collision avoidance algorithm, it is observed that as the scaling factor increase the probability of collision increases (Fig. 4(a)). This happens because the tools become more likely to share the same grid point when the tools are near and the velocity of one of the tool is high in the direction of the other.

Figure 4(a) clearly shows that, with the obstacle avoidance algorithm, the probability of collision decreases but does not approach zero. The properties are also verified for different widths of slow zones. The resultant probabilities are shown in Fig. 4(b). It is observed that the width of slow zone does not affect the collisions of tools and the probabilities of collision are almost the same.

6   Testing on Al-Zahrawi

In order to validate our verification results, we tested the considered virtual fixture control algorithm on a minimal invasive surgery (MIS) robot Al-Zahrawi [9], named after a renowned arab surgeon Abu al-Qasim Khalaf ibn al-Abbas Al-Zahrawi (936–1013), who is also known as the father of modern surgery. The Al-Zahrawi robot consists of a Master Console (MC) and Slave Console (SC) as shown in Fig. 5. The master console is used to track the force applied by the surgeon and transfer it to the slave console. The surgeon operates the tool using the master manipulator and a screen to display the camera output. The master manipulator, shown in Fig. 5(a), is made up of a mechanical mechanism and

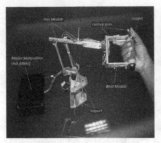 

(a) **Master Manipulator**　　(b) **Slave Manipulator**

Fig. 5. Consoles of the Al-Zahrawi surgical robot [9]

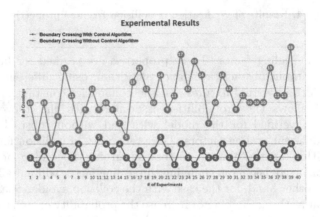

Fig. 6. Experimental results

optical encoders to track the movements of the hand of the surgeon. It offers 6 degree of freedom, i.e., Pitch, Yaw, Roll, back/forth and individual forceps jaw open/close. The slave console, shown in Fig. 5(b), is used to reproduce the force applied by the surgeon on the patient and is mainly composed of a servo motor based mechanical structure to replicate the movements of the surgeon's hand on the patient side. The slave console provides the same degrees of freedom as the master console.

We implemented the virtual fixture based control algorithm on the Al-Zahrawi surgical robot for our experiment. The master manipulator sets the value of attenuation for the velocities based on the feedback of the positions of slave manipulators and sends them to the slave manipulator. The slave manipulator is equipped with a clamper, which is a widely used surgical instrument. Our testbed consists of five different positions, one at the center and four at the boundaries of a rectangular region.

In our experiment, 40 different subjects, with various levels of expertise in robotic surgery, are asked one-by-one to pick an object, placed in the center, using the telesurgical tool and move it to any edge box and try to place it at the center of that box. The user then picks the object and places it in the box located at the opposite corner of the testbed.

The resultant boundary crossings of all the operators are logged and plotted in Fig. 6 for both the cases, i.e., with the virtual fixture control algorithm and without the algorithm. The results show that the number of boundary crossings of the robotic tool without the algorithm are much greater than the ones of with the algorithm. They also show that the tool does cross the boundary with the algorithm but the crossings in that case are very less compared to ones without the algorithm. This validates our verification results, given in Sect. 6, stating that the algorithm is not completely safe with respect of restricting the robot within the operating area and crossovers will occur if significant force is applied near the edge of the boundary.

7   Conclusions

This paper presents a formal verification technique for a virtual fixture based control algorithm used in a surgical robot [24]. In order to consider the randomized nature of the environment, such as the force, applied by the surgeon, and its direction, we propose to use probabilistic model checking for the verification. The main idea is to first develop a formal Discrete-Time Markov chain (DTMC) model of the given algorithm and its environment. This model can then be used to analyze the corresponding probabilistic properties. The paper describes the details about modelling a well-known virtual fixture based control algorithm and also identifies the corresponding probabilistic properties. Our results confirm that the properties of out-of-boundary are failing but under certain conditions the probability of failure is very small, and thus it is quite safe to use the robot under these conditions. Since traditional model checking cannot be used to verify probabilistic properties so these insights about the safe conditions cannot be obtained.

References

1. Alur, R., Courcoubetis, C., Henzinger, T.A., Ho, P.-H.: Hybrid automata: an algorithmic approach to the specification and verification of hybrid systems. In: Grossman, R.L., Nerode, A., Ravn, A.P., Rischel, H. (eds.) HS 1991-1992. LNCS, vol. 736, pp. 209–229. Springer, Heidelberg (1993). doi:10.1007/3-540-57318-6_30
2. Alur, R., Henzinger, T.A.: Reactive modules. Formal Methods Syst. Des. 15(1), 7–48 (1999)
3. Bresolin, D., Guglielmo, L.D., Geretti, L., Muradore, R., Fiorini, P., Villa, T.: Open problems in verification and refinement of autonomous robotic systems. In: Euromicro Conference on Digital System Design, pp. 469–476 (2012)
4. Fainekos, G.E., Gazit, H.K., Pappas, G.J.: Temporal logic motion planning for mobile robots. In: Robotics and Automation, pp. 2020–2025 (2005)
5. Groote, J.F., Mateescu, R.: Verification of temporal properties of processes in a setting with data. In: Haeberer, A.M. (ed.) AMAST 1999. LNCS, vol. 1548, pp. 74–90. Springer, Heidelberg (1998). doi:10.1007/3-540-49253-4_8

6. Groote, J.F., Mathijssen, A., Reniers, M., Usenko, Y., Weerdenburg, M.V.: The formal specification language mCRL2. Citeseer (2007)
7. Haidegger, T., Benyó, B., Kovács, L., Benyó, Z.: Force sensing and force control for surgical robots. In: Symposium on Modeling and Control in Biomedical Systems, pp. 401–406 (2009)
8. Hasan, O., Tahar, S.: Formal Verification Methods. In: Encyclopedia of Information Science and Technology, pp. 7162–7170. IGI Global (2014)
9. Hassan, T., Hameed, A., Nasir, S., Kamal, N., Hasan, O.: Al-Zahrawi: a telesurgical robotic system for minimal invasive surgery. IEEE Syst. J. **10**(3), 1035–1045 (2016)
10. Kazanzides, P., Zuhars, J., Mittelstadt, B., Taylor, R.H.: Force sensing and control for a surgical robot. In: Robotics and Automation, pp. 612–617 (1992)
11. Kim, M., Kang, K.C., Lee, H.: Formal verification of robot movements-a case study on home service robot SHR100. In: Robotics and Automation, pp. 4739–4744 (2005)
12. Kouskoulas, Y., Renshaw, D., Platzer, A., Kazanzides, P.: Certifying the safe design of a virtual fixture control algorithm for a surgical robot. In: Hybrid Systems: Computation and Control, pp. 263–272 (2013)
13. Kwiatkowska, M., Norman, G., Parker, D.: PRISM 4.0: verification of probabilistic real-time systems. In: Computer Aided Verification, pp. 585–591 (2011)
14. Lahijanian, M., Wasniewski, J., Andersson, S.B., Belta, C.: Motion planning and control from temporal logic specifications with probabilistic satisfaction guarantees. In: Robotics and Automation, pp. 3227–3232 (2010)
15. Li, L., Shi, Z., Guan, Y., Zhao, C., Zhang, J., Wei, H.: Formal verification of a collision-free algorithm of dual-arm robot in HOL4. In: Robotics and Automation (ICRA), pp. 1380–1385 (2014)
16. Mack, M.J.: Minimally invasive and robotic surgery. J. Am. Med. Assoc. **285**(5), 568–572 (2001)
17. Mikaël, L.: Formal verification of flexibility in swarm robotics. Thesis, Department of Computer Science, Universit libre de Bruxelles (2012)
18. Oldenkamp, H.A.: Probabilistic model checking: a comparison of tools. Master's thesis, University of Twente, Enschede, Netherlands (2007)
19. Platzer, A., Quesel, J.-D.: KeYmaera: a hybrid theorem prover for hybrid systems (system description). In: Armando, A., Baumgartner, P., Dowek, G. (eds.) IJCAR 2008. LNCS, vol. 5195, pp. 171–178. Springer, Heidelberg (2008). doi:10.1007/978-3-540-71070-7_15
20. Rosenberg, L.B.: Virtual fixtures: Perceptual tools for telerobotic manipulation. In: Virtual Reality Annual International Symposium, pp. 76–82 (1993)
21. Saberi, A.K., Groote, J.F., Keshishzadeh, S.: Analysis of path planning algorithms: a formal verification-based approach. In: Robotics and Automation ICRA, pp. 232–239 (2013)
22. Scherer, S., Lerda, F., Clarke, E.M.: Model checking of robotic control systems. In: International Symposium on Artificial Intelligence, Robotics and Automation in Space (i-SAIRAS), pp. 5–8 (2005)
23. Webster, M., Dixon, C., Fisher, M., Salem, M., Saunders, J., Koay, K., Dautenhahn, K.: Formal verification of an autonomous personal robotic assistant. In: Formal Verification and Modeling in Human-Machine Systems: Papers from the AAAI Spring Symposium (FVHMS 2014), pp. 74–79 (2014)
24. Xia, T., Baird, C., Jallo, G., Hayes, K., Nakajima, N., Hata, N., Kazanzides, P.: An integrated system for planning, navigation and robotic assistance for skull base surgery. J. Med. Robot. Comput. Assist. Surg. **4**(4), 321–330 (2008)

Performance Analysis of Multi-services Call Admission Control in Cellular Network Using Probabilistic Model Checking

Sana Younes[1,2]([⊠]) and Momtez Benmbarek[1]

[1] Tunis El Manar University, Tunis, Tunisia
sana.younes@fst.utm.tn, momtez.benmbarek@etudiant-fst.utm.tn
[2] LIP2 Laboratory, Campus Universitaire El-Manar, 2092 Tunis, Tunisia

Abstract. This paper deals with formal verification to evaluate performances of Call Admission Control (CAC) schemes in cellular mobile network. Call Admission Control is a mechanism regulating cellular network access to ensure QoS provisioning. From the fact that cellular networks have many classes of services and each class has different QoS requirements, we study CAC schemes supporting two classes of services, real time (RT) and non-real time (NRT), and for each class we distinguish two types of calls, handoff calls (HCs) and new calls (NCs). The studied CAC schemes give priority to RT calls over NRT calls and to HCs over NCs. Traditionally, performance analysis of CAC schemes is performed using analytic and/or simulation models by computing the main steady-state performance measures: new call blocking probability, handoff call dropping probability and mean channels occupation rate. In this work we propose to employ Continuous-time Stochastic Logic (CSL) to specify QoS requirements using transient and steady-state formulas supported by this formalism. Indeed, CSL is a specification language that can be used for Continuous Time Markov Chains (CTMCs) and offers the flexibility to express both transient and steady-state measures including probabilistic path and steady-state formulas. We model the studied CAC schemes with labelled CTMCs then we formalize QoS requirements of each traffic class with CSL. We perform the verification of the considered formulas with PRISM model checker. A performance comparison of the studied CAC schemes is provided based on verification results.

Keywords: Probabilistic model checking · CTMC · CSL · CAC schemes · PRISM

1 Introduction

Probabilistic model checking is a formal verification technique for modelling and analysis systems which exhibit stochastic behavior. It has been employed in different application domains such as wireless communication protocols, security, power management [9,10]. Probabilistic model checking, using Continuous Time Markov Chains, is widely employed to perform quantitative measurements of

© Springer International Publishing AG 2017
K. Barkaoui et al. (Eds.): VECoS 2017, LNCS 10466, pp. 17–32, 2017.
DOI: 10.1007/978-3-319-66176-6_2

properties such as performance and reliability. In this context we use this formalism to evaluate performances of Call Admission Control (CAC) schemes in cellular network.

In cellular network, base station (BS) is a radio access point covering certain geographic area (cell). Each cell is equipped with a limited number of channels to serve different user's connections. If there is no available channel the connection request will be rejected. Call admission control is the mechanism handling the acceptance or rejection of arriving calls. Several CAC schemes are proposed and can be classified based on different criteria [1]. One criterion is the number of services/classes. Indeed, traffic arriving to BS can be classified to RT such as voice, streaming applications or NRT such as web services or file transfers. For each class two types of calls can be differentiated, NCs originating from the underlying cell and HCs coming from neighboring cells. Each traffic class has different Quality of Service (QoS) requirements. Indeed, RT traffic has stringent QoS requirements because it can contains interactive applications compared to NRT traffic which contains non-interactive applications. Moreover, HCs are prioritized over NCs because dropping a HC in progress is more annoying than blocking a NC request.

Several CAC schemes have been discussed in the literature [5,6,8,17] to provide priority to HC without significantly forgoing NC requests. These schemes can be categorized into two basic methods: The first is by reserving, statistically or dynamically, a number of channels exclusively for handoff calls called guard channels [6]. The second by queuing handoff request [8] if all channels are not available, waiting that channel be free.

Recently much research work has been done on call admission control for multi-service mobile networks by favoring RT calls over NRT calls. In [16], the authors propose a multi-service CAC schemes improving bandwidth utilization in case of bandwidth asymetry (between uplink and downlink) environment. In [5], the authors propose a CAC schema based on the classification of channels to bad and good. This classification is done by estimating the quality of channel according to received signal strength. Calls with high priority are favored by taking good channels. In [17], an adaptive CAC schema based on degradation procedure is presented. The authors propose to reduce the width of channels allocated to calls having lower priority in order to maximize the number of calls having higher priority. We refer reader to these surveys [1,11] that explain and classify different CAC schemes.

The main QoS requirements that a CAC schema should satisfy are: HC dropping probability and NC blocking probability should be below certain predefined value and the channels occupation rate should be greater than some threshold to obtain a good bandwidth utilization. Different works have studied performance evaluation of CAC schemes. To the best of our knowledge, all studies are performed using simulation technique [5,8,17] and/or analytic approaches [6,15,16]. In this paper, we propose to use probabilistic model checking to check and compare performances of different CAC schemes. This work contains two contributions: Firstly we propose two multi-service CAC schemes prioritizing RT calls over NRT calls, secondly we compare their performances with two classic ones using probabilistic model checking. We model CAC schemes with labelled CTMCs then we formalize QoS requirements of each traffic class with CSL. The verification of the considered formulas is performed with PRISM model checker which has been used in wide range of case studies [9,10]. A performance comparison of the studied CAC schemes is provided based on verification results.

This paper is organized as follows. In Sect. 2 we briefly give an overview of labelled CTMC and CSL. Section 3 provides a modeling of studied CAC schemes. In Sect. 4, we formalize QoS requirements with CSL. We give in Sect. 5 numerical results of verification. Finally, Sect. 6 concludes the paper.

2   Probabilistic Model Checking

In this section we present briefly formalisms (labelled Continuous-Time Markov Chain (CTMC) and CSL [3]) that we use to evaluate performance measures for the studied CAC schemes. We refer to the book [13] for more details on Markov chains. Recall that in this paper, we model CAC schemes by labelled CTMCs and we formalize QoS constraints with CSL.

2.1   Labelled CTMC

A labelled CTMC $\mathcal{M}$ is a tuple $(S, \mathbf{R}, L)$ where S is a finite set of *states*, $\mathbf{R} : S \times S \to \mathcal{R}^+$ is the *rate matrix* and $L : S \to 2^{AP}$ is the *labelling* function which assigns to each state $s \in S$, the set $L(s)$ of atomic propositions $a \in AP$ that are valid in s, AP denotes the finite set of atomic propositions. Remark that the infinitesimal generator $\mathbf{Q}$ can be easily deduced as $\mathbf{Q}(s, s') = \mathbf{R}(s, s')$ if $s \neq s'$ and $\mathbf{Q}(s, s) = -\sum_{s' \in S} \mathbf{R}(s, s')$. A path through a CTMC is an alternating sequence $\sigma = s_0 t_0 s_1 t_1 \cdots$ with $\mathbf{R}(s_i, s_{i+1}) > 0$ and $t_i \in \mathcal{R}^+$ for all $i \geq 0$. t_i represents the amount of time spent in state s_i. Let us denote by $path_s$ the set of paths through $\mathcal{M}$ starting from the state s. For a CTMC, there are two types of state probabilities: transient probabilities where the system is considered at time t and steady-state probabilities when the system reaches an equilibrium if it exists. In the sequel, we denote by $\mathbf{\Pi}_s^{\mathcal{M}}(t)$ the transient distribution at time t of Markov chain $\mathcal{M}$ starting at $t = 0$ from the initial state s. The probability to be in state s' at time t starting initially from s will be denoted by $\mathbf{\Pi}_s^{\mathcal{M}}(s', t)$. $\mathbf{\Pi}_s^{\mathcal{M}}(s') = \lim_{t \to \infty} \mathbf{\Pi}_s^{\mathcal{M}}(s', t)$ is the steady-state probability to be in state s'. If $\mathcal{M}$ is ergodic, $\mathbf{\Pi}_s^{\mathcal{M}}(s')$ exists and it is independent of the initial distribution that we will denote by $\mathbf{\Pi}^{\mathcal{M}}(s')$. We denote also by $\mathbf{\Pi}^{\mathcal{M}}$ the steady-state probability vector. For $S' \subseteq S$, we denote by $\mathbf{\Pi}_s^{\mathcal{M}}(S', t)$ (resp. $\mathbf{\Pi}^{\mathcal{M}}(S')$) the transient probability to be in states of S', $\mathbf{\Pi}_s^{\mathcal{M}}(S', t) = \sum_{s' \in S'} \mathbf{\Pi}_s^{\mathcal{M}}(s', t)$ (the steady-state probability to be in states of S', $\mathbf{\Pi}^{\mathcal{M}}(S') = \sum_{s' \in S'} \mathbf{\Pi}^{\mathcal{M}}(s')$).

2.2   Temporal Logic CSL

Continuous Stochastic Logic is an extension of CTL (Computational Tree Logic) [7] with two probabilistic operators that refer to steady-state and transient behaviors of the underlying system.

Let p be a probability threshold, $\lhd$ be a comparison operator such that $\lhd \in \{\leq, \geq, <, >\}$ and I be an interval of real numbers. In the sequel, we denote by S_ϕ or ϕ-states the set of states that satisfy ϕ property and by $\models$ the satisfaction relation. The syntax of CSL is defined by:

$$\phi ::= true \mid a \mid \phi \wedge \phi \mid \neg\phi \mid \mathcal{P}_{\lhd p}(\phi\, \mathcal{U}^I \phi) \mid \mathcal{S}_{\lhd p}(\phi)$$

In this paper, we will use probabilistic operators $\mathcal{P}_{\lhd p}(\phi_1\, \mathcal{U}^I \phi_2)$ and $\mathcal{S}_{\lhd p}(\phi)$ to define and quantify performance measures of studied systems. In fact these operators are refering to transient and steady state behavior of the considered system.

$\mathcal{P}_{\lhd p}(\phi_1\, \mathcal{U}^I \phi_2)$ asserts that the probability measure of paths satisfying $\phi_1\, \mathcal{U}^I \phi_2$ meets the bound given by $\lhd p$. Whereas, the path formula $\phi_1\, \mathcal{U}^I \phi_2$ asserts that ϕ_2 will be satisfied at some time $t \in I$ and that at all preceding time ϕ_1 holds. $\mathcal{S}_{\lhd p}(\phi)$ asserts that the steady-state probability for ϕ-states meets the bound $\lhd p$.

Let us present briefly the semantics of these formulae [4]:

$s \models true$ for all $s \in S$

$s \models a$ iff $a \in L(s)$

$s \models \neg\phi$ iff $s \not\models \phi$

$s \models \mathcal{P}_{\lhd p}(\phi_1\, \mathcal{U}^I \phi_2)$ iff $Prob^{\mathcal{M}}(s, \phi_1\mathcal{U}^I\phi_2) \lhd p$

$s \models \mathcal{S}_{\lhd p}(\phi)$ iff $\mathbf{\Pi}_s^{\mathcal{M}}(S_\phi) \lhd p$

Where $Prob^{\mathcal{M}}(s, \phi_1\mathcal{U}^I\phi_2)$ denotes the probability measure of all paths σ starting from s ($\sigma \in paths_s$) satisfying $\phi_1\, \mathcal{U}^I \phi_2$ i.e. $Prob^{\mathcal{M}}(s, \phi_1\mathcal{U}^I\phi_2) = Prob\{\sigma \in paths_s \mid \sigma \models \phi_1\, \mathcal{U}^I \phi_2\}$.

In this paper we will use also two reward operators belonging to CSRL logic. Continuous Stochastic Reward Logic (CSRL) [12] is an extension of Continuous Stochastic Logic (CSL) by adding constraints over rewards. The steady-state operator $\mathcal{E}_J(\phi)$ asserts that the expected (long run) reward rate for ϕ-states lies in J (J is an interval of real numbers). The transient operator $\mathcal{E}_J^t(\phi)$ asserts that the expected instantaneous reward rate at time t for ϕ-states lies in J. $\rho : S \rightarrow \mathcal{R}^+$ is a *reward structure* that assigns to each state $s \in S$ a reward $\rho(s)$. The verification of these reward formulas $\mathcal{E}_J(\phi)$ (resp. $\mathcal{E}_J^t(\phi)$) requires the computation of the steady-state (resp. transient at t) distribution of the considered CTMC $\mathcal{M}$.

$$\begin{aligned} s &\models \mathcal{E}_J^t(\phi) \text{ iff} \sum\nolimits_{s' \in S_\phi} \mathbf{\Pi}_s^{\mathcal{M}}(s', t) \cdot \rho(s') \in J \\ s &\models \mathcal{E}_J(\phi) \text{ iff} \sum\nolimits_{s' \in S_\phi} \mathbf{\Pi}^{\mathcal{M}}(s') \cdot \rho(s') \in J \end{aligned} \tag{1}$$

3 Formal Modelling of CAC Schemes

In this section we describe and model with labelled CTMC four CAC schemes. We compare next their performances in Sect. 5 using probabilistic model checking. Let us first describe the system under consideration.

We consider a single cell and the arrival traffic to the base station (BS) is categorized in two classes of services: RT class and NRT class. The RT class is prioritized over the NRT class. This latter is assumed best effort traffic. For each class of service, we distinguish two types of calls: NCs originating from the underlying cell and HCs coming from neighboring cells. BS channels are divided into two parts: NRT channels and RT channels. RT channels serve only RT calls whereas NRT channels can serve both NRT and RT calls depending on the CAC schema. In this paper we study performances of four CAC schemes. The first two schemes named B-CAC (Basic CAC) and Q-CAC (Queuing CAC) are classics and their performances are studied in many works [2,8]. The two other schemes RTP-CAC (Real Time Priority CAC) and RTPQ-CAC (Real Time Priority Queuing) schemes are proposed in this paper in order to enhance QoS of RT calls by carrying out mechanisms that give priority to this class of calls.

All the investigated CAC schemes use guard channels in order to prioritize HC over NC since dropping handoff calls is less tolerable than blocking new calls. In fact, from user's point of view, a call being forced to terminate during a service (HC) is more annoying than a call being blocked at its start (NC). B-CAC is a static admission control schema. It does not consider the priority between classes of calls and only prioritize HCs over NCs for each class by reserving exclusively guard channels used only by HCs. Similarly, the second schema Q-CAC uses guard channels and further adds, for each class of traffic, a queue used by HC if all channels are occupied. In RTP-CAC, we give RT priority by permitting RT calls to use NRT channels if there is no idle RT channels. For the last CAC schema RTPQ-CAC, we combine mechanisms of RTP-CAC and Q-CAC in order to improve QoS of Calls with high priority (RT calls and HCs).

Let C_1 (resp. C_2) be the total number of NRT (resp. RT) channels. Let g be the number of guard channels reserved exclusively for HCs. We assume that the arrival processes for different traffic are independent and follow Poisson distribution with the following rates: λ_{Nh} for NRT HCs, λ_{Nn} for NRT NCs, λ_{Rh} for RT HCs and λ_{Rn} for RT NCs. We denote by $\lambda_N = \lambda_{Nh} + \lambda_{Nn}$ (resp. $\lambda_R = \lambda_{Rh} + \lambda_{Rn}$) arrival rate of NRT (resp. RT). We suppose that the holding time of channels is exponentially distributed with mean $1/\mu$.

In order to check CSL formulas that specify QoS requirements in terms of NC blocking probability and HC dropping probability for both NRT and RT classes, we need to label CTMC states with atomic propositions that characterize the state. Let us consider the following set of atomic propositions AP.

$$AP = \{\text{RT\_Drop}, \text{RT\_Block}, \text{NRT\_Drop}, \text{NRT\_Block}\} \tag{2}$$

RT_Drop (resp. NRT_Drop) is assigned to states in which RT (resp. NRT) HC is dropped. RT_Block (resp. NRT_Block) is assigned to states in which RT (resp. NRT) NC is blocked.

Let us detail the corresponding labelled CTMC of studied CAC schemes. We start by classical and existing schemes (B-CAC and Q-CAC) and then we detail proposed schemes in this work (RTP-CAC and RTPQ-CAC).

3.1   Basic CAC (B-CAC) Schema

B-CAC is a static admission schema that does not take into account the priority between classes of traffic. For both classes NRT and RT, the priority is given only to HCs over NCs by assigning g channels used exclusively by HCs. HCs and NCs for NRT (resp. RT) class are sharing $C_1 - g$ (resp. $C_2 - g$ channels). The channel allocation in B-CAC is presented in Fig. 1(a). A NRT (resp. RT) NC is blocked if the number of available channels in NRT (resp. RT) channel part is less or equal to $(C_1 - g)$ (resp. $C_2 - g$). Whereas, A NRT (resp. RT) HC is dropped if the number of occupied channels in NRT (resp. RT) channel part is equal to C_1 (resp. C_2).

Based on assumptions for arrival and service rates described previously, we obtain a two dimensional homogeneous CTMC (see Fig. 1(b)). The state space is given by:

$$S_{B-CAC} = \{(c_1, c_2) | 0 \le c_1 \le C_1; 0 \le c_2 \le C_2\} \tag{3}$$

In state (c_1, c_2), c_1 (resp. c_2) represents the number of busy NRT (resp. RT) channels. The transition rate $\mathbf{R}_{B-CAC}(c_1, c_2; \bar{c}_1, \bar{c}_2)$ from state (c_1, c_2) to state

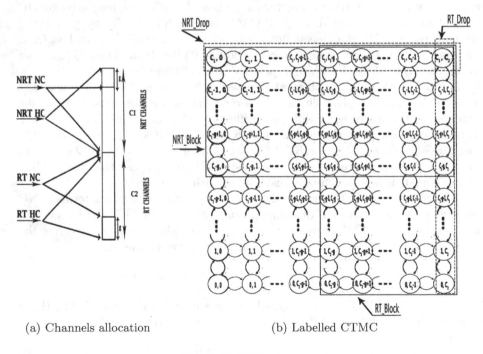

(a) Channels allocation   (b) Labelled CTMC

Fig. 1. B-CAC schema

$(\bar{c}_1, \bar{c}_2)$ in B-CAC schema is defined as follows:

$$\mathbf{R}_{B-CAC}(c_1, c_2; c_1 + 1, c_2) = \begin{cases} \lambda_N & \text{if } (0 \leq c_1 < C_1 - g; 0 \leq c_2 \leq C_2) \\ \lambda_{Nh} & \text{if } (C_1 - g \leq c_1 < C_1; 0 \leq c_2 \leq C_2) \end{cases}$$

$$\mathbf{R}_{B-CAC}(c_1, c_2; c_1, c_2 + 1) = \begin{cases} \lambda_R & \text{if } (0 \leq c_1 \leq C_1; 0 \leq c_2 < C_2 - g) \\ \lambda_{Rh} & \text{if } (0 \leq c_1 \leq C_1; C_2 - g \leq c_2 < C_2) \end{cases}$$

$$\mathbf{R}_{B-CAC}(c_1, c_2; c_1 - 1, c_2) = \mu c_1 \qquad \text{if } (0 < c_1 \leq C_1; 0 \leq c_2 \leq C_2)$$

$$\mathbf{R}_{B-CAC}(c_1, c_2; c_1, c_2 - 1) = \mu c_2 \qquad \text{if } (0 \leq c_1 \leq C_1; 0 < c_2 \leq C_2)$$

We label states by atomic propositions of AP set defined in Eq. 2. The obtained satisfaction sets are marked in Fig. 1(b) and defined formally by:

$$S_{NRT\_Drop} = \{(c_1, c_2) \mid c_1 = C_1 \text{ and } 0 \leq c_2 \leq C_2\}$$
$$S_{NRT\_Block} = \{(c_1, c_2) \mid C_1 \geq c_1 \geq C_1 - g \text{ and } 0 \leq c_2 \leq C_2\}$$
$$S_{RT\_Drop} = \{(c_1, c_2) \mid c_2 = C_2 \text{ and } 0 \leq c_1 \leq C_1\}$$
$$S_{RT\_Block} = \{(c_1, c_2) \mid C_2 \geq c_2 \geq C_2 - g \text{ and } 0 \leq c_1 \leq C_1\}$$

3.2   Queuing CAC (Q-CAC) Schema

In order to improve the QoS of HCs, two queues Q_{NRT} (resp. Q_{RT}) can be added to put HC for NRT (resp. RT) traffic. If a HC arrives and there is no idle channels, it is pushed in the corresponding queue. A HC is deleted from the queue when it moves out handoff area before getting channel (it is forced to terminate) or if the conversation is completed before living handoff area. The HC is dispatched from the queue to as soon as any channel is released. It is clear that this schema offers the same QoS for NCs as B-CAC but improve the QoS of HCs. The description of the channels allocation of this schema is given in Fig. 2(a).

We suppose that queues Q_{NRT} (resp. Q_{RT}) is finite with capacity Q_1 (resp. Q_2). We assume that the overtime in each queue is exponentially distributed with mean $1/\mu_{to}$. Based on these assumptions, the underlying model is a homogeneous two dimensional CTMC and the state space is defined by Eq. 4 where i is the sum of number of NRT busy channels and number of NRT HC requests in the queue Q_{NRT}, j is the sum of number of RT busy channels and number of RT HC requests in the queue Q_{RT}. The obtained CTMC is presented in Fig. 2(b).

$$S_{Q-CAC} = \{(i, j) \mid 0 \leq i \leq C_1 + Q_1; 0 \leq j \leq C_2 + Q_2\} \qquad (4)$$

The transition rate from state (i, j) to state $(\bar{i}, \bar{j})$ is defined by:

$$\mathbf{R}_{Q-CAC}(i, j; i + 1, j) = \begin{cases} \lambda_N & \text{if } (0 \leq i < C_1 - g; 0 \leq j \leq C_2 + Q_2) \\ \lambda_{Nh} & \text{if } (C_1 - g \leq i < C_1 + Q_1; 0 \leq j \leq C_2 + Q_2) \end{cases}$$

$$\mathbf{R}_{Q-CAC}(i, j; i, j + 1) = \begin{cases} \lambda_R & \text{if } (0 \leq i \leq C_1 + Q_1; 0 \leq j < C_2 - g) \\ \lambda_{Rh} & \text{if } (0 \leq i \leq C_1 + Q_1; C_2 - g \leq j < C_2 + Q_2) \end{cases}$$

$$\mathbf{R}_{Q-CAC}(i, j; i - 1, j) = \begin{cases} \mu i & \text{if}(0 < i \leq C_1; 0 \leq j \leq C_2 + Q_2) \\ \mu C_1 + \mu_{to}(i - C_1) & \text{if}(C_1 < i \leq C_1 + Q_1; 0 \leq j \leq C_2 + Q_2) \end{cases}$$

$$\mathbf{R}_{Q-CAC}(i, j; i, j - 1) = \begin{cases} \mu j & \text{if}(0 \leq i \leq C1 + Q_1; 0 < j \leq C_2) \\ \mu C_2 + \mu_{to}(j - C_2) & \text{if}(0 \leq i \leq C_1 + Q_1; C_2 < j \leq C_2 + Q_2) \end{cases}$$

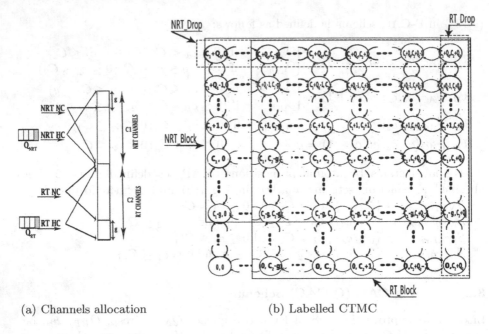

(a) Channels allocation   (b) Labelled CTMC

Fig. 2. Q-CAC schema

By the same mean, we label states of obtained CTMC corresponding to Q-CAC by atomic propositions of set AP (Eq. 2). The obtained satisfaction sets are marked in Fig. 2(b) and formally defined by:

$$S_{NRT\_Drop} = \{(i,j) \mid i = C_1 + Q_1 \text{ and } 0 \leq j \leq C_2 + Q_2\}$$
$$S_{NRT\_Block} = \{(i,j) \mid C_1 - g \leq i \leq C_1 + Q_1 \text{ and } 0 \leq j \leq C_2 + Q_2\}$$
$$S_{RT\_Drop} = \{(i,j) \mid 0 \leq i \leq C_1 + Q_1 \text{ and } j = C_2 + Q_2\}$$
$$S_{RT\_Block} = \{(i,j) \mid 0 \leq i \leq C_1 + Q_1 \text{ and } C_2 - g \leq j \leq C_2 + Q_2\}$$

We have described and modelled two classics CAC schemes B-CAC and Q-CAC that give priority to HC over NC without priortising RT calls over NRT calls. Next, we propose two CAC schemes in which we take into account the prioritization of RT calls over NRT calls and preserve priority given to HCs. We show in Sect. 5 that these proposed schemes improve QoS of RT calls and satisfy requirements expressed with CSL formulas.

3.3   Real Time Priority CAC (RTP-CAC) Schema

In this schema, to decrease the blocking/dropping of RT calls, we permit RT calls to use channels of NRT part. Hence, NRT calls are served only by NRT channels whereas RT calls can use NRT channels if there is no RT available channels. If $C_2 - g$ channels are occupied and a RT NC arrives to BS, it is not blocked and can

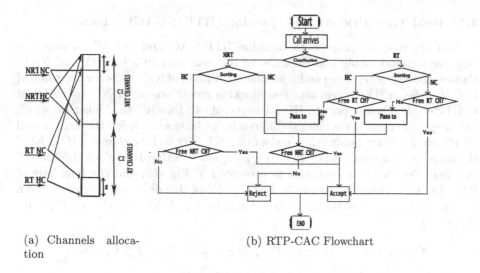

(a) Channels alloca-
tion

(b) RTP-CAC Flowchart

Fig. 3. RTP-CAC schema

take a NRT channel. In case of occupation of $C_1 - g$ channels (number authorized for NRT NC) then the RT NC will be blocked. A RT HC can take NRT channel if all C_2 channels are occupied. But if the number of busy NRT channels is equal to C_1 then it will be dropped. The channels allocation is presented in Fig. 3(a) and a flowchart that details mechanism of acceptation/rejection of calls is provided in Fig. 3(b).

Obviously, the CTMC state space of RTP-CAC and B-CAC is the same. And transition rates of these two CACs are the same except the arrival rate to NRT channels $\mathbf{R}_{RTP-CAC}(c_1, c_2; c_1 + 1, c_2)$ defined by:

$$\mathbf{R}_{RTP-CAC}(c_1, c_2; c_1 + 1, c_2) = \begin{cases} \lambda_N & \text{if}(0 \leq c_1 < C_1 - g; 0 \leq c_2 < C_2 - g) \\ \lambda_N + \lambda_{Rn} & \text{if}(0 \leq c_1 < C_1 - g; C_2 - g \leq c_2 < C_2) \\ \lambda_N + \lambda_R & \text{if}(0 \leq c_1 < C_1 - g; c_2 = C_2) \\ \lambda_{Nh} & \text{if}(C_1 - g \leq c_1 < C_1; 0 \leq c_2 < C_2) \\ \lambda_{Nh} + \lambda_{Rh} & \text{if}(C_1 - g \leq c_1 < C_1; c_2 = C_2) \end{cases}$$

We give now the satisfaction sets of AP atomic propositions. It is clear that S_{NRT_Drop} and S_{NRT_Block} sets are equals for RTP-CAC and B-CAC because NRT HC dropping and NRT NC blocking conditions are the same. Based on the dropping and blocking conditions for RT calls proposed in this CAC schema, S_{RT_Drop} and S_{RT_Block} are defined by:

$$S_{RT\_Drop} = \{(c_1, c_2) \mid c_1 = C_1 \text{ and } c_2 = C_2\}$$
$$S_{RT\_Block} = \{(c_1, c_2) \mid C_1 - g \leq c_1 \leq C_1 \text{ and } C_2 - g \leq c_2 \leq C_2\}$$

Clearly, the improvement in terms of RT class QoS that we expect with this RTP-CAC schema is fulfilled through the reduction of NRT class QoS.

3.4   Real Time Priority and Queuing (RTPQ-CAC) Schema

In this schema, we propose to combine RTP-CAC and Q-CAC in order to improve simultaneously performances of RT calls and HCs for (RT and NRT) classes. Indeed, acceptance and rejection conditions of NRT calls are the same of Q-CAC schema. The acceptance and blocking conditions of RT NC are identical to RTP-CAC schema. For RT HC (the type of call that has the higher priority), the dropping condition is defined differently. In fact, when a RT HC arrives and all RT channels are occupied, it passes to NRT part to take channel. If all NRT channels are occupied, it is put into Q_{RT} queue waiting the release of one RT channel. The channels allocation is presented in Fig. 4(a) and the flowchart of RTPQ-CAC is described in Fig. 5. The CTMC of this proposed schema is given in Fig. 4(b) and the state space is defined by the following set (see Eq. 4 for S_{Q-CAC}):

$$S_{RTPQ-CAC} = S_{Q-CAC} \setminus \{(i,j) | 0 \le i < C_1; C_2 < j \le C_2 + Q_2\} \qquad (5)$$

As we can see in Fig. 4(b) that the CTMC of this schema contains two parts. Transition rates of the lower part are equal to transition rates of CTMC in RTP-CAC and the transition rates of higher part are equal to transition rates of CTMC in Q-CAC schema. Hence, we have:

$$\begin{aligned}
\mathbf{R}_{RTPQ-CAC} &= \mathbf{R}_{RTP-CAC} & \text{if } (0 \le i < C_1; 0 \le j \le C_2) \\
\mathbf{R}_{RTPQ-CAC} &= \mathbf{R}_{Q-CAC} & \text{if } (C_1 \le i \le C_1 + Q_1; 0 \le j \le C_2 + Q2)
\end{aligned}$$

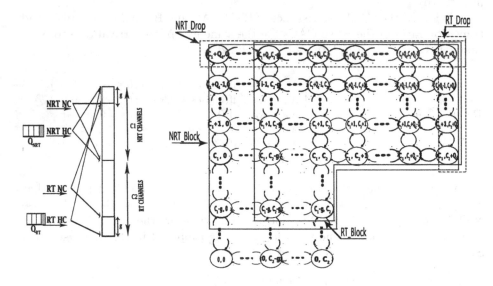

(a) Channels allocation   (b) Labelled CTMC

Fig. 4. RTPQ-CAC schema

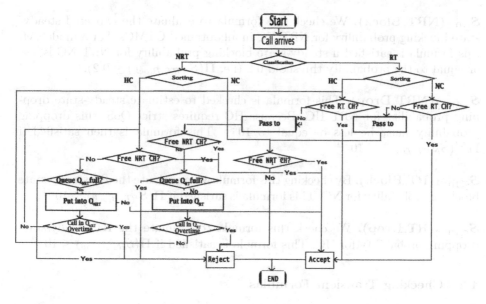

Fig. 5. RTPQ-CAC flowchart

Satisfaction sets of AP atomic propositions are marked in Fig. 4(b) and formalized by:

$$S_{NRT\_Drop} = \{(i,j) \mid i = C_1 + Q_1 \text{ and } 0 \le j \le C_2 + Q_2\}$$
$$S_{NRT\_Block} = \{(i,j) \mid C_1 - g \le i < C_1 \text{ and } 0 \le j \le C_2\}$$
$$\cup \{(i,j) \mid C_1 \le i \le C_1 + Q_1 \text{ and } 0 \le j \le C_2 + Q_2\}$$
$$S_{RT\_Drop} = \{(i,j) \mid C_1 \le i \le C_1 + Q_1 \text{ and } j = C_2 + Q_2\}$$
$$S_{RT\_Block} = \{(i,j) \mid C_1 - g \le i < C_1 \text{ and } C_2 - g \le j < C_2\}$$
$$\cup \{(i,j) \mid C_1 \le i \le C_1 + Q_1 \text{ and } C_2 - g \le j \le C_2 + Q_2\}$$

4   Formal Specification of Performance Properties by CSL Formulas

In this section, we formalize QoS requirements of each type of call with CSL in order to check if these requirements are satisfied by different CAC schemes. We express requirements using steady-state formulas, transient path formulas and reward formulas.

4.1   Checking Steady-State Formulas

The verification of steady-state formulas needs the computation of steady-state distribution $\Pi^{\mathcal{M}}$ of the considered CTMC $\mathcal{M}$. It is clear that obtained CTMCs of different CAC schemes presented in Sect. 3 are ergodic (finite and irreducible) so the steady-state probability vector $\Pi^{\mathcal{M}}$ of each CTMC $\mathcal{M}$ exists and is unique.

$\mathcal{S}_{\leq 0.2}$(**NRT_Block**). We check this formula to evaluate the expected steady-state blocking probability for NRT NC in all obtained CTMCs. For a model $\mathcal{M}$, this formula is satisfied if steady-state blocking probability for NRT NC is less or equal to the probability threshold 0.2 (i.e. $\mathbf{\Pi}(S_{NRT\_Block}) \leq 0.2$).

$\mathcal{S}_{\leq 10^{-2}}$(**NRT_Drop**). This formula is checked to estimate steady-state dropping probability for NRT HC. Because HC requires strict QoS, this dropping probability must be less or equal to 10^{-2}. This formula is then satisfied if $\mathbf{\Pi}^{\mathcal{M}}(S_{NRT\_Drop}) \leq 10^{-2}$.

$\mathcal{S}_{\leq 10^{-1}}$(**RT_Block**). By checking this formulas, we evaluate the RT steady-state blocking probability for NC. This formula is satisfied if $\mathbf{\Pi}(S_{RT\_Block}) \leq 10^{-1}$.

$\mathcal{S}_{\leq 10^{-3}}$(**RT_Drop**). We check this formula to estimate the RT steady-state dropping probability for HC. This formula is satisfied if $\mathbf{\Pi}(S_{RT\_Drop}) \leq 10^{-3}$.

4.2   Checking Transient Formulas

The verification of transient formulas requires the computation of the transient distribution $\mathbf{\Pi}_s^{\mathcal{M}}(t)$ which depends on the initial distribution. We choose to evaluate transient formulas at time 2 because after making some tests we observe that studied CTMCs reach equilibrium state at around $t = 4$. We suggest to check transient QoS requirements at the middle of time before reaching the steady-state of considered CTMCs. We suppose that at $t = 0$ all channels are empty (i.e. $s = (0,0)$).

$\mathcal{P}_{\leq 10^{-1}}$(**true** $\mathcal{U}^{[2,2]}$ **NRT_Block**). We check this formula to evaluate the NRT transient blocking probability of NC at time 2 in the considered model $\mathcal{M}$. This formula is satisfied if (i.e. $\mathbf{\Pi}_s^{\mathcal{M}}(S_{NRT\_Block}, t) \leq 10^{-1}$)

$\mathcal{P}_{\leq 10^{-3}}$(**true** $\mathcal{U}^{[2,2]}$ **NRT_Drop**). This formula is checked to evaluate the transient dropping probability at time 2 for NRT HC. If this probability is less or equal to 10^{-3} then it is satisfied. We have to check if $\mathbf{\Pi}_s^{\mathcal{M}}(S_{NRT\_Drop}, 2) \leq 10^{-3}$.

$\mathcal{P}_{\leq 10^{-2}}$(**true** $\mathcal{U}^{[2,2]}$ **RT_Block**). By checking this formulas, we evaluate the RT transient blocking probability of NC. This formula is satisfied if $\mathbf{\Pi}_s^{\mathcal{M}}(S_{RT\_Block}, 2) \leq 10^{-2}$ in the underlying model $\mathcal{M}$.

$\mathcal{P}_{\leq 10^{-4}}$(**true** $\mathcal{U}^{[2,2]}$ **NRT_Drop**). We check this formula to estimate the RT transient dropping probability at time 2 for HC. This formula is satisfied if $\mathbf{\Pi}_s^{\mathcal{M}}(S_{RT\_Drop}, 2) \leq 10^{-4}$.

Let us note that RT HCs have the most strict QoS requirements that's why the dropping probability threshold in the transient (resp. steady-state) formula must be the lowest, 10^{-4} (resp. 10^{-3}).

4.3   Checking Reward Formulas

We use CSRL [12] logic to express requirements related to the occupation rate of channels. Hence, we define three reward function ρ_1, ρ_2 and ρ to evaluate respectively the occupation rate of NRT channels, RT channels and the whole BS channels. ρ_1 (resp. ρ_2) associates to each state of the CTMC a reward value equal to percentage of occupied NRT (resp. RT) channels. ρ associates to each state of the CTMC a reward value equal to percentage of occupied BS station. Therefore, for each state $s = (c_1, c_2)$ of CMTCs in B-CAC and RTP-CAC schemes, the reward value associated to s is:

$$\rho_1(s) = 100c_1/C_1 \quad \rho_2(s) = 100c_2/C_2 \quad \rho(s) = 100(c_1 + c_2)/(C_1 + C_2)$$

For each state $s = (i, j)$ of CMTCs in Q-CAC and RTPQ-CAC, the reward value assigned to s is:

$$\rho_1(s) = 100\min(i, C_1)/C_1 \qquad\qquad \rho_2(s) = 100\min(C_2, 100)/C_2$$
$$\rho(s) = 100(\min(i, C_1) + \min(j, C_2))/(C_1 + C_2)$$

Now, for each reward function (ρ_1, ρ_2 and ρ), we check the two following reward formulas related to the transient and the steady-state behavior in each obtained CTMC.

$\mathcal{E}_J^2(\mathbf{true})$. We check this formula for each reward function ρ_1, ρ_2 and ρ to evaluate respectively the mean occupation rate of NRT, RT and BS channels. For a given reward function, this formula is satisfied if the mean occupation rate at time 2 lies in J. To check this formula we compute transient distributions at time 2 and then we sum over the probabilities of all CTMC states (because all CTMC states are *true*) multiplied with the corresponding rewards and finally we check if the obtained reward lies in J or not (see Eq. 1).

$\mathcal{E}_J(\mathbf{true})$. This formula is checked to evaluate the expected steady-state occupation rate of NRT, RT and BS channels by considering respectively the reward function ρ_1, ρ_2 and ρ. These reward measures are derived from steady-state distributions of studied CTMCs and reward functions (see Eq. 1).

5   Model Checking Results of CSL Formulas

The aim of this study is to compare performances of proposed CAC schemes (RTP-CAC and RTPQ-CAC) with classical schemes (B-CAC and Q-CAC). In this section, we give numerical results obtained based on the following parameters: we suppose that the number of RT channels ($C_2 = 50$) is greater than the number of NRT channels ($C_1 = 30$) and traffic intensity of RT class ($\lambda_{Rn} = \lambda_{Rh} = 25$) is higher than the traffic intensity of NRT class ($\lambda_{Nn} = \lambda_{Nh} = 10$). The time unit is 1 minute, we suppose that the channel holding time $\mu = 1$, $Q_{NRT} = Q_{RT} = 5$ and $\mu_{to} = 0.75$. In this scenario, the

Table 1. Model checking results of CSL transient formulas

Transient formulas	B-CAC		Q-CAC		RTP-CAC		RTPQ-CAC	
	Prob.	Sat?	Prob.	Sat?	Prob.	Sat?	Prob.	Sat?
$\mathcal{P}_{\leq 10^{-1}}(true\ \mathcal{U}^{[2,2]}\ \text{NRT\_Block})$	$4,4\ 10^{-3}$	Yes	$4,4\ 10^{-3}$	Yes	$2,0\ 10^{-2}$	Yes	$2,0\ 10^{-2}$	Yes
$\mathcal{P}_{\leq 10^{-3}}(true\ \mathcal{U}^{[2,2]}\ \text{NRT\_Drop})$	$2,9\ 10^{-4}$	Yes	$6,7\ 10^{-7}$	Yes	$1,0\ 10^{-3}$	Yes	$3,1\ 10^{-6}$	Yes
$\mathcal{P}_{\leq 10^{-2}}(true\ \mathcal{U}^{[2,2]}\ \text{RT\_Block})$	$1,1\ 10^{-1}$	No	$1,1\ 10^{-1}$	No	$6,0\ 10^{-3}$	Yes	$6,1\ 10^{-3}$	Yes
$\mathcal{P}_{\leq 10^{-4}}(true\ \mathcal{U}^{[2,2]}\ \text{RT\_Drop})$	$3,8\ 10^{-3}$	No	$6,3\ 10^{-5}$	Yes	$8,7\ 10^{-5}$	Yes	$2,6\ 10^{-7}$	Yes

Table 2. Model checking results of steady-state CSL formulas

Steady-state formulas	B-CAC		Q-CAC		RTP-CAC		RTPQ-CAC	
	Prob.	Sat?	Prob.	Sat?	Prob.	Sat?	Prob.	Sat?
$\mathcal{S}_{\leq 0.2}(\text{NRT\_Block})$	$1,3\ 10^{-2}$	Yes	$1,3\ 10^{-2}$	Yes	$7,1\ 10^{-2}$	Yes	$7,1\ 10^{-2}$	Yes
$\mathcal{S}_{\leq 10^{-2}}(\text{NRT\_Drop})$	$1,0\ 10^{-3}$	Yes	$3,7\ 10^{-6}$	Yes	$6,1\ 10^{-3}$	Yes	$2,1\ 10^{-5}$	Yes
$\mathcal{S}_{\leq 10^{-1}}(\text{RT\_Block})$	$1,5\ 10^{-1}$	No	$1,5\ 10^{-1}$	No	$1,9\ 10^{-2}$	Yes	$1,9\ 10^{-2}$	Yes
$\mathcal{S}_{\leq 10^{-3}}(\text{RT\_Drop})$	$5,5\ 10^{-3}$	No	$1,8\ 10^{-4}$	Yes	$2,6\ 10^{-4}$	Yes	$1,1\ 10^{-6}$	Yes

traffic load of RT class (25 requests per minute) is higher than the traffic load to NRT class (10 requests per minute). This choice is justifiable because the number of user's requests with high exigence in terms of QoS (RT calls) is continually increasing.

We use the probabilistic model checker PRISM [14] to construct and solve considered CTMCs. This tool is a high-level modeling language and formulas are checked automatically. Recall that the main relevant QoS requirements are NC blocking probabilities, HC dropping probabilities and the channels occupation rate. The best CAC schema is which provides: the lowest values of call dropping probabilities, the lowest values of call blocking probabilities and the highest value of channels occupation rate.

In Table 1 (resp. Table 2) we present model checking results of transient at time $t = 2\,\text{min}$ (resp. steady-state) formulas described in Sect. 4. For each CAC schema we give the probability value and the satisfaction results of considered formulas. As observed, RTP-CAC and RTPQ-CAC satisfy all underlying formulas and therefore requirements in terms of HC dropping probabilities and NC blocking probabilities for both NRT and RT classes are fulfilled. Whereas, these probability measures in B-CAC and Q-CAC are greater than the probability thresholds measures given in formulas related to RT traffic. This implies that QoS requirements for RT traffic (which must has the best QoS) are not satisfied with these classical CACs.

We note that the size of obtained CTMCs is 1581 for B-CAC and RTP-CAC, 2016 for Q-CAC and 1866 for RTPQ-CAC. The checking time of each formula presented in the following tables is less than 2 s.

Table 3 provides model checking results of transient (at $t = 2\,\text{min}$) and steady-state reward formulas. These formulas are checked by considering reward functions defined previously: ρ_1 for NRT channels occupation rate, ρ_2 for RT

Table 3. Model checking results of Reward CSRL formulas

Reward formulas	B-CAC		Q-CAC		RTP-CAC		RTPQ-CAC	
	Mean occupation rate of NRT channels							
	Mean ρ_1	Sat?	Mean ρ_1	Sat?	Mean ρ_1	Sat?	Mean ρ_1	Sat?
$\mathcal{E}^2_{[60,100]}(true)$	57,51%	No	57,48%	No	63,98%	Yes	63,99%	Yes
$\mathcal{E}_{[75,100]}(true)$	65,28%	No	65,15%	No	77,35%	Yes	77,36%	Yes
	Mean occupation rate of RT channels							
	Mean ρ_2	Sat?	Mean ρ_2	Sat?	Mean ρ_2	Sat?	Mean ρ_2	Sat?
$\mathcal{E}^2_{[80,100]}(true)$	81,95%	Yes	81,98%	Yes	81,95%	Yes	81,95%	Yes
$\mathcal{E}_{[84,100]}(true)$	84,56%	Yes	84,60%	Yes	84,56%	Yes	84,50%	Yes
	Mean occupation rate of BS channels							
	Mean ρ	Sat?	Mean ρ	Sat?	Mean ρ	Sat?	Mean ρ	Sat?
$\mathcal{E}^2_{[75,100]}(true)$	72,79%	No	72,79%	No	75,22%	Yes	75,21%	Yes
$\mathcal{E}_{[80,100]}(true)$	77,33%	No	77,30%	No	81,86%	Yes	81,82%	Yes

channels occupation rate and ρ for BS channels occupation rate. As observed, proposed CACs (RTP-CAC and RTPQ-CAC) provides the highest transient and steady-state values of NRT and BS occupation rates which implies that proposed schemes provide a good utilization ratio of BS bandwidth. We can observe also that the occupation rate of RT channels is the same in all CAC schemes which are predictable because RT channels allocation mechanism is the same in all studied CAC schemes.

6   Conclusion

In this paper, we have presented a formal modeling and verification of different CAC multi-service schemes. We have proposed two CAC schemes that consider the prioritization of RT traffic over NRT traffic and HC over NC. We model CAC schemes with labeled CTMC. In order to compare their performances, we use CSL logic to specify QoS requirements of each class of call. We perform numerical results using the PRISM model checker. Results show that the proposed CAC schemes (RTP-CAC and RTPQ-CAC) satisfy QoS requirements of different classes of traffic compared to classical schemes (B-CAC and Q-CAC). This work can be extended by checking other CSL formulas providing further performance measures like queue occupation rate and queue waiting time. We can verify also the satisfaction of other QoS requirements over the execution paths of the considered model using the until path formula $\mathcal{P}$. Moreover, we envisage to consider vertical handoffs by taking into account traffic coming from networks having different access technologies as WLAN.

References

1. Ahmed, M.H.: Call admission control in wireless networks: a comprehensive survey. In: IEEE Communications Surveys and Tutorials, pp. 49–68 (2005)
2. Alagu, S., Meyyappan, T.: An efficient call admission control scheme for handling handoffs in wireless mobile networks. IJANS **2**(3) (2012)
3. Aziz, A., Sanwal, K., Singhal, V., Brayton, R.: Model checking continuous time Markov chains. ACM Trans. Comput. Log. **1**(1), 162–170 (2000)
4. Baier, C., Haverkort, B., Hermanns, H., Katoen, J.-P.: Model checking continuous-time Markov chains by transient analysis. In: Emerson, E.A., Sistla, A.P. (eds.) CAV 2000. LNCS, vol. 1855, pp. 358–372. Springer, Heidelberg (2000). doi:10.1007/10722167_28
5. Belghith, A., Mohamed, M.B., Obaidat, M.S.: Efficient bandwidth call admission control in 3Gpp. LTE networks. In: GLOBECOM (2016)
6. Bisdikian, C., Choi, Y., Kwon, T., Naghshineh, M.: Call admission control for adaptive multimedia in wireless/mobile networks. In: Proceedings of the IEEE Wireless Communications and Networking Conference, vol. 2, pp. 540–544 (1999)
7. Clarke, E.M., Emerson, A., Sistla, A.P.: Automatic verification of finite-state concurrent systems using temporal logic specifications. ACM Trans. Program. Lang. Syst. **8**(2), 244–263 (1986)
8. Cornefjord, M., Gaasvik, P.-O., Svensson, V.: Different methods of giving priority to handoff traffic in a mobile telephone system with directed retry. In: Proceedings of the 41st IEEE Vehicular Technology Conference, pp. 549–553 (1991)
9. Dubslaff, C., Klppelholz, S., Baier, C.: Probabilistic model checking for energy analysis in software product lines. In: Proceedings of the 13th International Conference on Modularity, pp. 169–180. ACM (2014)
10. Duflot, M., Kwiatkowska, M., Norman, G., Parker, D.: A formal analysis of Bluetooth device discovery. Int. J. STTT **8**(6), 621–632 (2006)
11. Ghaderi, M., Boutaba, R.: Call admission control in mobile cellular networks: a comprehensive survey. Wirel. Commun. Mob. Comput. **6**, 69–93 (2006)
12. Haverkort, B., Cloth, L., Hermanns, H., Katoen, J.P., Baier, E.C.: Model checking performability properties. In: Proceedings of DSN. IEEE CS Press (2002)
13. Kulkarni, V.G.: Modeling and Analysis of Stochastic Systems. Chapman & Hall, London (1995)
14. Kwiatkowska, M., Norman, G., Parker, D.: PRISM 4.0: verification of probabilistic real-time systems. In: Gopalakrishnan, G., Qadeer, S. (eds.) CAV 2011. LNCS, vol. 6806, pp. 585–591. Springer, Heidelberg (2011). doi:10.1007/978-3-642-22110-1_47
15. Wang, J., Qiu, Y.: A new call admission control strategy for LTE femtocell networks. In: International Conference on Advances in Computer Science and Engineering, Sydney (2013)
16. Yang, X., Feng, G., Siew, C.K.: Call admission control for multi-service wireless networks with bandwidth asymmetry between uplink and downlink. IEEE Trans. Veh. Technol. **55**, 360–368 (2006)
17. Zarai, F., Ben Ali, K., Obaidat, M.S., Kamoun, L.: Adaptive call admission control in 3GPP LTE networks. Int. J. Commun. Syst. **27**(10), 1522–1534 (2014). Wiley

Application of Generalized Stochastic Petri Nets to Performance Modeling of the RF Communication in Sensor Networks

Sedda Hakmi[✉], Ouiza Lekadir, and Djamil Aïssani

Research Unit LaMOS (Modeling and Optimization of Systems),
Bejaia University, 06000 Béjaïa, Algeria
sed.hakmi@gmail.com, ouizalekadir@gmail.com, lamos_bejaia@hotmail.com

Abstract. In this paper we model and analyse the radio frequency (RF) transmission in wireless sensor networks using Generalized Stochastic Petri Nets (GSPN). In our model two types of priority requests are considered. In the first type, high priority requests are queued and served according to FIFO discipline. In the second type (case of blocking) low priority requests join the orbit before retrying the request until they find the server free. We consider the preemptive priority to the requests. Indeed, in this study, we highlight the impact of the presence of priority requests on network performances via GSPN formalism. Firstly, we study the case where the high priority requests have non-preemptive priority over lower ones. While, in the second case, we apply the preemptive discipline to the high priority requests. Finally, some numerical examples are given to illustrate our analysis.

Keywords: Radio Frequency (RF) transmission · Wireless sensor network · Generalized Stochastic Petri Nets · Modeling · Performance evaluation · Priority requests

1 Introduction

Wireless sensor networks are rapidly emerging as an important new area in the research community. Their applications are numerous and growing, and range from indoor deployment scenarios in the home and the office to outdoor deployment scenarios in natural, military and embedded settings such as temperature, pressure, fire alarms, motion etc. [8]. Wireless sensor sends such sensed data, usually via radio frequency. Signal processing and communication activities are the main parts of sensor networks. Therefore, optimal organization and management of the sensor network is very crucial in order to perform the desired function with an acceptable level of quality [13]. In order to study the performance of wireless sensor networks, many researchers rely mainly on queueing theory especially retrial or priority queues [9,22].

In the last decades there has been significant contribution in the area of retrial queueing theory. The particularity of these kinds of queueing systems is that arriving requests, which find a server busy, go to some virtual place called

© Springer International Publishing AG 2017
K. Barkaoui et al. (Eds.): VECoS 2017, LNCS 10466, pp. 33–47, 2017.
DOI: 10.1007/978-3-319-66176-6_3

orbit and try their request after some random time. These queueing models arises in many communication protocols, local area networks, and some other life situations. For a detailed survey one can see [1, 2, 5–7, 10, 11, 23] and the references therein. Furthermore, there are some situations in sensor networks where some requests are generally considered more important than others such as: fire, explosion sounds in the military field, etc., so the modeling by retrial queue with priority requests arises. In this context of modeling with priority retrial queues, Berczes et al. introduce a non preemptive priority retrial model for the transmission in wireless sensor networks which is based on vacation of the server in [3]. This work is primary based on the works of [9, 22]. Later, in [4], Berczes et al. extend this model by adding the fact that at the arrival of high priority requests wake up the Radio Frequency (RF) unit (server) while the low priority requests can not do it.

Motivated by the need for performance models suitable for modeling and evaluating of the Radio transmission in wireless sensor networks, we consider a preemptive priority in order to extend the model of [4]. So, in our model, two types of requests (high priority and low priority requests) arrive at the system and if they find the server unavailable, the high priority requests join the ordinary queue, while the low priority requests have to join the orbit and reattempt after a random period. The server departs for a vacation when there are no requests in the queue or in the orbit upon a service completion. Under this scheme, when a vacation period expires, the server wakes up. If the queue or the orbit are non-empty, the server starts serving requests according to the order of priority. Otherwise, it remains awake for a limited time period, waiting for a possible other request. If no requests arrive during this period, it goes for another vacation. The particularity of our proposed model resides in the fact that any high priority request, upon arrival, interrupts the service of low priority one and begins its service. To analyse this model we used the generalized stochastic Petri nets formalism (GSPN).

To highlight priority impact of priority requests on sensor networks performances, we have considered two models. In the first model we considered the case where the requests are served under the non-preemptive priority policy. Whereas in the second model, the requests are served under the preemptive priority. For the numerical application, we compared the performance indices of the models above for different parameters values. We considered the non preemptive case where the high and the low priority requests have the same service rates to compare our results with those in [4]. Furthermore, we considered different service rates in the preemptive priority case to illustrate the influence of these parameters on the performance indices of our model.

This paper is organized as follows: In Sect. 2, we introduce the proposed models of the RF transmission in wireless sensor networks in detail. In Sect. 3, we give an overview of Petri Nets. The generalized Stochastic Petri Net models describing the RF transmission in wireless networks for the two cases: non preemptive and preemptive priority are investigated in Sect. 4. Section 5 is devoted to the performance characteristics where we give the main steady-state characteristics of the studied models. In Sect. 6, we provide various numerical results which are presented and discussed in detail. We finally conclude and give some envisaged further works.

2   The Basic Models

Our motivation is the need for performance models suitable for modeling and evaluating of the Radio Frequency transmission in wireless sensor networks. Thus, we consider in the RF transmission two types of requests: high priority and low priority requests. The sources represent two classes of sensors: the emergency class like fire alarms (high priority requests) while the second one refers to the standard case like temperature measurement (low priority requests). The basic operation of the model can be described as:

- **Arrival and retrial process:** Two types of requests high priority (resp. low priority) requests arrive from two groups of finite sources with capacity N_1, resp. N_2. The high priority (resp. low priority) requests follow Poisson process with mean arrival rate λ_1 (resp. λ_2). Upon blocking, low priority requests immediately join a pool of unsatisfied requests, called the orbit. Any orbiting request tries to connect with the RF (server) after an exponential time period with rate $\nu > 0$, until it finds the server free.
- **Service process:** The RF unit (server) can be in two states: in ON state (accessible), it is able to start processing the incoming requests, or in OFF state, the RF unit can be asleep. The distribution of this ON state times is exponential with parameter α. If there are no incoming requests during this time period, the RF unit switches to OFF state. The distribution of this OFF state times is exponential with parameter β. A listening session starts when the server is in ON state and there are not requests waiting in the queue or in the orbit.

  If the server RF is in ON state at the arrival time of a low priority request, it will be served according to exponential distribution with rate μ_2. Any high priority request in non preemptive case, which upon arrival finds the server busy is queued up in an ordinary queue and will be served according to exponential distribution with rate μ_1. In the case of preemptive priority, the service of a lower-priority request will be interrupted and begins its service immediately with rate μ_3. The interrupted request joins the orbit and will restart service later. Indeed, in these two priorities cases, when the high priority request arrives when the server is at the OFF state, it wakes up the RF unit and starts its service with an exponentially distributed initialization time with parameter γ. In the following, we present the GSPN models describing the RF transmission in wireless sensor networks for the two cases of non preemptive and preemptive priority.

3   An Overview of Generalized Stochastic Petri Nets

Petri nets (PNs) are a powerful modeling tool, introduced in 1962 by Carl Adam [21]. In fact, they combine a well defined mathematical theory with a graphical representation of the systems dynamic behavior. PNs are widely studied and successfully applied in different discrete event dynamic systems in computers networks, real-time computing systems, telecommunication networks, etc. [12, 14–17]. The strong mathematical foundation of Petri nets and the amiability of a wide range of supporting tools have made them popular among academic researchers. A Petri Net is a collection of directed arcs connecting places and transitions. Places may hold tokens, so the state or marking of a net is its assignment of tokens to places. A transition is enabled when the number of tokens in each of its input places is at least equal to the arc weight going from the place to the transition. When fired, the tokens in the input places are moved to output places, according to arc weights and place capacities.

In this paper, we use Generalized Stochastic Petri Nets (GSPN) formalism [19, 20], which is a modeling formalism that can be conveniently used for analyzing the complex models of discrete event dynamic systems and study their performances or reliability evaluations. This formalism allows us to define two classes of transitions: immediate transitions and timed transitions. Immediate transitions fire in zero time, this means they occur instantaneously, so they always have priority over any enabled timed transitions. While timed transitions fire after a random exponentially distributed enabling time. A marking in which immediate transitions are enabled is known as a vanishing marking, while a marking in which only timed transitions are enabled is known as a tangible marking. The use of GSPN has several advantages due to the memoryless property of the exponential distribution of firing times. [19, 20] has shown that the stochastic Petri nets are isomorphic to a Continuous-Time Markov Chain (CTMC). Thus, solving GSPN models consists first to eliminate the vanishing states in order to obtain an equivalent CTMC which contains only tangible states. In this way, the performance measures of this GSPN model can be evaluated by a simple computation of the steady-state distribution $\pi = (\pi_1, \pi_2, \pi_3, \cdots, \pi_n)$, which is the solution of the following linear system:

$$\begin{cases} \pi.Q = 0; \\ \sum_{i \in E} \pi_i = 1; \end{cases} \tag{1}$$

where: π_i denotes the steady-state probability that the process is in the state M_i and E is the set of the tangible states. Q is the infinitesimal generator matrix of the Markov process and its elements are computed as a function of the timed transitions firing rates [18].

4   GSPN Models of the RF Transmission in Wireless Sensor Networks

The two GSPN models that we proposed to describe the RF transmission with non preemptive (resp. preemptive) priority are depicted in Fig. 1 (resp. Fig. 2).

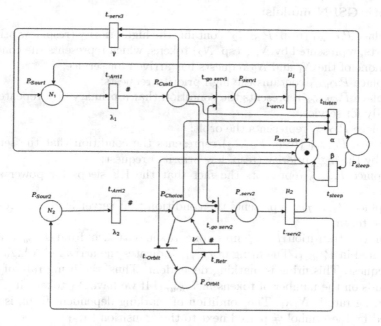

Fig. 1. The non preemptive GSPN Model of the RF transmission in wireless sensor networks.

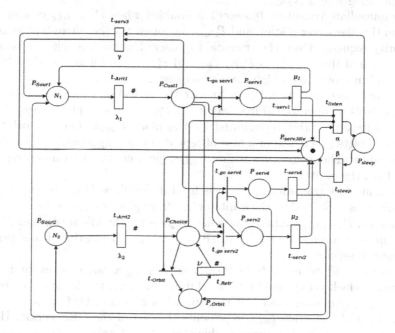

Fig. 2. The preemptive GSPN Model of the RF transmission in wireless sensor networks.

▶ **In both GSPN models:**

- The place $P._{Sour1}$ (resp. $P._{Sour2}$) contains the high priority (resp. low priority) requests, represented by N_1 (resp. N_2) tokens, which represents the condition that none of the N_1 and N_2 requests has arrived for service;
- The place $P._{Cust1}$ contains the high priority requests;
- The place $P._{Choice}$ represents the condition that a primary or a repeated call is ready for service;
- The place $P._{Orbit}$ represents the orbit;
- The place $P._{serv1}$ (resp. $P._{serv2}$) represents the condition that the server is busy by the high priority (resp. low priority) request;
- The place $P._{sleep}$ represents the fact that the RF sleeps for power saving purposes.
- The place $P._{serv.Idle}$ represents the condition that server is idle, represented by one token.
- When the transition t_{Arri1} fires, one token is taken from P_{Sour1} and is deposited in P_{Cust1}. The firing of t_{Arri1} indicates the arrival of a high priority request. This firing is marking dependent. Thus, the firing rate of t_{Arri1} depends on the number of tokens in P_{Sour1}. If we have N_1 tokens in P_{Sour1}, the firing rate is $N_1\lambda_1$. The condition of marking dependent firing is represented by the symbol $\#$ placed next to the transition t_{Arr1}.
- If the arrived request is a low priority one, the transition t_{Arri2} will fire, then P_{Choice} receives a token. Because the transition t_{Arri2} is a marking dependent, so the firing rate is $N_2\lambda_2$.
- The immediate transition $tgo.serv1$ is enabled when $P_{Serv.Idle}$ contains one token (i.e. the server is idle), and P_{Cust1} is not empty (i.e. there is at least one priority request). Once the transition $tgo.serv1$ is fired, a token is removed from each of the two places $P_{Serv.Idle}$ and P_{Cust1}, and it is placed in P_{Serv1}. This token represents a high priority request in service.
- The immediate transition $t._{Orbit}$ fires at the arrival of a low priority request which finds no operational free server i.e. $P_{Serv.idle}$ is empty. Hence, it joins immediately the orbit represented by the place P_{Orbit}. Once in orbit, the request starts generation of a flow of repeated calls exponentially distributed with rate ν. The firing of transition t_{Retr} represents the arrival of a repeated call from the orbit.
- The immediate transition $t_{go.serv2}$ is fired if the place P_{Cus1} is empty (This condition is expressed by the inhibitor arc from place P_{Cust1} to the transition $t_{go.serv2}$.), $P_{Serv.idle}$ contains one token represents the idle server and P_{Choice} contain one token. So, P_{Serv2} receives a token representing a low priority request in service.
- When there are no requests in P_{Cus1} and P_{Choice} a listening session is commencing which is expressed by the inhibitor arcs. So, the firing of the transition t_{listen} represents the event that an idle server is in OFF state.
- The firing of transition t_{sleep} represents the end of the OFF period. Hence, the server is returned to the available state (ON state).
- Once in the OFF state, the server can serve the high priority requests if there is at least one high priority request in P_{Cus1}.

- The timed transition t_{Serv2} (resp. t_{Serv1} and t_{Serv3}) is fired to determine the end of the low priority (resp. high priority) requests period service. Thus, P_{sour2} (resp. in P_{sour1}) receives a token which represents the condition that a low priority request or a high priority one will be returned to be idle, and a second token is deposited in $P_{Serv.idle}$ which represents the condition that the server is ready to serve another request.

▶ **In the preemptive GSPN model:**

- $P_{.serv4}$ represents the condition that the server is busy by the high priority request after interruption of low priority request service. So, the interrupted request joins the orbit and will restart service later.
- At the end of a service period of the preemptive requests, timed transition $t_{go.Serv4}$ fires. The request under service returns to free state P_{sour2} and the server becomes idle.

5 Performance Measures

The aim of this section is to derive the formulas of the most important stationary performance indices corresponding to a RF transmission. As all the proposed models are bounded their initial markings are home states. Accordingly, their steady-state probability distributions exist. In this case, several performance indices can be computed by the formulas given in the following subsections.

▶ **The mean arrival rate of the high priority requests η_1 (resp. low priority requests η_2 are:**

$$\eta_1 = \sum_{j \in (SM_j)_1} \lambda_1(M_j)\pi_j, \quad \eta_2 = \sum_{j \in (SM_j)_2} \lambda_2(M_j)\pi_j; \tag{2}$$

with: $(SM_j)_k$ is the set of markings where the transition t_{Arri_k} is enabled, and $\lambda_k(M_j)$ is the firing rate associated with the transition t_{Arri_k} in the marking M_j, with $k = \overline{1,2}$.

▶ **The mean retrial rate of low priority requests:**
The throughput of the transition t_{Retr} gives the mean retrial rate of low priority requests:

$$\eta_o = \sum_{j \in (SM_j)_o} \nu(M_j).\pi_j; \tag{3}$$

with: $(SM_j)_o$ is the set of markings where the transition t_{Aretr} is enabled, and $\nu(M_j)$ is the firing rate associated with the transition t_{retr} in the marking M_j.

▶ **The mean rate of listening period:**
This represents the throughput of the transition t_{listen}:

$$\bar{\alpha} = \sum_{j \in (SM_j)} \alpha(M_j).\pi_j; \tag{4}$$

with: (SM_j) is the set of markings where the transition t_{listen} is enabled, and $\alpha(M_j)$ is the firing rate associated with the transition t_{listen} in the marking M_j.

▶ **The mean rate of sleeping period:**
This represents the throughput of the transition t_{listen}:

$$\bar{\beta} = \sum_{j \in (SM_j)} \beta(M_j).\pi_j; \tag{5}$$

with: (SM_j) is the set of markings where the transition t_{sleep} is enabled, and $\beta(M_j)$ is the firing rate associated with the transition t_{sleep} in the marking M_j.

▶ **The mean number of the high priority requests η_{01} (resp. low priority requests η_{02}) in the queue:**

$$\eta_{01} = \sum_j M_j(P_{Cust1}) + M_j(P_{Serv4})\pi_j, \quad \eta_{02} = \sum_j M_j(P_{Orbit}).\pi_j; \tag{6}$$

where, $M_j(P_{Cust1})$ is the number of tokens in place P_{Cust1} in the marking M_j and $M_j(P_{Orbit})$ is the number of tokens in place P_{Orbit} in the marking M_j. The sum in this formula is made on all the accessible markings.

▶ **The mean number of high priority requests η_{S1} (resp. low priority requests η_{S2}) in the system:**

$$\eta_{S1} = \sum_j [M_j(P_{Cust1}) + M_j(P_{Serv1}) + M_j(P_{Serv4})]\pi_j; \tag{7}$$

$$\eta_{S2} = \sum_j [M_j(P_{Orbit}) + M_j(P_{Serv2})]\pi_j. \tag{8}$$

The sum in this formula is made on all the accessible markings.

▶ **The mean waiting time of high priority W_1 (resp. low priority W_2) the requests:**

$$W_1 = \frac{\eta_{01}}{\eta_1}; \qquad W_2 = \frac{\eta_{02}}{\eta_2}. \tag{9}$$

▶ **The mean response time of high priority τ_1 (resp. low priority τ_2) requests:**

$$\tau_1 = \frac{\eta_{S1}}{\eta_1}; \qquad \tau_2 = \frac{\eta_{S2}}{\eta_2}. \tag{10}$$

▶ **The blocking probability of low priority requests:**

$$B_p = \sum_i Prob\{M(P_{Orbit}) \geq 1 \ and \ M(P_{.serv.Idle}) = 0\}. \tag{11}$$

▶ **The probability that the server is busy by high priority request P_{s1} (resp. low priority requests P_{s2}):**

$$P_{s1} = \sum_i Prob\{(M(P_{serv1}) = 1) \ or \ (M(P_{serv4}) = 1)\}; \tag{12}$$

$$P_{s2} = \sum_i Prob\{M(P_{serv2}) = 1\}. \tag{13}$$

▶ **The probability of sleeping period:**

$$Pr_s = \sum_i Prob\{M(P_{sleep}) \geq 1\}. \tag{14}$$

6 Numerical Results

In the present section, we study the effect of several parameters on the performance measures in the sensor networks for the two cases: preemptive and non preemptive priority. The results of this study are displayed in different figures. On each figure the blue lines correspond to the non preemptive priority and the red lines correspond to the preemptive priority. In Table 1, we considered the same parameters as those used by Berczes et al. [4] in order to compare the results.

Figure 3 displays the mean queue length versus the λ. We see that as the arrival rate increases, the mean queue length increases. We note that the mean queue length for the preemptive priority is less than in the non preemptive priority. In the case of preemptive priority, the requests spend less time compared to non preemptive case.

On Fig. 4 the mean orbit size of low priority requests is displayed as a function of λ. We see that the mean number of requests in the orbit is an increasing function of arrival rate. However, the mean orbit size in preemptive priority is almost close to the mean orbit size in non preemptive priority. For high request generation rates mean orbit size approaches N_2 i.e. the low priority requests are blocked. These results are useful for choosing the parameters that fine tuning the size of the orbit.

In Fig. 5, mean waiting time spent in the queue are plotted versus arrival rates. We remark that increasing of the arrival rates increases the mean waiting time spent in the queue by the high priority requests. But the mean waiting time in preemptive case is smaller than mean waiting time in the non preemptive

Table 1. Network parameters.

Parameter	Symbol	Value
Population size	(N_1, N_2)	$(50, 50)$
Arrival rates	(λ_1, λ_2)	$(\frac{\lambda}{10}, \frac{9\lambda}{10})$
Service rates	(μ_1, μ_2)	$(20, 20), (20, 10), (10, 20)$
Retrial rate	ν	2
Initialization rate	γ	10
Mean time of sleeping period	$\frac{1}{\beta}$	0.5
Mean time of listening period	$\frac{1}{\alpha}$	1.5

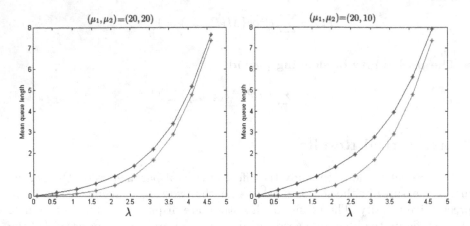

Fig. 3. Mean queue length versus λ.

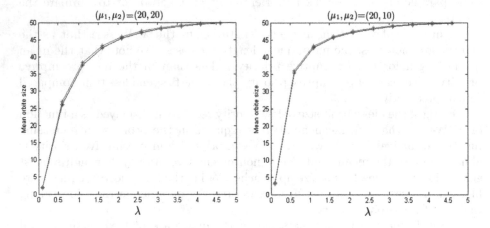

Fig. 4. Mean orbit size versus λ.

case. We remark also that the waiting time in the case of non preemptive priority increases with the decreases of the service rate of low priority requests, contrary to the case of preemptive priority where waiting time remains almost the same.

Figure 6 illustrates the behavior of mean waiting time in the orbit versus the arrival rates. The curves show the increases of the waiting time in the orbit with the increases of λ. We can see that for small values of $\lambda \leq 2$ mean waiting time in the orbit given by the preemptive case is close to mean waiting time in the orbit given by the non preemptive one. But after this value, the requests spend more time in the orbit. This is because the server interrupt the non preemptive requests (which join the orbit) and serve the high priority requests.

Figures 7 and 8 show how much the increases of the arrival rate affects the mean response time, especially for the low priority requests. We can also see

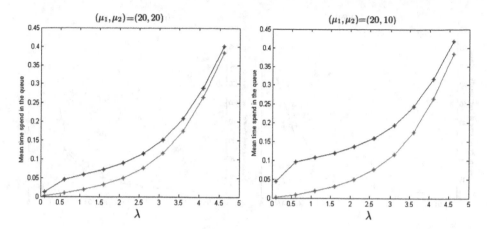

Fig. 5. Mean waiting time in the queue versus λ.

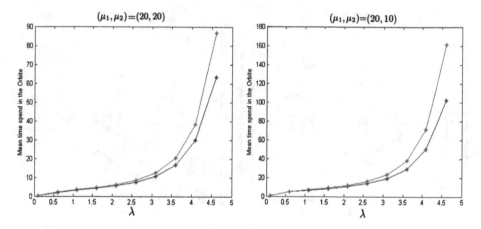

Fig. 6. Mean waiting time in the orbit versus λ.

the influence of service rates, for example, the difference between the response times for $\lambda = 4.5$ in the case of $(\mu_1, \mu_2) = (20, 20)$ and $(\mu_1, \mu_2) = (20, 10)$ is significant. Furthermore, we remark that the mean response time of low priority requests in non preemptive case is almost close to the mean response time in the preemptive case for a lower values of the arrival rates ($\lambda \leq 2.3$). But priority requests response time in the case of preemptive case gives the best results. This is because the server is busy a lot more with priority requests.

In Fig. 9 the blocking probability of retrial requests curves are plotted versus the arrival rate λ. From this figure it is shown that this probability increases as λ increases and approaches one. The increasing of this blocking probability is rapid for a small value of μ_2. This figure also shows that the optimal choice of

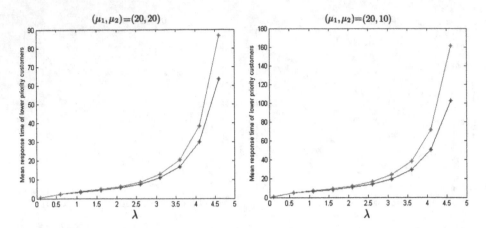

Fig. 7. Mean response time of low priority requests versus λ.

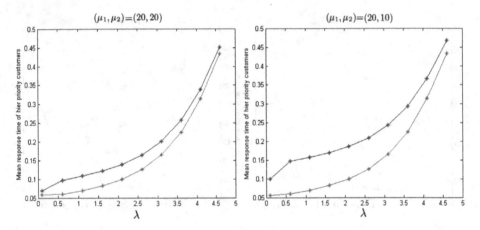

Fig. 8. Mean response time of high priority requests versus λ.

blocking probability for the retrial requests corresponds to the case of preemptive discipline.

Figure 10 illustrates the behavior of the probability that the server is busy versus the arrival rate λ. We have presented two curves which correspond to the probability that the server is busy by the high priority (resp. low priority) requests. These curves show the probability that RF is busy by the low priority request increases until the maximum and decreases to approaches zero. The observed peak in curve indicates that from the $\lambda = 0.5$ corresponding to this point, the high-priority requests are strongly constrained to be preferred over low-priority requests. We notice that this probability approaches zero with the increases of λ. The zero is reached rapidly for a lower values of μ_1. We can

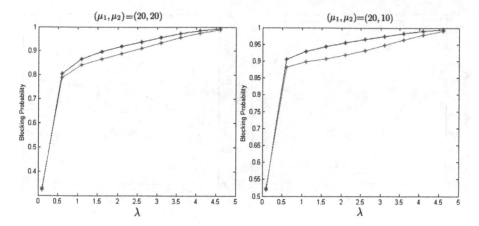

Fig. 9. Blocking probability of retrial requests versus λ.

see also that in the case of preemptive discipline this probability is less than in preemptive case.

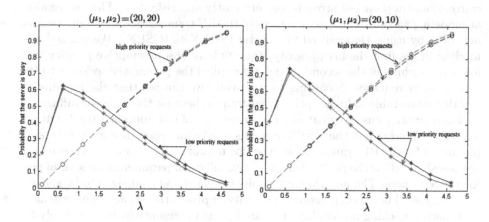

Fig. 10. The probability that the server is busy versus λ.

Figure 11 shows that the increases of the sleeping period rate doesn't influences a lot for the mean queue length and for the orbit size. For example, the mean number of waiting requests is around 0.02 in the case of preemptive priority and around 0.11 in the case of non preemptive priority. Otherwise, the average number of requests in the orbit is between $[21.4, 22.4]$ in the case of preemptive priority, and between $[22.1, 23.4]$ in the case of non preemptive priority. We constat that the number of priority requests in the queue does not depend on the sleeping period rate, this is due the wake up of the server and the preemptive priority of the requests.

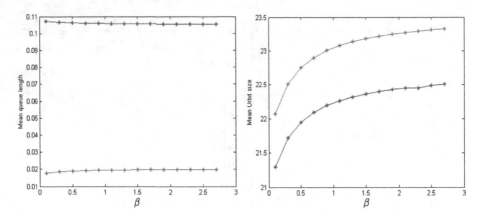

Fig. 11. Mean queue length and mean orbit size versus β.

7 Conclusion

Sensor networks can increase the efficiency of many military and civil applications, such as combat field surveillance, security and disaster management where conventional approaches prove to be very costly and risky [13]. This paper aims at modeling and studying performances of the RF transmission in wireless sensor networks by using Generalized Stochastic Petri Nets (GSPN). We studied two models: in the first the high priority requests have non-preemptive priority over lower ones while, in the second model, we applied the preemptive priority to the high priority requests. According to this study we can see that the preemptive priority is favorable to higher priority customers, because they are not influenced by lower priority customers at all. The advantage of our approach resides in the expressive power that the GSPN formalism offer in order to construct a simple model for the RF transmission in sensor networks. The numerical results are discussed and show the positive and negative effects of parameters on several performance Indices. The performance results obtained and compared to [4] showed that our model based on preemptive priority improves the network performances with better blocking probability compared to non preemptive one, especially for high priority requests. The results show significant performance improvements in the processing of high priority requests. The conclusion is that the proposed model can be implemented in sensor networks situations where some requests are considered more important than others such us: fire, explosions sound in the military field.

In future, we plan to extend our model to mixed priority with more sleeping period schemes.

References

1. Artalejo, J.R.: A classified bibliography of research on retrial queues: progress in 1990–1999. Top **7**, 187–211 (1999)

2. Artalejo, J.R.: Accessible bibliography on retrial queues: progress in 2000–2009. Math. Comput. Model. **51**, 1071–1081 (2010)
3. Bérczes, T., Sztrik, J., Orosz, P., Moyal, P., Limnios, N., Georgiadis, S.: Tool supported modeling of sensor communication networks by using finite-source priority retrial queues. Carpathian J. Electron. Comput. Eng. **5**, 13–18 (2012)
4. Bérczes, T., Almási, B., Sztrik, J., Kuki, A.: Modeling the RF communication in sensor networks by using finite-source retrial queueing system. Trans. Autom. Control Comput. Sci. **58**(72), 2–4 (2013). Scientific Bulletin of the Politehnica University of Timisoara, Romania
5. Choi, B.D., Park, K.K.: The M/G/1 retrial queue with Bernoulli schedule. Queueing Syst. **7**, 219–227 (1990)
6. Choi, B.D., Choi, K.B., Lee, Y.W.: M/G/1 retrial queueing system with two types of calls and finite capacity. Queueing Syst. **19**, 215–229 (1995)
7. Choi, B.D., Chang, Y.: Single server retrial queues with priority calls. Math. Comput. Model. **30**(3–4), 7–32 (1999)
8. Deng, J., Han, R., Mishra, S.: A performance evaluation of intrusion-tolerant routing in wireless sensor networks. In: Zhao, F., Guibas, L. (eds.) IPSN 2003. LNCS, vol. 2634, pp. 349–364. Springer, Heidelberg (2003). doi:10.1007/3-540-36978-3_23
9. Dimitriou, I.: Analysis of a priority retrial queue with dependent vacation scheme and application to power saving in wireless communication systems. Comput. J. **56**(11), 1363–1380 (2012)
10. Falin, G.I., Templeton, J.G.C.: Retrial Queues. Chapman and Hall, London (1997)
11. Falin, G.I.: A survey of retrial queues. Queueing Syst. **7**(2), 127–167 (1990)
12. Gharbi, N., Charabi, L.: Comparing random server and fastest free server disciplin. Int. J. Adv. Netw. Serv. **5**(1–2), 102–115 (2012)
13. Gupta, G., Younis, M.: Performance evaluation of load-balanced clustering of wireless sensor networks. In: 10th International Conference on Telecommunication, vol. 2 (2003)
14. Hakmi, S., Lekadir, O., Aïssani, D.: A GSPN formalism to obtain service-time probability of finite source-queue with different customers. In: International Conference on Natural Science and Applied Mathematics, ICNSAM, Dubai (2016)
15. Ikhlef, L., Lekadir, O., Aïssani, D.: MRSPN analysis of semi-Markovian finite source retrial queues. Ann. OR **247**, 141–167 (2016)
16. Liu, F., Blätke, M.A., Heiner, M., Yang, M.: Modelling and simulating reaction diffusion systems using coloured Petri nets. Comput. Biol. Med. **53**, 297–308 (2014)
17. Marsan, M.A., Balbo, M.G., Conte, G.: Models of Multiprocessor Systems, vol. 11, p. 294. The MIT Press, Massachusetts (1986)
18. Marsan, M.A., Balbo, G., Conte, G., Donatelli, S., Franceschinis, G.: Modelling with Generalized Stochastic Petri Nets. Wiley, New York (1995)
19. Molloy, M.K.: On the integration of delay and throughput measures in processing models, Ph.D. Thesis. University of California, Los Angeles (1981)
20. Molloy, M.K.: Performance analysis using stochastic petri nets. IEEE Trans. Comput. **C–31**, 913–917 (1982)
21. Petri, C.A.: Kommunikation mit automaten, Ph.D. dissertation, Institut für Instrumentelle Mathematik, University of Bonn, West Germany, pp. 65–377 (1962)
22. Wüchner, P., Sztrik, J., Meer, H.: Modeling wireless sensor networks using finite-source retrial queues with unreliable orbit. In: Hummel, K.A., Hlavacs, H., Gansterer, W. (eds.) PERFORM 2010. LNCS, vol. 6821, pp. 73–86. Springer, Heidelberg (2011). doi:10.1007/978-3-642-25575-5_7
23. Yang, T., Templeton, J.G.C.: A survey on retrial queues. Queueing Syst. **2**(3), 201–233 (1987)

Regression-Based Statistical Bounds on Software Execution Time

Peter Poplavko[1], Ayoub Nouri[1(✉)], Lefteris Angelis[2,3], Alexandros Zerzelidis[2], Saddek Bensalem[1], and Panagiotis Katsaros[2,3]

[1] Univ. Grenoble Alpes, VERIMAG, CNRS, 38000 Grenoble, France
ayoub.nouri@univ-grenoble-alpes.fr
[2] Information Technologies Institute, Centre of Research & Technology - Hellas,
6th km Xarilaou - Thermi, 57001 Thessaloniki, Greece
[3] Department of Informatics, Aristotle University of Thessaloniki,
Thessaloniki, Greece

Abstract. Our work aims at facilitating the schedulability analysis of non-critical systems, in particular those that have soft real-time constraints, where WCETs can be replaced by less stringent probabilistic bounds, which we call Maximal Execution Times (METs). In our approach, we can obtain adequate probabilistic execution time models by separating the non-random input data dependency from a modeling error that is purely random. To achieve this, we propose to take advantage of the rich set of available statistical model-fitting techniques, in particular linear regression. Although certainly the proposed technique cannot directly achieve extreme probability levels that are usually expected for WCETs, it is an attractive alternative for MET analysis, since it can arguably guarantee safe probabilistic bounds. We demonstrate our method on a JPEG decoder running on an industrial SPARC V8 processor.

1 Introduction

We propose a new statistical measurement-based method, for the timing analysis of software programs. Such methods aim at highly-probable execution time overestimations, as opposed to the 100% certain upper bounds given by common worst-case execution times (WCET) techniques. This option can be justified in many practical situations. For systems that do not have safety requirements (*e.g.*, car infotainment) that are characterized by weak, soft or firm real-time constraints, we can rely on statistical (over-)estimations based on extensive measurements that we call probabilistic *maximal* execution times (MET).

The methods used to estimate arguably reliable METs are referred to as *measurement-based timing analysis* (MBTA) techniques. In the recent research literature, the reliability of MBTA techniques has been improved, even to the level of considering them eligible for WCET estimates for hard real-time systems, under some restrictive hardware assumptions (*e.g.*, cache randomization).

The research leading to these results has received funding from the European Space Agency project MoSaTT-CMP, Contract No. 4000111814/14/NL/MH.

K. Barkaoui et al. (Eds.): VECoS 2017, LNCS 10466, pp. 48–63, 2017.
DOI: 10.1007/978-3-319-66176-6_4

Such estimates are the so-called probabilistic WCETs, *i.e.*, METs that hold at an extremely high probability $(1 - \alpha)$ with $\alpha = 10^{-15}$ per program execution [CSH+12] or 10^{-9} per hour, which corresponds to the most stringent requirements in safety-critical standards.

Analyses aiming to 'true' WCET (with $\alpha = 0$) are costly to adapt to new application domains and processor architectures, as they require the construction of complex exact models that have to be verified. The techniques based on extreme value theory (EVT) can ensure the levels of probability that render them suitable for WCET. However, these techniques assume that the execution times are random and identically distributed, a strong assumption that does not generally hold in practice. Execution times typically show significant autocorrelations and their probability distribution varies due to the input data dependencies.

For non safety-critical systems, one can settle for METs characterized by α a few orders of magnitude larger than that claimed by EVT methods (10^{-15}). In this case, it is possible to rely on a rich set of mature statistical model fitting tools, such as *linear regression*, which can handle the input data dependencies. In this paper, we propose a novel probabilistic MET analysis technique that builds upon linear regression and the associated statistical analyses.

The contributions of the paper are the following. In Sect. 2, we discuss MBTA and recall linear regression basics. In Sect. 3, we introduce a regression model, called Maximal Regression Model, that yields probabilistic upper bounds for METs estimation, using confidence intervals. A great challenge for building a regression model is to come up with the most influential explanatory variables of the execution time. For this, we propose, in the same section, step-wise regression, an iterative method for building a compact model including the most relevant variables. Since the proposed method is measurement-based, we also propose a statistical technique for assessing the input data in order to obtain pertinent measurements. In Sect. 4, we rely on all these techniques to propose a complete design flow for METs estimation. In Sect. 5, we demonstrate our flow using a JPEG decoder case study with a significant input data dependency, which runs on a state-of the art industrial SPARC V8 architecture with caches, reset at every execution start. The related work is further discussed along with the conclusions, in Sect. 6.

In [LS09], it was proposed to use linear regression for conservative execution time analysis, but without profiting from the rich statistics associated with it. More specifically, that work aims at 100% conservative estimates (without probabilities) and for this reason it focuses on non-statistical linear model fitting techniques. However, targeting 100% conservative estimates may result in a costly analysis, losing the advantage of regression. Moreover, their technique for calculating the regression parameters is rather *ad hoc* and is not described in detail. On the other hand, in [LS09], an important connection is established between linear regression and WCET analysis methodologies, which is based on implicit path enumeration.

In that work, some interesting possibilities are also shown for the explicit modeling of hardware effects, *e.g.*, pipelining, which could be used in our work.

However, for simplicity, in the present paper we do not address the hardware modeling issue directly, but undoubtedly this is an important future work matter. Nevertheless, since our analysis is based on measurements on real hardware and since the variability attributed to hardware is consequence of the variability of input data, we believe that hardware effects are covered indirectly up to a level of accuracy that may be appropriate for non safety-critical applications.

2 Common Probabilistic Techniques

In this section, we first review the general MBTA setting, and we recall the basics of linear regression while providing an interpretation in the context of MBTA.

2.1 Probabilistic Measurement-Based Timing Analysis

MBTA consists of initially performing multiple measurements of the program execution times and/or the execution times for its blocks of code, and a subsequent analysis to combine the results and thereafter to calculate the MET bound. The probabilistic variant of MBTA utilizes statistical methods [CSH+12] for the analysis phase.

We denote by Y the execution time, which in general depends on some other variables, X_i. An MET bound with probability $(1-\alpha)$ can be obtained by finding the minimal y such that $Pr\{Y < y\} \geq (1 - \alpha)$. Suppose that Y is random with a known continuous distribution f, denoted $Y \sim f$. A possible solution is given through the *quantile function* of that distribution: $y = Q_f(1 - \alpha)$, such that, by definition, $Pr\{Y < y\} = (1 - \alpha)$.

In the case when Y is normally distributed, *i.e.*, $Y \sim \mathcal{N}(\mu_Y, \sigma_Y)$, we have $y = \mu_Y + \sigma_Y \Phi^{-1}(1 - \alpha)$, where Φ^{-1} is the quantile function for $\mathcal{N}(0, 1)$. In order to calculate METs using this formula, the 'mean' μ_Y and the 'standard deviation' σ_Y have to be estimated from measurements with enough precision, which requires a large enough number of measured Y samples. The normal distribution can describe many random physical variables, especially noise and measurement errors in model parameters. Furthermore, it provides access to a rich set of mature statistical tools for reliably estimating parameters from measurements.

Unfortunately, neither normal nor any other distribution law can be justified to describe execution times *directly*. Therefore probabilistic MBTA techniques do not consider execution time itself as a random variable, but only some of its characteristics. For example, the normal distribution can be adequate if we suppose that we dispose of an 'oracle model' that for each program run can predict its execution time Y almost perfectly, but still makes a small error due to various independent factors ignored by the 'oracle'. Then it is reasonable to apply the normal distribution law to characterize the error of the 'oracle'. This is, in fact, the underlying idea of our method. It should be mentioned, though, that normal distribution is only adequate for the values of α that are not too small, and thus this idea can be applied only for soft real-time systems.

To sustain very small α, MBTA analyses use EVT [CSH+12]. They apply EVT probability distribution laws, again, not to the execution times directly but to their upper bounds. However, as noted in [CSH+12], to justify the EVT-based techniques an important requirement is that the execution times should be independent and identically distributed (*iid*) random variables. However, this requirement is typically violated due to the dependency on input data via multiple conditional branches and loops in the program. The input data parameters are not *iid* and in a certain sense they are even 'non-random' (no practically adequate distribution law can characterize them). Therefore for programs with complex control flow the applicability of EVT-based techniques is difficult to justify. By contrast, using linear regression, our method separates the non-random factors from the modeling error. The regression is our 'oracle model'.

2.2 Linear Regression in the Nutshell

Linear regression is mostly used to predict *average* execution times [EFH04, HJY+10]. Though our goal is to produce *upper bounds*, we use the same approach as the starting point. The main goal of linear regression is to model a variable of interest Y, called dependent variable, with explanatory variables (or predictors) X_i. The fundamental requirements for the validity of such an analysis is that (i) X_i should have approximately linear contribution to Y and (ii) the approximation error should be normally distributed. The first requirement is realistic since one can always decompose execution time as a linear combination of code block contributions. The second requirement validity is motivated in the previous subsection and is further confirmed by experiments (see Sect. 5).

The concrete values of X_i represent the possibility to 'explain' (or 'predict'), with some precision, the concrete value of Y. For MET, an important implication is that if we can obtain bounds for X_i this helps us to derive a bound on Y as well. In linear regression [DS81], the dependence of Y on X_i is given by

$$Y(n) = \beta_0 + \beta_1 X_1(n) + \ldots + \beta_{p-1} X_{p-1}(n) + \epsilon(n) \tag{1}$$

In the context of MBTA, the dependent variable Y is the program execution time, and $Y(n)$ is its nth observation in a series of measurements. Coefficients β_i are *parameters* that have to be *fitted* to measurements $Y(n)$ to minimize the *regression error* $\epsilon(n)$. The dependent variable Y, the error ϵ, and the parameters β_i are components of the execution time and therefore they can be modeled as real numbers. Their probability distributions are assumed to be continuous, as it is usually the case for timing metrics in statistical MET methods [CSH+12, BCP02]. On the contrary, the predictors X_i are discrete; they are in fact non-negative integers that count the number of times that some important branch or loop iteration in the program is taken or skipped. The corresponding parameter β_i can be either positive, to reflect the processor time spent per unit of X_i, or negative, to reflect the economized time.

From a probabilistic MBTA perspective, Eq. (1) has a concrete meaning. It captures the 'non-randomness' of Y by building a model $\sum_i \beta_i X_i(n)$ which 'explains' its dependence on some factors X_i, with different weights β_i, reflecting the complexity of the program. Ideally, the remaining 'non-explained' part is a random variable $\beta_0 + \epsilon(n)$ with β_0 representing the mean value and $\epsilon(n)$ the random deviation, whereby $\epsilon(n)$ are hopefully independent and normally distributed, by $\mathcal{N}(0, \sigma_\epsilon)$.

The probability bounds proposed in this work are accurate only if this assumption is valid. However, they are generally believed to be robust with respect to deviations from the normal distribution. We can justify the 'randomness' of ϵ by the hypotheses that all non-random factors have been captured by X_i. Also, the normality of ϵ can be justified using the central limit theorem based on the intuitive observation that the sources of execution time variation, e.g., non-linearity of X_i, are additive in nature and independent.

The parameters β_i are 'ideal' abstractions whose exact values are unknown. They can only be estimated based on measurement data, e.g., with the *least-squares method*. We denote by b_i the estimate of β_i and by $\widehat{Y}$ the estimate of Y. Hence, when ϵ is 0, we get an *unbiased regression model*

$$\widehat{Y}(n) = b_0 + b_1 X_1(n) + \ldots + b_{p-1} X_{p-1}(n) \tag{2}$$

whereas the difference $e_{\text{res}}(n) = Y(n) - \widehat{Y}(n)$, called *residual*, serves as an estimation of the error $\epsilon(n)$: $\epsilon(n) \approx e_{\text{res}}(n)$.

For more convenience, we use a vector notation. Let $\mathbf{x} = (X_i \mid i = 0 \ldots (p-1))$, where $X_0 = 1$ is an artificial constant predictor that corresponds to b_0, and $\mathbf{b}$ the vector of parameters estimators. The regression model can thus be seen as the product of $\mathbf{b}$ and $\mathbf{x}$.

The model parameters are obtained from a set of measurements - the so-called training set - through a process known as *model training* (or *fitting*). In our case, the training set consists of N measurements of $Y(n)$ and $\mathbf{x}(n)$, with N recommended in practice to be $N \gg p$, i.e. at least $N > 5p$ [LS09]. We consider a training-set with predictors measurements organized into a $p \times N$ matrix $\mathbf{X}^{\text{train}} = [\mathbf{x}(1) \ldots \mathbf{x}(N)]$, and the corresponding N-dimensional vector of execution time measurements $\mathbf{y}^{\text{train}} = (Y(n) \mid n = 1 \ldots N)$.

3   Linear Regression for MET

In this section, we introduce the maximal regression model for conservative estimation of MET. Then, we propose a technique to identify the most relevant predictors for the model. Since we rely on measurements, we also present a technique for collecting enough input data to ensure a good coverage.

3.1   The Maximal Regression Model

The least-squares method provides a closed form formula to compute the vector $\mathbf{b}$ from $\mathbf{X}^{\text{train}}$ and $\mathbf{y}^{\text{train}}$ (see [DS81]). However, each least-square model parameter b_i is itself a random variable, because it is obtained from a training-set $\mathbf{y}^{\text{train}}$

'perturbed' with a random error ϵ. It turns out from theoretical studies that each estimate b_i can be seen itself as a sample from a normal distribution, since different training sets would lead to distinct samples b_i from the distribution shown in Fig. 1. This distribution has as mean value the unknown parameter β_i and therefore, the estimator samples b_i are likely to be close to β_i.

For the estimation of METs, the model parameters b that are simply '*close*' to β are not adequate. We prefer a conservative model consisting of parameters b^+ that are likely to be *larger* than β. Such parameters can be obtained using the notion of confidence interval, which is an interval $\Delta b = [b^-, b^+]$ that likely contains β (see Fig. 1), such that

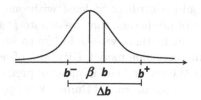

Fig. 1. Parameter confidence interval

$$Pr\{\beta \in \Delta b\} = (1 - \alpha) \tag{3}$$

where α is some small value, usually specified in percents, *e.g.*, $\alpha = 5\ \%$. By symmetry with the distribution of b, if we use b^+, the upper bound of Δb, as coefficient estimator, then our model in the above example is conservative, *i.e.*, with probability $(1 - \alpha/2)$. Therefore, our *maximal regression model* is not the usual unbiased regression model of Eq. (2), but

$$\widehat{Y}^+(n) = b_0^+ + b_1^+ X_1(n) + \ldots + b_{p-1}^+ X_{p-1}(n) + \epsilon^+ \tag{4}$$

where we assume that ϵ^+ is the (probabilistic) maximal error. By analogy to b^+, we set it to a value, such that $Pr\{\epsilon(n) < \epsilon^+\} \geq (1 - \alpha/2)$. Because $\epsilon \sim \mathcal{N}(0, \sigma_\epsilon)$ we could use $\sigma_\epsilon \cdot \Phi^{-1}(1 - \alpha/2)$. However, just as the case where we did not know the exact value of β_i and had to obtain an estimate b_i instead, we do not know the value of σ_ϵ and have to use $\epsilon^+ = \widehat{\sigma}_\epsilon^+ \cdot \Phi^{-1}(1 - \alpha)$. The estimate $\widehat{\sigma}_\epsilon^+$ should be pessimistic, *i.e.*, it should be biased to be larger than the value of σ_ϵ with a high probability. When obtaining its unbiased estimate, $\widehat{\sigma}_\epsilon$, the sum of squares of regression 'residual' is involved, $e_{\text{res}}^2(n) = (Y(n) - \widehat{Y}(n))^2$, which is calculated from the training set. Based on the properties of the residual [DS81], we can show that for $\widehat{\sigma}_\epsilon^+ = \sqrt{\sum_{n=1}^{N} (Y(n) - \widehat{Y}(n))^2 / Q_{\chi^2(N-p)}(\alpha/2)}$, we have $Pr\{\sigma_\epsilon < \widehat{\sigma}_\epsilon^+\} = (1 - \alpha/2)$, where $Q_{\chi^2(N-p)}$ is the quantile function of a χ^2 distribution with $(N - p)$ degrees of freedom.

By comparison of Eqs. (1) and (4) we can see that all the terms of the first are likely to be inferior to the corresponding terms of the second, and therefore $\widehat{Y}^+(n)$ is a probabilistic bound of $Y(n)$. Moreover, we have

$$Pr\{Y(n) < \widehat{Y}^+(n)\} \geq \left(1 - \frac{(p+2)\alpha}{2}\right) \tag{5}$$

since we have $(p + 2)$ parameter estimates.

3.2   Identifying the Predictors: Stepwise Regression

When modeling execution times using a regression model, the simplest way to construct the set of predictors is to create a predictor for every block of code of the program that counts the number of block's executions, see *e.g.*, [LS09]. In this case, every program operator that introduces branching, *e.g.*, loop, 'if' operator, would contribute at least with one predictor. This results in a relatively large set of predictors, that we denote P and we call it the set of *potential* predictors. In our method, we would like to *identify* only a small sufficient subset of P for our regression model. By abuse of notation, we call it p (*i.e.*, the same notation for the set and the number of predictors).

By simple rule of thumb $N > 5p$, we see that by ignoring one predictor we can save 5 measurements. However, the rationale is not merely a less costly model, but also the so-called *principle of parsimony*: a model should not contain redundant variables. Many predictors are interdependent, as, for example, in nested loops, where the (total) number of inner-loop iterations is likely to have a strong dependence on the number of outer-loop iterations. From a pair of dependent variables we can try to keep only one, while attributing the small additional effect of the other variable to random error ϵ. If we keep too many variables in P, we will have overfitting, which means that our model will perfectly fit the training set, but it will not be able to reliably predict any program execution outside this set. The reason for this is that an overfitted model would exactly fit not only the 'true' linear dependence $\beta_i X_i$, but also the particular sample of non-linear random noise 'ϵ' encountered in the training set, but not in other samples.

In most of the previous literature on execution time modeling, the identification of predictors is either manual or *ad hoc*. Here we point to a practical and mathematically sound algorithm for identifying the subset p of P. In applied mathematical studies, the identification of a subset of useful predictors in a set of candidates is an important problem to solve (see Ch. 15 of [DS81]).

An overall strategy of most such methods is based on starting with one predictor and observing the reduction of the model error when adding new predictors. It is thus expected that at a certain number of predictors, the error reaches saturation and new variables do not reduce it significantly anymore. At this point, we stop by adopting the hypothesis that the remaining error represents a 'random noise'. One of the most well-established methods is *stepwise regression*, which we propose for use in the MET analysis. This algorithm is outlined here by the following simple procedure (see [DS81] for details). A tentative set p of identified predictors is maintained, containing initially (for $p = 1$) only the constant predictor $X_0 = 1$, which is always kept in the set. The algorithm first tries to add a variable that is 'worthwhile' to add and then to remove a variable that is not worthwhile to keep; the same step is repeated until no progress can be made. A variable is added when it is moved from P to p and it is removed when moving it backwards. When there is no variable that can be added or removed, the algorithm stops.

The criterion for considering a predictor 'worth' to be included depends on the other variables that are already in p; the decision is based on evaluating the least-squares regression $\widehat{Y}$ with and without the candidate predictor. Intuitively, a predictor is 'worth' if its 'signal to noise ratio' is significantly large. The 'noise' here is the total model error, which is evaluated based on the residual sum of squares and the 'signal' is the contribution of the variable to the variance of $\widehat{Y}$. If the variance does not change significantly (compared to the total error) when the predictor is kept, then the predictor is not 'worth'. The whole procedure is controlled by a parameter α^{sw} that sets a threshold for variable acceptance and rejection, and is based on statistical hypothesis-testing procedures under the assumption that modeling error is normally distributed.

3.3   Quality of Input Data: Cook's Distance

The set of measurements should represent all important scenarios that may occur at runtime. To ensure this, the engineer should discover the most influential algorithmic complexity parameters of the program that may vary at run time. Then, it is essential to obtain an input data set, where every *combination* of these factors is represented *fairly*.

For the linear regression, a useful mathematical metric of input-data quality is *Cook's distance*. Given a set of measurements, this metric ranks every measurement n by a numeric 'distance' value $D(n)$ that indicates the amount to which the measurement influences the whole regression model. The regression model should not be dominated by 'odd' measurements; it is generally recommended to have $D(n) < 1$ or even $D(n) < 4/N$. For convenience, let us refer to the measurements with $D(n) > \theta$ as the *bad samples*, for some threshold θ. These samples should be examined, and one should either add more similar samples (so that they are not exceptional anymore) or remove them from the training set (keep them for testing).

4   A Design Flow for MET

We build upon the techniques presented in the previous section to present a complete design flow for MET estimation[1]. In this section, we give a simplified view of the flow and we discuss its steps (see Fig. 2). The first phase of the flow is the instrumentation of the input program in order to obtain measurements. Then, the most relevant predictors p are identified. Finally, the model to estimate MET is produced in the model construction phase.

4.1   Instrumentation and Measurements

In some MBTA approaches, multiple blocks of code may have to be instrumented and measured [BCP02]. Such instrumentation can be intrusive, whereas it is

---

[1] Sources (Octave) can be found at www-verimag.imag.fr/~nouri/exec-time-lra.

Fig. 2. A simplified view of the MET design flow

likely to obtain inaccurate results when adding the block contributions, due to various hardware effects (e.g. pipelining).

However, the instrumentation is not intrusive in a regression-based approach, where measurements are end-to-end, *i.e.*, they include the entire program. For the end-to-end measurements, $Y(n)$, the program has to be instrumented only at the start and the end. As for the measurements needed to construct the set of potential predictors P and to obtain their values $X_i(n), i \in P$ the instrumented program does not have to run on the target platform; a workstation can be used instead, but it is essential to run the program with the same input data, as those used for the $Y(n)$ measurements. We refer to these measurements as functional simulations[2].

The instrumentation for functional simulations consists of inserting *instrumentation points (i-points)* into the source code of the program. The i-points are inserted at every point, where the control flow diverges or converges, *e.g.*, at the start/end of the conditional and loop blocks, at the branches of the conditional statements *et cetera*. An i-point is a subroutine call passing the i-point identifier 'q', *e.g.*, in Fig. 3 we have points with $q = 1, 2, \ldots, 5$. The goal is to get a measurement record about the path followed in an simulation run. This information consists of the sequence of i-points visited during the simulation run, which is called *i-point trace* and it is denoted as $Tr(n) = (q_1, q_2, q_3, \ldots)$. Examples of traces for Fig. 3 are (1,2,4), (1,2,3,4,5), and (1,2,4,5,5,5).

From the traces we automatically detect the set of basic blocks, which correspond one-to-one to predictors in P. We count the number of their occurrences in the trace, denoted $f(q_1, q_2)$, where q_1

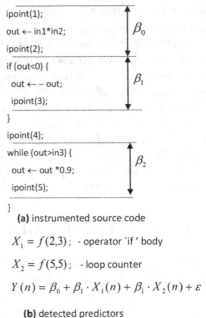

(a) instrumented source code

$X_1 = f(2,3)$; - operator 'if' body

$X_2 = f(5,5)$; - loop counter

$Y(n) = \beta_0 + \beta_1 \cdot X_1(n) + \beta_1 \cdot X_2(n) + \varepsilon$

(b) detected predictors

Fig. 3. Instrumentation and predictors

---

[2] For a higher precision, instead of instrumenting the source code one could instrument the binary code for the target platform and run it on an ISS simulator for construction of P, while still using non-instrumented version for the end-to-end execution time measurements on the target platform.

and q_2 are the i-point boundaries of the block. We have $\forall k, X_k = f(q_i, q_j)$ for some i, j. For the example in Fig. 3 we would detect a predictor $f(2,3)$, which corresponds to the 'if' operator body, and predictor $f(5,5)$, which corresponds to one loop iteration. For a general procedure, we refer the reader to [PAN+16].

4.2 Final Flow Steps

As sketched in Fig. 2, having done the measurements and detected the set of potential predictors P, we identify the final set of predictors $p \subseteq P$, as described in Sect. 3.2. It is worth mentioning that measurements are separated into two sets, a training set $(\mathbf{X}^{\text{train}}, \mathbf{y}^{\text{train}})$ and a test set $(\mathbf{X}^{\text{test}}, \mathbf{y}^{\text{test}})$[3], and that only the former is used to construct the model, whereas the latter is used to evaluate its quality. The next step of the flow is the construction of the maximal regression model, as described in Sect. 3.1. This phase will instantiate the model, *i.e.*, given the set of predictors and their associated measurements $\mathbf{X}^{\text{train}}, \mathbf{y}^{\text{train}}$, it will estimate their coefficients, *et cetera*. In this phase, we also evaluate the quality of input data as described in Sect. 3.3. Finally, we calculate a MET bound.

Pragmatic MET. Our maximal regression model could be used within the context of the *implicit path enumeration technique* (IPET) [LS09]. In this case, the MET would be computed by

$$\epsilon^+ + \max_{\mathbf{x} \in \mathbb{X}} \left(\sum_{i=0}^{p-1} b_i^+ X_i \right),$$ with $\mathbb{X}$ the set of all vectors $\mathbf{x}$ that can result from feasible program paths. This is achieved by solving the integer linear programming (ILP) problem with a set of constraints on the variables X_i. The constraints are derived from a *static program analysis*, which requires sophisticated tools, as well as from user provided hints, such as loop bounds. We have not yet implemented the IPET method in our flow. Currently, we assume that for each predictor we have (either from measurements or user hint) its minimal and maximal bound, X^- and X^+ and we calculate the pessimistic estimate: $\epsilon^+ + b_0^+ + \sum_{i=1}^{p-1} (bX)_i^+$, where $(bX)^+$ is $b^+ X^+$ if $b^+ > 0$ or $b^+ X^-$ otherwise. We refer to this estimate as the *pragmatic MET*.

It is true that the pragmatic MET can be very pessimistic; for example, in switch-case branching it may associate with every case a separate predictor and then assume that they all take the maximal value simultaneously. Nevertheless, the pragmatic MET is safe with the probability bound (5) if the regression model itself is safe with this bound.

5   A JPEG Decoder on a SPARC Platform

We use a JPEG decoder program written in C[4] to illustrate our method. The JPEG decoder processes the header and the main body of a JPEG file. Basically,

---

[3] A common practice is to consider 70% for the training set and 30% for the test set.
[4] Downloaded from Internet, presumably authored by P. Guerrier and G. Janssen 1998.

the main body consists of a sequence of compressed MCUs (Minimum Coded Units) of 16×16 or 8×8 pixels. An MCU contains pixel blocks also referred to as 'color components', as they encode different color ingredients. In the color format '4:1:1' an MCU contains six blocks. For monochromatic images, the MCU contains only one pixel block. The pixel blocks are represented by a matrix of Discrete Cosine Transform (DCT) coefficients, which are encoded efficiently over few bits, so that a whole pixel block can fit in only a few bytes.

The hardware for the execution time measurements was an FPGA board featuring a SPARC V8 processor with a 7-stage pipeline, a double-precision FPU, a 4 KB instruction cache, a 4 KB data cache, a 256 KB Level-2 cache, and an SDRAM. The data caches were reset at every new program run (*i.e.*, after loading a new JPEG image), so that the data caches are always empty at the beginning.

5.1 Instrumentation and Measurements

We used 99 different JPEG images of different sizes and color formats, which yields 99 execution traces including the predictors X_i and the execution time Y.[5] From the generated traces we detected 103 potential predictors. We then randomly split the complete set of 99 measurements into $N = 70$ for the training set, and 29 for the test set used to verify the regression model. In the training set, 8 predictors showed up as constants and they were therefore eliminated, thus ending up with $P = 95$ potential predictors, plus one constant $X_0 = 1$ added by default. Since we had a training set size $N = 70$, by the rule of thumb, we should not exceed $N/5 = 14$ variables, to avoid overfitting.

It is worth mentioning that the maximal observed execution time (over the whole set of measurements) corresponds to an image of a particularly large size, yielding *maximal measured time* of 23643 Mcycles, while the *mean time* was only 1000 MCycles. In the remaining discussion, all timing values (*e.g.*, errors) are reported in Megacycle units. We use $\alpha = 0.05$ for the maximal regression parameters and MET, but we also present the final estimate for $\alpha = 0.00005$.

5.2 Predictors Identification and Model Construction

Basic Model. The simplest model to build is when $p = 1$, *i.e.*, when the execution time is modeled as a purely random variable $\beta_0 + \epsilon(n)$ without non-random contributors. This case corresponds to a naïve measurement-based method where the execution time does not capture the non-random factors. In this case, we cannot expect good results with such a strong input data dependency as in JPEG decoders. Indeed, we carried out a normality test for Y using the Kolmogorov-Smirnov test that reported only a mere 2% likelihood, which was not surprising as the histogram for Y was considerably skewed and had a few extreme values due to images of exceptionally large size.

---

[5] We could not obtain more measurements because the FPGA card was available for a limited period of time, and loading data into it required some manual work.

The obtained error in this case is large (compared to the mean) $\epsilon^+ = 6650$ and the *pragmatic MET* is ≈8000, which underestimates the maximal measured time; this adversity is the consequence of the relatively large model error whose distribution was essentially not normal and which was actually not random (it could be easily controlled, *e.g.*, made large by using large JPEG images).

In line with our methodology, these observations point to a need of adding more predictors into the model (*e.g.*, those characterizing the image size) in order to ensure a smaller, random and normally distributed error, so that the computation of MET is more accurate.

Our Method. We first tune the α^{sw} (≈20%) to obtain $p = 6$, *i.e.*, to have 5 predictors. Table 1 shows the identified variables – in the order of their identification – and the corresponding MET calculation on the training set. The meaning of the identified variables is the following. The first predictor $f(271, 244)$ corresponds to the *byte count* in the 'main body' of JPEG. The second basic-block counter $f(90, 30)$ gives the *pixel block count* specifically for those blocks that had correct prediction of the 0-th DCT coefficient. Typically, such blocks are not costly in terms of needed bytes for encoding. At the same time, the contribution of the costly blocks can be captured by the first predictor. Hence, the $f(90, 30)$ as second predictor can account for the additional computations that were not accounted for by the first predictor; a similar variable in P, the *total* pixel block count, $f(406, 26)$, would give less additional information and hence was not identified by our method.

The remaining predictors have less impact on the execution time. The third predictor, $f(101, 101)$, corresponds to the number of *elements in the color format* minus one, *e.g.*, $5 = 6 - 1$ for the 4:1:1 format and 0 for monochromatic images. Equivalently, it gives the number of pixel blocks per MCU block minus one. We note that this predictor has a negative regression coefficient. The JPEG decoding is characterized by two related cost components: a cost per pixel block (reflected by the first two predictors) and a highly correlated cost per MCU block. The more pixel blocks fit into one MCU, the less overhead per pixel block has the MCU processing and this presumably explains why the found coefficient is negative. The fourth identified predictor, $f(80, 81)$, counts the number of *'padded'* *image dimensions*, X and Y, *i.e.*, the dimensions which are not exactly proportional to the MCU size (16 or 8 pixels). When an image has such dimensions, less processing is required and less data copying for 'partial' MCU blocks, which presumably explains the negative coefficient for this predictor. Finally, the predictor $f(409, 410)$ is zero for colored images. This predictor counts the total number of MCUs in monochromatic images and its impact is presumably complementary to that of $f(101, 101)$.

The obtained *pragmatic MET* is 26696, which, as we expected, exceeds 23643, the *observed maximal time*. For the MET, we used the X^+ and X^- observed in the measurements. We recall that the pragmatic MET is likely to incur extra overestimation by including unfeasible paths. In fact, this is presumably the case for the presented model, as the calculation in Table 1 may combine a relatively

Table 1. Stepwise regression results in the training set

p	b^-	b^+	X^-	X^+	$(bX)^+$
(Constant)	409.660	637.29	1	1	637
$f(271, 244)$	0.010	0.011	3688	1818500	19752
$f(90, 30)$	0.055	0.070	28	27215	1917
$f(101, 101)$	−49.506	−11.530	0	5	0
$f(80, 81)$	−113.010	−26.009	0	2	0
$f(409, 410)$	0.013	0.022	0	192280	4150
ϵ^+	−	−	−	−	240
Pragmatic MET	−	−	−	−	26696

large byte and block count that is typically required for colored images with pessimistic contributions of the predictors representing monochromatic images. With the IPET approach this possibility would be excluded and a more realistic worst-case vector **x** would have been obtained. A lower bound on hypothetical IPET results with the given model is 25764, which is calculated as the observed maximum value of $\widehat{Y}^+(n)$. Compared to $p = 1$, we see a significantly smaller error $\epsilon^+ = 240$. In the test set, we saw reasonably tight overestimations from $\widehat{Y}^+(n)$, however, two underestimations were detected. Analyzing these two samples, we saw that they had Cook's distance significantly larger than all other samples.

Our quality of input data assurance procedure has moved the two samples from the training to the test set and we re-constructed the model for $p = 6$. The obtained error was $\epsilon^+ = 52$ and we observed a tight overestimation for all samples. The normality test of the residual returned 26% likelihood on the training set. The MET has become less accurate, reaching 28048. This is presumably explained by the degraded stability of regression accuracy for the bad samples; the sample that provided X^+ and maximal Y was among such samples. This corresponded to a monochromatic image of exceptionally large size, whereas a vast majority of other samples were color images of much smaller size. In practice, such a situation should be avoided by well prepared measurement data. For technical reasons we could not repair the situation by adding more measurements but we decided to keep the bad samples for illustrative purposes. An observation that should be made, though, is that the instability did not result in unsafe underestimation, but instead in a safe overestimation.

By experimenting with larger values of p, we found that the model with $p = 8$ was optimal. The error ϵ^+ was reduced to 35 and stopped improving, thus showing saturation. With more variables, a degradation of model tightness was observed, probably because the new parameters b started getting 'blurred', showing a Δb much larger than b. The optimal $p = 8$ yielded 97% error normality likelihood, with tight overestimations for all measured samples except for the bad ones; the resulting MET was 56538, not particularly tight due to bad samples, but safe. By (5) this estimate corresponded to $\mathcal{P}r > 0.725$ – for $\alpha = 0.05$. The

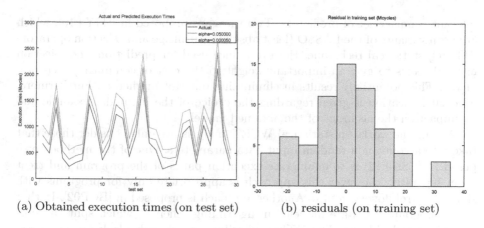

(a) Obtained execution times (on test set)   (b) residuals (on training set)

Fig. 4. Maximal regression model results for $p = 8$

MET estimations using the same model at $\mathcal{P}r > 0.999725$ amounts to 58859. As it is shown in Fig. 4a, the corresponding maximal regression model showed tight overestimations over the measurements not only for $\alpha = 0.05$ but also for $\alpha = 0.00005$. In Fig. 4b, the histogram of residual error is shown that is close to the normal distribution. This is in line with the 97% estimate of normality test and it justifies the use of statistical formulas associated with linear regression.

6   Related Work

Historically, linear regression and other model fitting techniques have been mostly used to predict *average*, not conservative, software performance in terms of execution time, *e.g.,* [EFH04], and energy consumption. A regression for *maximal* execution time was proposed in [LS09], but, unlike our work, their regression model is not based on statistical techniques. Instead, the authors sketch an *ad hoc* linear programming based approach and they admit that additional future work is still required. In contrast to our work, *all* potential predictors are included in the model, instead of a small subset of the significant ones, and therefore their techniques presumably require many more measurements to avoid overfitting, and more costly calculations to estimate all parameters. The coverage criteria are based on existence of an hypothetical exact model with a large enough number of variables, which should be known, whereas we tolerate presence of error and estimate the coverage probabilistically. On the other hand, they have showed how a maximal regression model, such as ours, could be combined with existing complementary WCET techniques for calculating tighter execution time bounds than our pragmatic MET formula.

In [HJY+10], regression analysis is used in the context execution time prediction. The proposed method, called SPORE, considers polynomial regression models, as opposed to our work. Although it fundamentally differs from our work, the SPORE method is faced with similar challenges, namely, identifying a relevant compact set of predictors. Two ways are proposed in [HJY+10], which are both variants of the LASSO (least absolute shrinkage and selection operator) [HTF09] statistical technique. However, since used for prediction, the selection method seems to give an important weight to the cost of computing each predictor. This potentially results in eliminating relevant predictors. Furthermore, no clear indication is given regarding the choice of the input data sample and its impact on the accuracy of the obtained model.

Among the works on statistical WCET analysis, we only consider those that take into account non-random input data parameters. One of the methods proposed in [CSH+12] is to enumerate execution paths of the program and treat them separately, however this approach is appropriate only for programs with simple control flow structure. Another approach is proposed in [BCP02]. In that work, program paths are modeled using 'timing schema', which split the program into code blocks. The WCET distributions of each block are measured separately and then the results for the different blocks are combined. However, this approach requires executing instrumentation points together with timing measurements, which introduces the unwanted probe effect.

7   Conclusions

In this paper, we have presented a new regression-based technique for the estimation of probabilistic execution time bounds. Unlike WCET analysis techniques, it cannot ensure safe estimates at very high probability levels, but it can be utilized for preliminary WCET estimates and in the context of non safety-critical systems. We have described a complete methodology for model construction, which includes an algorithm for identifying the proper model variables and an algorithm for finding conservative model parameters. So far, this technique was tested with only one program, a JPEG decoder, through a limited set of measurements. Nevertheless, it has shown promising results, by giving tight overestimations in the tests.

In future work, it would be interesting to combine the presented regression technique with a complete WCET analysis flow using implicit path enumeration techniques and to study how to model hardware effects using specially defined predictors, similarly to [LS09]. An investigation of possible connections between regression and extreme value theory is also needed, in order to produce high-probability bounds, as in [CSH+12]. Finally, we observed that by putting too many variables into the multi-variate regression analysis the estimation of model parameters is weakened, which manifests in 'blurred' parameter confidence intervals. Therefore, it is interesting to investigate splitting the program into blocks characterized by a smaller set of variables and combining the results by their joint distributions, as in [BCP02].

References

[BCP02] Bernat, G., Colin, A., Petters, S.M.: WCET analysis of probabilistic hard real-time system. In: Proceedings of RTSS 2002, pp. 279–288. IEEE (2002)

[CSH+12] Cucu-Grosjean, L., Santinelli, L., Houston, M., Lo, C., Vardanega, T., Kosmidis, L., Abella, J., Mezzetti, E., Quiñones, E., Cazorla, F.J.: Measurement-based probabilistic timing analysis for multi-path programs. In: Proceedings of ECRTS 2012, pp. 91–101. IEEE (2012)

[DS81] Draper, N.R., Smith, H.: Applied Regression Analysis, 2nd edn. Wiley, New York (1981)

[EFH04] Eskenazi, E., Fioukov, A., Hammer, D.: Performance prediction for component compositions. In: Crnkovic, I., Stafford, J.A., Schmidt, H.W., Wallnau, K. (eds.) CBSE 2004. LNCS, vol. 3054, pp. 280–293. Springer, Heidelberg (2004). doi:10.1007/978-3-540-24774-6_25

[HJY+10] Huang, L., Jia, J., Yu, B., Chun, B.-G., Maniatis, P., Naik, M.: Predicting execution time of computer programs using sparse polynomial regression. In: Proceedings of NIPS 2010, pp. 883–891. Curran Associates Inc., USA (2010)

[HTF09] Hastie, T., Tibshirani, R., Friedman, J.: The Elements of Statistical Learning: Data Mining, Inference and Prediction, 2nd edn. Springer, New York (2009)

[LS09] Lisper, B., Santos, M.: Model identification for WCET analysis. In: Proceedings of RTAS 2009, pp. 55–64. IEEE (2009)

[PAN+16] Poplavko, P., Angelis, L., Nouri, A., Zerzelidis, A., Bensalem, S., Katsaros, P.: Regression-based statistical bounds on software execution time. Technical report TR-2016-7, Verimag Research Report (2016)

WCET Analysis by Model Checking
for a Processor with Dynamic Branch Prediction

Armel Mangean, Jean-Luc Béchennec[(✉)], Mikaël Briday, and Sébastien Faucou

CNRS, École Centrale de Nantes, Université de Nantes, LS2N,
44000 Nantes, France
jean-luc.bechennec@ls2n.fr

Abstract. In this paper, we investigate the case for model checking
in the WCET analysis of pipelined processors with dynamic branch and
target prediction. We consider a microarchitecture inspired by the e200z4
Power 32-bit architecture, with an instruction cache, a dynamic branch
prediction mechanism, a branch target buffer (BTB) and an instruction
prefetch buffer. The conjoint operation of all these components produce
a very complex behaviour that is difficult to analyse with tight and sound
static analysis techniques. We show that model checking techniques can
actually be used to compute WCET bounds for this kind of architectures.

1   Introduction

Embedded control systems found in domains like automotive, industrial automation, or robotics, have to satisfy real-time requirements stemming from the
dynamics of the physical plant they control. To design these systems, the worst
case execution time (WCET) of the tasks must be computed. The execution time
of a task is a function of its inputs and the initial state of the microarchitecture.
As it is usually not possible to run the real system with all possible combinations
of these variables, techniques have been developed to statically estimate upper
bounds on the WCET [17].

In this context, different approaches have been investigated. One of them is
model checking. Using model checking in the context of WCET analysis has been
debated in the scientific community. In [16] it is deemed as ineffective because
of the state space explosion problem. In [14], it is claimed that it can actually
improve the precision of WCET analysis by leveraging dynamic analysis[1] of
microarchitecture features. Both points actually hold: model checking allows to
compute more precise bounds but suffers from scalability issues. However, recent
results show that model checking sufficiently scales to tackle the WCET analysis
of systems based on core such as ARM7 or ARM9 [2,4].

In this paper, we investigate the case for model checking in the WCET analysis of architectures typically found in embedded control systems. We consider a
core architecture inspired by the e200z4 Power 32-bit architecture. More precisely,

---

[1] Metzner use dynamic analysis to designate techniques that analyze concrete paths
in the system, as opposed to static analysis that consider abstract paths.

© Springer International Publishing AG 2017
K. Barkaoui et al. (Eds.): VECoS 2017, LNCS 10466, pp. 64–78, 2017.
DOI: 10.1007/978-3-319-66176-6_5

we consider a microarchitecture with an instruction cache (ICache), a dynamic branch prediction mechanism, a branch target buffer (BTB), a prefetch instruction buffer, and a 5-stage pipeline[2]. The conjoint operation of all these components produce a very complex behaviour that is difficult to analyse with tight and sound static analysis techniques. We show that model checking techniques can actually be used to compute WCET bounds for this kind of architectures.

Contribution and Outline. To the best of our knowledge, this paper is the first to propose an analysis integrating at the same time the ICache, the branch target buffer, and the instruction prefetch buffer. Among the work exploring model checking for WCET analysis, it is the first to tackle a dynamic branch prediction mechanism. Based on this analysis, we also provide an evaluation of the impact of dynamic branch prediction and BTB on the estimation of WCET for embedded control systems.

The paper is organized as follows. In Sect. 2 we provide some background and summarize related works. In Sect. 3 we describe our target microarchitecture. In Sect. 4 we describe our WCET analysis framework. In Sect. 5 we give some insights on the models developed for the dynamic analysis of the target microarchitecture. In Sect. 6 we report an evaluation based on benchmarks. In Sect. 7 we conclude the paper.

2 Background and Related Works

2.1 Branch Prediction Basis

In modern processors, pipelines are used to improve the instruction execution rate by executing simultaneously different stages of several instructions at the same time. Each cycle, one (or more in the case of superscalar processor) instruction is fetched sequentially from the memory and fed into the pipeline. When a branch instruction is executed, the outcome (whether the branch is taken or not, and what is the actual target) is usually not known in the lower stages of the pipeline. Thus, bubbles[3] are inserted in these stages until the address of the next instruction is available. These delays are control hazards and have an impact on the execution time.

Branch prediction is a set of techniques used to minimize the occurrence of this situation. It consists in trying to predict the outcome of a branch instruction when it gets into the pipeline in order to fetch the correct following instruction with a high probability. The simplest form of branch prediction is static branch prediction based on the program code only. A straightforward prediction algorithm is to predict all branches as always not taken. If the prediction is correct, no cycle is lost. If the prediction is incorrect, the lower stages of the pipeline

---

[2] The main difference is that the e200z4 is actually a two issues statically scheduled superscalar processor, whereas we consider a single issue processor.

[3] A bubble, or pipeline stall, is a delay cycle. When a bubble enters a stage, this stage has no activity during the current cycle.

have to be flushed to mimic the insertion of bubbles. A more efficient algorithm widely used is to predict forward branches (conditional statements) as always not taken and backward branches (loops) as always taken.

Dynamic branch prediction uses runtime information to further improve the prediction accuracy. There is a wide variety of dynamic branch prediction algorithms that cannot be covered here (see [5] for an overview). From now on, we will focuses on the algorithm analysed in this paper. It is based on a set of 2-bit saturating counter as illustrated on Fig. 1. From left to right, the four states are usually called: taken (11), weakly taken (10), weakly not taken (01), not taken (00). A counter is associated with a branch instruction. It is initialized either statically or after the first execution of the branch. Then, the state evolves according to the actual outcomes of the execution of the instruction: it is incremented when the branch is taken and decremented otherwise.

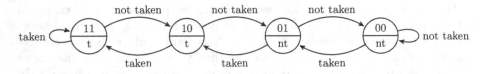

Fig. 1. State machine of a 2-bit saturating counter. Outputs: t for taken, nt for not taken. The initial state is implementation dependant.

Each of these counters is usually stored along with the target of the branch instruction in an entry of a small cache memory: the BTB. A BTB entry is commonly retrieved with a combination of index and tag computed from the branch instruction. When the BTB is full, a replacement policy is applied to free an entry.

2.2 Analysis of Branch Prediction Techniques

An important body of work is related to WCET analysis for processor with dynamic branch prediction (see for instance [1,3,8,12,15]). Most of these works focus on the analysis of branch prediction (whether a branch is taken or not) but except for [3,8], do not take into account branch target prediction (whether the target of the branch is in the BTB or not). Only [8] analyzes the interactions between the BTB and the instruction prefetch buffer which is mandatory to take into account fine grain penalty for misprediction. When this interaction is not analyzed, a uniform penalty must be used to account for misprediction, and the hypothesis of the timing compositionality of the architecture must be implicitly assumed (*i.e.* the analysis can safely follow local worst case path only [18]). Lastly none of these works tackle the problem of analyzing the interactions between the ICache and the branch prediction mechanism. Our approach integrates in a single analysis the ICache, the BTB, and the pipeline using an instruction prefetch buffer.

2.3 Model Checking and WCET Analysis of Processors

There is a limited body of work on model checking techniques for the WCET analysis of processors [2,4,10,14]. In [2,4], it is shown that UPPAAL, a state-of-the-art symbolic model checker for (networks of) timed automata, can be used to model and analyze real-life processors. The target processor of these works feature instruction and data caches and an in-order 5-stage pipeline without dynamic branch prediction. Our target processor features an ICache and an in-order 5-stage pipeline with a BTB and an instruction prefetch buffer. Our ICache model is original, but close to the model used in [2]. Our pipeline model is fully original, as it integrates an instruction prefetch buffer and interactions with an original BTB model.

Following [2], to improve scalability, our analysis framework uses program slicing to narrow the set of instructions and memory locations that must be accurately modeled in order to compute a sound bound. To improve modularity, we use a standalone, state-of-the-art, program slicer for binary code [13].

3 Description of the Target Microarchitecture

Our target microarchitecture is inspired by the Qorivva MPC5643L microcontroller [7]. It is a dual-core developed for safety critical applications of the automotive domain. The architecture is based on two e200z4 Power cores [6]. The e200z4 core is a 32-bits processor of the Power family, based on the PowerPC instruction set. In this paper, we focus on the model of one core.

3.1 Memory Hierarchy

The Qorivva SoC classically embeds internal (S)RAM and flash. The RAM uses a 32-bit data bus and no data cache is available on the e200z4 core. The flash stores the program instructions and is connected to the ICache using the AHB interface[4]. It supports 64-bit data bus for instruction fetch and 32-bit data bus for CPU loads and DMA access. A burst mode allows to fill cache lines faster by sending only the start address to the flash memory controller and get the data flow of sequential access to memory, instead of reading one 64-bit value at a time and then requesting the data at the following address and so on.

The ICache size is 4Kbyte with 32 bytes lines. It can be configured either has a 2- (64 sets) or 4-ways (32 sets) associative cache. The replacement policy is pseudo round-robin. A global register shared among sets points to the next way to replace. The register is incremented for each cache miss modulo the number of ways.

The cache is non-blocking so that the execution continues during a cache miss. On a cache miss, four 64-bits memory accesses are required to fill a cache line. These accesses are done starting with the required instruction to decrease access

---

[4] The Advanced High-performance Bus is part of the open standard ARM-AMBA on-chip interconnect specification.

latency. A line fill buffer stores the memory words retrieved from the memory and the cache line is updated as soon as the line fill buffer load completes. Moreover, a hit under fill feature is implemented to check the line fill buffer instead of waiting for the cache line update.

3.2   Execution Pipeline and Instruction Prefetch Buffer

The e200z4 is a 2-issue static scheduling superscalar core. Instructions are executed on a 5-stage pipeline. The *fetch stage* gets the instruction code from the cache using a 64-bits memory bus. It can retrieve up to two 32-bits instructions to feed them to the decode stage. Fetched instructions are stored in a 32 bytes instruction buffer (8 32-bits instructions). When an instruction enters the fetch stage, the program counter (PC) is updated with the address of the next instruction to fetch. If the instruction is a branch, a BTB lookup is performed. In case of a hit, dynamic branch prediction applies (see below). If the prediction is to take the branch, PC gets the predicted target. Otherwise, PC gets the next address in sequence.

The *decode stage* decodes up to two instructions from the instruction buffer, determine instructions requirements and check register dependencies[5]. In the case of a branch instruction, if it was not found in the BTB when entering the fetch stage, static prediction policy is applied. If the prediction is to take the branch, then the lower stages of the pipeline, including the instruction buffer, are flushed and PC is updated to the target of the branch. The instruction buffer will be refilled either at the next pipeline stall caused by a data or structural hazard (lack of hardware resources).

The next two stages are either the *execute stages* or *data memory accesses stages*. In the case of a branch instruction, the actual outcome of the branch is resolved here. According to the match between the prediction and the actual outcome, the BTB and PC are updated. If the prediction was incorrect, the lower stages of the pipeline, including the instruction fetch buffer, are flushed and PC is updated to the correct address. This is an in-order execution and the last stage is the *write back stage* to update registers.

3.3   Branch Prediction

The branch unit integrates a fully associative 8-entry BTB. The branch unit mixes static and dynamic prediction. Static prediction is used when the branch is not known, *i.e.* not allocated in the BTB. It can be configured to use either the *always not taken* (AN) policy, or the *backward taken forward not taken* (BTFN) policy presented in Sect. 2.1. Dynamic prediction uses a 2-bit saturating counter. Thus each entry of the BTB contains a tag (the full address of the branch

---

[5] In the case where the instruction in the decode stage requires a result produced by an instruction ahead in the pipeline, bubbles are inserted until the availability of the result. This is a data hazard. Bypasses are used between stages to propagate results and limits these bubbles.

instruction), a 2-bit saturating counter and the target address. In the case of a BTB miss, if the branch is resolved as taken, it is allocated in the BTB using a FIFO replacement policy and its counter is initialized to *weakly taken*. Its target address is also stored.

The reference manual of the e200z4 core does not provide information on the prediction of computed branches, *i.e.* branches for which the target is computed at runtime. This is typically the case of function return, switch statement, or function pointer. In this paper, we consider that these branches are handled in the same way as the other ones. According to this interpretation, for these branches, the branch prediction can be correct and at the same time the target prediction incorrect because the BTB stores the last target address of the branch.

All in all, there are 9 different outcomes for this branch prediction mechanism. They are summarized in Table 1. Notice that in case of misprediction, the instruction buffer has to be flushed. In this case, a memory access is triggered to refill this buffer. In turn, this access can add extra latency when the target instruction is not already in the ICache.

Table 1. The 9 different cases of branch prediction. The given penalties are lower bound corresponding to the case where all involved instructions are already in the ICache. $^+$: this case triggers a flush of the instruction buffer because the branch is predicted taken in the decode stage. *: this case triggers a flush of the instruction buffer because of misprediction detected in the execute stage.

BTB	Hit				Miss			
Prediction	Taken			Not taken	Taken		Not taken	
Correct prediction	Yes		No	Yes	No	Yes	No	Yes	No
Target prediction	Correct	Incorrect						
Penalty (in cycle)	0	2^*	2^*	0	2^*	1^+	$2^{+,*}$	0	2^*

3.4 Analyzability and Predictability

The main challenge concerning the WCET analysis of this architecture lays in the complex interactions between the ICache, the branch prediction unit, and the instruction prefetch buffer. To compute a safe and tight bound on the WCET, an integrated analysis of these 3 units is required. Indeed, only an integrated analysis allows to compute the actual sequence of memory accesses requests and pipeline stall states produced by a given run of the program.

4 Our WCET Analysis Framework

As shown in Fig. 2, our analysis framework is built around two tools: BEST [13] and UPPAAL [11].

BEST is a program slicing tool for binary code. It is interfaced with a disassembler library for the target instruction set architecture (PowerPC 32-bit in

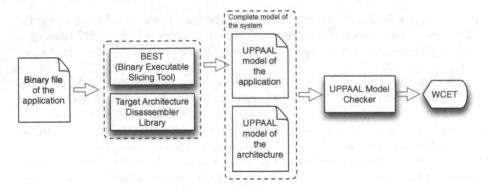

Fig. 2. The UPPAAL model of the application is generated by the BEST tool, from the application binary file. This model is synchronized with the hand-written model of the architecture (that does not depend on the application considered). The WCET is then computed by model checking.

this paper). For each instruction of the program, the disassembler provides a set of semantics information including the opcode, the arguments, the type (branch or not), the set of used and defined registers, etc. BEST uses this information to slice the program, with all the branch instructions as the slice criterion. The resulting sliced program contains all and only the instructions that have an impact on the execution flow. This sliced program is then used to produce a control flow graph where each instruction is tagged as either in or out of the slice. From the set of instructions in the slice, the set of useful memory locations to analyze the control flow of the program is computed. This information is then used to generate an UPPAAL model of the program (see Sect. 5.1). The program slicing is a mandatory phase to limit the state space explosion problem.

The second step consists in analyzing the system with UPPAAL. UPPAAL is a model design and verification tool for networks of timed automata (NTA). Timed automata (TA) are finite state automata augmented with real-valued clocks. The values of these clocks all increase at the same rate. Linear constraints on clocks can be used to guard transition, and clocks can be reset when a transition is taken. In UPPAAL syntax, TA can use boolean and bounded integer variables. These variables can be manipulated through functions specified in a language with a C-like syntax. Moreover, TA can be synchronized over synchronous channels to form a NTA.

In our framework, we have developed a set of TA corresponding to the components of the microarchitecture. These components interact through global variables and synchronizations. The corresponding models are briefly described in Sect. 5. The model of the program generated by BEST is synchronized with the models of the microarchitecture. The resulting NTA models the whole system, hardware and software. This model contains a specific clock reset one time only, at system startup. The model checker is then used to perform a symbolic exploration of the state space of the system and computes the maximal value reached by this clock over all paths. Our framework (BEST, UPPAAL models and script files) used to produce the experimental data are distributed in open-source[6].

5   Models

Figures 3, 4a, b and 5 show UPPAAL models. Location labels, invariants, guards, synchronisations and updates are displayed respectively in purple, pink, green, cyan and blue.

5.1   Modeling the Program

The model of a program is composed of two main parts: an array of data structures that will be fed to the model of the pipeline to mimic the timing behavior, and an automata to mimic the functional behavior.

A data structure is associated with an instruction of the program. It contains constant information like the instruction address, the number of cycles required to execute the instruction in the execute stage, a flag indicating whether the instruction is a branch instruction and if applicable its target address, a flag indicating whether the instruction is a memory access instruction and the set of defined and used registers.

It contains also a dynamic part called the instruction runtime data structure. For a standard instruction, it contains only the number of remaining execution cycles. In the particular case of a branching instruction, 3 flags are also used: whether the instruction has been predicted taken or not taken, whether the prediction was static or dynamic, and lastly, whether the branch has actually been taken or not taken.

The automata is built from the control flow graph of the program, as illustrated in Fig. 3. In this automata, each location models a breakpoint before the execution of the corresponding instruction and each outcoming transition is associated with the functional effect of the execution of the instruction.

The label identifies the instruction: thus BBx_Inst$y$ denotes the yth instruction of the xth basic block of the program. The guard InE(Inst$y$) tests if this instruction is currently in the execute stage of the pipeline. The Tick signal is used to synchronize the program model with the pipeline update. The update of the transition calls a UPPAAL function that execute the semantics of the instruction. It consists in updating the global variables that model the content of the memory and the status flags of the processor. If the instruction is not part of the slice, then the transition does no update as executing its semantics has no influence on the temporal behavior of the system (e.g. the outgoing transition of location BB10_Inst10 on Fig. 3). For conditional branches, two transitions are provided, corresponding to the two cases: taken or not taken. For these transitions, the guard is completed with a test to select the correct path according to the status of the processor (e.g. nz() or !nz() on the two outgoing transition of location BB10_Inst12 for Inst12 on Fig. 3).

---

[6] Available at https://github.com/TrampolineRTOS/BEST.

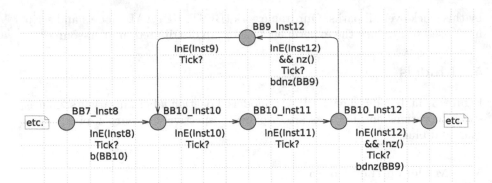

Fig. 3. Part of an automata modeling the functional behavior of a program. The bdnz instruction is a branch instruction that decrements a counter register (CTR) and branches if this counter is not null. (Color figure online)

5.2 Modeling the Pipeline

The model of the pipeline is composed of a set of data structures that capture the content of the internal memory of the components such as the pipeline stages, the instruction buffer and the BTB; and a set of automata used to synchronize the update of this data structures with the flow of time in order to mimic the timing behavior of the system.

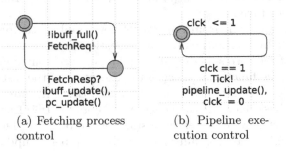

(a) Fetching process   (b) Pipeline exe-
control   cution control

Fig. 4. Automata controlling the pipeline. (Color figure online)

The first automaton (Fig. 4a) is associated with the (pre)fetching process. When the instruction buffer (IBuff) is not full, it tries to fetch an instruction from the instruction cache. When an instruction is fetched, the function ibuff_update updates the instruction buffer and the BTB. The instruction buffer is an array of instruction runtime data structures. The BTB is a circular buffer with each entry composed of a tag and a 2-bit saturating counter. Notice that the target adresses are not actually stored in the BTB because they are already in the

program automata. The `pc_update` updates the PC. It performs a BTB lookup
in the case of a branch instruction.

The second automaton (Fig. 4b) controls the execution of the pipeline.
Thanks to the invariant `clck <= 1` it generates a `Tick` signal every one unit
of time. This is used to synchronize the NTA to the frequency of the pipeline.
It also calls the `pipeline_update` function used to update the data structure
and variables associated with the pipeline stage following the fetch stage. Each
pipeline stage is associated with an instruction runtime data structure. Updating the stages consists in making instructions progress by updating the data
structures from stage to stage (including the instruction prefetch buffer), taking
into account the possible stall cycles due to data or structural hazards.

Static branch prediction is done when a branch instruction enters the decode
stage, if no dynamic branch prediction was available for this instruction at the
fetch stage. If the prediction is taken, the lower stages are flushed and PC is
updated.

Branch target resolution is done when a branch instruction enters the execute
stage. This encompass a potential BTB update, and, in case of misprediction, a
flush of the lower stages and a PC update.

5.3   Modeling the Memory Hierarchy

The model of the memory hierarchy is composed of a set of data structures
and global variables to track the content of the instruction cache and store the
content of the useful memory locations (as computed during the program slicing
step), and a set of automata to mimic the access times. In this paper, we focus
on branch prediction so for the sake of clarity we will not give too many details
on these models.

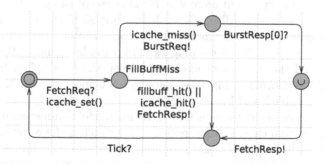

Fig. 5. Instruction cache access time model. (Color figure online)

The automata used to mimic the ICache access time is shown Fig. 5. When a
fetch request is received, a cache look up and update is performed by the function
`icache_set`. If the instruction is present in the cache or in the fill buffer, the
request is acknowledged. Otherwise, a request is sent to the Flash memory. As

explained in Sect. 3.1, the instruction cache line fill requires 4×64 bits memory transactions from the flash, using a burst access. The request is acknowledged before the end of the burst, as soon as the instruction is in the fill buffer. At the end, a synchronization on the `Tick` signal enforces the cycle required to transfer an instruction from the cache to the fetch stage.

6   Experimental Results

We have conducted a set of experiments with the framework described above. The main goals of these experiments are (i) to assess the applicability and scalability of model checking for computing WCET estimation for embedded control systems; and (ii) to evaluate the impact of the branch prediction policy on the WCET.

We used the Mälardalen WCET benchmarks [9] to generate the programs. We excluded certain programs to account for the current limitations of our framework:(i) TAs are not fit to model recursive programs; (ii) our model of the architecture does not manage floating point arithmetic instructions; (iii) BEST does not manage binary executables with indirect branch instructions other than function return instructions (*i.e.* switch-case statements and function pointers); (iv) BEST does not manage slices where instructions depend each others through local variables located on the program stack. This point will be addressed in the future.

We built the binaries with GCC 5.3.1. Without optimization, GCC generates code where local variables are loaded from and stored to the stack frame each time they are used. Such binary executables can not be processed by the current version of our framework. Options -O1 and -O2 force GCC to output optimized code that uses registers to load and store local variables. Thus we created two versions of each of the 14 Mälardalen benchmarks fitting our constraints, except for cnt.c, insertsort.c and ud.c which make use of the program stack when compiled with option -O1. All in all, we have built 25 binaries and for each one we ran our framework to compute its WCET on an Intel Core i7-3770 (4 cores, 3.40 GHz) with 8 GiB of RAM running Debian 9 (64-bit, Linux 4.9). Each time, we also collected the number of explored states, the time taken by UPPAAL to perform the exploration, and the amount of memory used. The results are summarized in Table 2 and Fig. 6.

Table 2 displays raw data from UPPAAL for models implementing the static always not taken branch prediction policy (AN) which is the worst wrt. resource consumption during the analysis. The worst case for each column is highlighted in bold. It is obtained for the binary built from the program fir.c compiled with -O1. Even in this case, both the analysis time (less than 5 s) and the amount of memory used (less than 640 MiB) are very reasonable. Our conclusion is that model checking seems to be a promising solution to compute WCET for this type of system. Further experiments should be performed to identify the limits of the scalability of the approach.

Figure 6 presents the impact of the branch prediction policy on the WCET (Fig. 6a) and the state space (Fig. 6b). Each bar represents the ratio between

Table 2. Consumption of resources by the analysis for the AN prediction policy.

Program	States explored	CPU time (ms)	Memory (KiB)
bs-O1	586	10	12684
bs-O2	451	0	12140
bsort100-O1	12457	130	29192
bsort100-O2	11982	130	27868
cnt-O2	11279	110	30504
crc-O1	157612	1600	550048
crc-O2	144653	1570	494760
expint-O1	5967	40	22236
expint-O2	4118	40	13860
fdct-O1	6823	50	23804
fdct-O2	7080	50	25532
fibcall-O1	949	10	12104
fibcall-O2	590	0	11000
fir-O1	**728321**	**4770**	**655628**
fir-O2	692704	4430	608412
insertsort-O2	2995	20	14116
janne_complex-O1	779	10	12512
janne_complex-O2	594	0	12572
jfdctint-O1	11121	100	31636
jfdctint-O2	11349	100	33796
ns-O1	32482	250	44964
ns-O2	31229	230	40276
prime-O1	12072	80	26560
prime-O2	12056	80	25564
ud-O2	11305	380	491300

two policies: BTFN over AN in dark gray, BTFN+BTB over BTFN in light gray, and BTFN+BTB over AN in medium gray. For instance the ratio between the WCET computed for program `expint-O1.c` with the policy BTFB+BTB (1944 cycles) and the WCET computed for the same program with the policy AN (2304 cycles) is 84% (medium gray bar in slot `expint-O1` of Fig. 6a). When a bar is above 100%, it means that the numerator policy performs worst than the denominator policy. On the contrary, if the bar is below 100%, it means that it performs better.

Concerning the WCET, we first remark that most ratios are smaller than 100%. It means that branch prediction policies designed to improve the average case also have a positive impact on the WCET. Second, we remark that no branch prediction policy dominates the others: for each case, we have at least

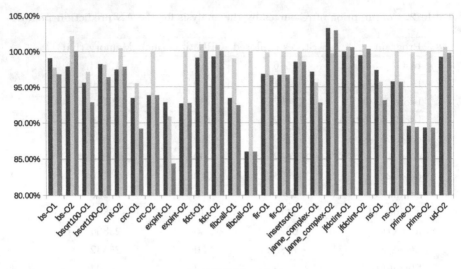

(a) WCET ratios

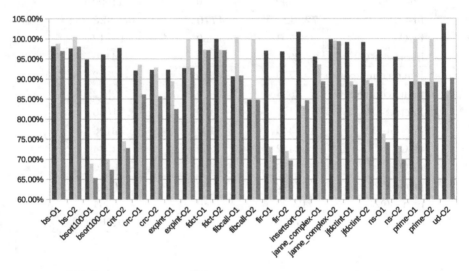

(b) State space ratios

Fig. 6. Impact of the branch prediction policy on the WCET and the size of the state space. Each bar represent the ratio between two policies for a given binary: BTFN over AN in dark gray, BTFN+BTB over BTFN in light gray, BTFN+BTB over AN in medium gray.

one bar below the 100% threshold and one bar above. In the context of WCET analysis, it means that there is no worst policy that could be used to always estimate a worst case upper bound.

Concerning the state space, we remark that adding the BTB to the model of the architecture does not results in an increase of its size. On the contrary we note that the average number of states decreases while using a model simulating a more complex behavior. For example, Fig. 6b shows a decrease of the state space when using BTFN+BTB over AN policies (medium gray bars) up to 35% (for `bsort100-01`), with an average around 15%. A better prediction policy decreases the number of control hazards and thus the number of configurations of the lower stages of the pipeline, thus reducing the size of the state space. In addition, we note that the WCET bound and the size of the state space do not always change in the same direction. For instance, in the case of `fdct-02`, using BTFN+BTB over BTFN (light gray bar) increases the WCET bound (bar above 100%) but decreases the size of the state space (bar below 100%). Further experiments should be performed to collect lower level events (eg. cache accesses, memory accesses, flushes of the prefetch buffer, etc.) to better understand this type of phenomenon.

7 Conclusion

In this paper we show that model checking can be used to analyze the complex interactions between the components of a microarchitecture used in safety critical embedded control systems. We focus on the interaction between the instruction cache, the branch prediction unit, and a pipeline with an instruction buffer. Model checking provides a solution to perform an integrated analysis of the whole system. This integrated analysis allows to explore only feasible traces of the system and to compute the actual sequence of memory access requests and pipeline stall states corresponding to each trace. Our result are promising concerning the scalability of the approach for such systems.

In future works, we shall extend our analysis framework to support programs that use the stack to store data that impact the control flow. We also want to produce results using more complex benchmarks, and explore the impact of non-determinism concerning the initial state of the micro-architecture (eg. cache and BTB state). We will also tend toward having a model aligned with the actual e200z4 core (*i.e.* adding a second way to the pipeline) in order to validate our model against a real system through microbenchmarks. Our long term objective is to model and analyze a multiprocessor architecture based on e200z4 core such as the MPC5643L.

References

1. Bate, I., Reutemann, R.D.: Worst-case execution time analysis for dynamic branch predictors. In: 16th Euromicro Conference on Real-Time Systems, ECRTS, pp. 215–222 (2004)
2. Cassez, F., Béchennec, J.: Timing analysis of binary programs with UPPAAL. In: 13th International Conference on Application of Concurrency to System Design, ACSD, pp. 41–50 (2013)

3. Colin, A., Puaut, I.: Worst case execution time analysis for a processor with branch prediction. Real-Time Syst. **18**(2/3), 249–274 (2000)
4. Dalsgaard, A.E., Olesen, M.C., Toft, M., Hansen, R.R., Larsen, K.G.: META-MOC: modular execution time analysis using model checking. In: 10th International Workshop on Worst-Case Execution Time Analysis, WCET, pp. 113–123 (2010)
5. Engblom, J.: Analysis of the execution time unpredictability caused by dynamic branch prediction. In: 9th IEEE Real-Time and Embedded Technology and Applications Symposium, RTAS, pp. 152–159 (2003)
6. Freescale semiconductors/NXP: e200z4 Power Architecture™ Core Reference Manual, rev. 0 edn., October 2009
7. Freescale semiconductors/NXP: MPC5643L Microcontroller Reference Manual, rev, 10 edn., June 2013
8. Grund, D., Reineke, J., Gebhard, G.: Branch target buffers: WCET analysis framework and timing predictability. J. Syst. Architect. **57**(6), 625–637 (2011)
9. Gustafsson, J., Betts, A., Ermedahl, A., Lisper, B.: The Mälardalen WCET benchmarks - past, present and future. In: International Workshop on Worst-Case Execution Time Analysis (WCET) (2010)
10. Gustavsson, A., Ermedahl, A., Lisper, B., Pettersson, P.: Towards WCET analysis of multicore architectures using UPPAAL. In: 10th International Workshop on Worst-Case Execution Time Analysis, WCET, pp. 101–112 (2010)
11. Larsen, K.G., Pettersson, P., Yi, W.: UPPAAL in a nutshell. STTT **1**(1–2), 134–152 (1997)
12. Maiza, C., Rochange, C.: A framework for the timing analysis of dynamic branch predictors. In: 19th International Conference on Real-Time and Network Systems, RTNS, pp. 65–74 (2011)
13. Mangean, A., Béchennec, J.L., Briday, M., Faucou, S.: BEST: a binary executable slicing tool. In: 16th International Workshop on Worst-Case Execution Time Analysis, WCET, pp. 7:1–7:10 (2016)
14. Metzner, A.: Why model checking can improve WCET analysis. In: Alur, R., Peled, D.A. (eds.) CAV 2004. LNCS, vol. 3114, pp. 334–347. Springer, Heidelberg (2004). doi:10.1007/978-3-540-27813-9_26
15. Puffitsch, W.: Efficient worst-case execution time analysis of dynamic branch prediction. In: 28th Euromicro Conference on Real-Time Systems, ECRTS, pp. 152–162 (2016)
16. Wilhelm, R.: Why AI + ILP Is Good for WCET, but MC Is Not, Nor ILP Alone. In: Steffen, B., Levi, G. (eds.) VMCAI 2004. LNCS, vol. 2937, pp. 309–322. Springer, Heidelberg (2004). doi:10.1007/978-3-540-24622-0_25
17. Wilhelm, R., Engblom, J., Ermedahl, A., Holsti, N., Thesing, S., Whalley, D.B., Bernat, G., Ferdinand, C., Heckmann, R., Mitra, T., Mueller, F., Puaut, I., Puschner, P.P., Staschulat, J., Stenström, P.: The worst-case execution-time problem - overview of methods and survey of tools. ACM Trans. Embedded Comput. Syst. **7**(3), 36:1–36:53 (2008)
18. Wilhelm, R., Grund, D., Reineke, J., Schlickling, M., Pister, M., Ferdinand, C.: Memory hierarchies, pipelines, and buses for future architectures in time-critical embedded systems. IEEE Trans. CAD Integr. Circuits Syst. **28**(7), 966–978 (2009)

Factor-Based C-AMAT Analysis for Memory Optimization

Qi Yu, Libo Huang$^{(\boxtimes)}$, Cheng Qian, Jianqiao Ma, and Zhiying Wang

College of Computer, National University of Defense Technology, Changsha, China
{yuqi13,libohuang,qiancheng,majianqiao12,zywang}@nudt.edu.cn

Abstract. The "memory problem" promotes researches on improving performance of memory systems, as well as researches on proposing more accurate memory metrics. C-AMAT, an extension of AMAT that takes memory concurrency into consideration, can evaluate the performance of modern memory systems more accurately. However, compared to AMAT, the method for calculating C-AMAT is more complicated, besides, additional detecting logic and registers are required to measure parameters of C-AMAT, which incur high hardware overhead for this metric. In this paper, we propose Factor-Based C-AMAT (FC-AMAT), an analysis model based on C-AMAT. FC-AMAT divides a memory system into factors according to actual research demands, and uses factor's-first C-AMAT to evaluate effects of optimizations applied to the memory system. By selecting factor's C-AMAT, FC-AMAT can reduce the hardware overhead for measuring its parameters, meanwhile, it guarantees an acceptable evaluation accuracy through a rigorous check. Simulations with varied cache configurations were conducted to verify the usefulness of FC-AMAT. Experimental results show that FC-AMAT can simplify the detecting logic and reduce the storage cost for recording memory access phases, without sacrificing obvious evaluation accuracy, demonstrating the effectiveness of FC-AMAT.

Keywords: FC-AMAT · C-AMAT · Correlation coefficient · Evaluation accuracy

1 Introduction

With expanding disparities between processor and memory speeds, the "memory wall" problem [9,13] emerges and memory rather than processor has become the leading performance bottleneck in modern computing systems. A number of techniques, including conventional techniques and advanced methods, have been proposed to alleviate the "memory wall" problem. Conventional techniques are mainly designed to reduce the memory access latency, while advanced methods like pipelined cache [1], nonblocking cache [4], mainly focus on improving memory system concurrency. These methods allow tens or even hundreds of memory accesses to coexist in the memory hierarchy simultaneously, thus, a single cache miss is no longer a key performance factor of the overall memory system [10].

© Springer International Publishing AG 2017
K. Barkaoui et al. (Eds.): VECoS 2017, LNCS 10466, pp. 79–91, 2017.
DOI: 10.1007/978-3-319-66176-6_6

As the performance of memory systems has a dominant impact on the overall performance (represented by IPC), how to measure and evaluate memory systems has become an important issue in the high performance computing community. Conventional memory performance metrics, such as MR (Miss Rate), AMP (Average Miss Penalty) and AMAT (Average Memory Access Time), are designed to measure a particular component in the memory system or measure accesses based on sequential single-access activities [3]. Therefore, they are inadequate for evaluating concurrent memory access activities, which are common in modern memory systems that adopt designs like pipelined cache, nonblocking cache, et cetera.

To tackle the evaluation problem, X.H. Sun *et al.* proposed a new memory metric called C-AMAT (Concurrent Average Memory Access Time) [10]. It is an extension of AMAT that takes memory concurrency into consideration. C-AMAT introduces two new parameters, namely hit concurrency and miss concurrency, as well as a new concept called pure miss. Pure miss is defined as a miss access that contains at least one miss cycle with no hit access activity [10]. As C-AMAT considers both memory locality and memory concurrency, it can evaluate modern memory systems more accurately and comprehensively.

The advantage of C-AMAT lies in its effectiveness for evaluating memory system designs. However, compared to AMAT, the method for measuring its parameters is more complicated. According to [10], to calculate C-AMAT, additional hardware resources are needed to measure its two parameters, namely hit concurrency and miss concurrency. More specifically, a hit concurrency detector and a miss concurrency detector are required. The hit concurrency detector is a monitoring unit that counts total hit cycles and records each hit phase (the starting cycle and the ending cycle of each hit event), and the miss concurrency detector has similar functionality. The hit/miss concurrency detector is composed of some detecting logic and registers. Detecting logic detects hit/miss events, while registers are used to count total hit/pure miss cycles as well as record each hit/miss phase, which may incur high hardware overhead for this metric. Based on the above analysis, we propose Factor-Based C-AMAT (FC-AMAT), an analysis model based on C-AMAT. FC-AMAT divides a memory system into factors and uses factor's-first C-AMAT to evaluate effects of optimizations applied to the memory system. By selecting factor's C-AMAT, FC-AMAT can reduce the hardware overhead for measuring its parameters, meanwhile, it guarantees an acceptable evaluation accuracy by checking whether the factor's C-AMAT meets certain requirement. Simulations with varied cache configurations were conducted to verify the usefulness of FC-AMAT. Experimental results show that FC-AMAT can simplify the detecting logic and reduce the storage cost for recording memory access phases, without sacrificing obvious evaluation accuracy, demonstrating the effectiveness of FC-AMAT.

The rest of this paper is organized as follows. We introduce the principle of FC-AMAT in Sect. 2. In Sect. 3, we introduce experiment methodology and setup. The analysis of experimental results is shown Sect. 4. Related work is briefly discussed in Sect. 5 and conclusion is discussed in Sect. 6.

2 FC-AMAT Analysis Model

As our work is directly based on C-AMAT, we first introduce the definition of C-AMAT. It is defined as total memory access cycles divided by total number of memory accesses:

$$C\text{-}AMAT = \frac{T_{MemCycle}}{C_{MemAcc}} \qquad (1)$$

$T_{MemCycle}$ represents total memory access cycles, C_{MemAcc} represents total number of memory accesses. Note that the memory access cycles are different from CPU cycles, only those CPU cycles in which there is at least one outstanding memory access can be counted as memory access cycles. Besides, $T_{MemCycle}$ is counted in overlapping mode, in other words, when several memory accesses coexist during the same cycle, $T_{MemCycle}$ increases by only one [10]. A more useful and detailed equation of C-AMAT is expressed as follows:

$$C\text{-}AMAT = \frac{H}{C_H} + pMR \times \frac{pAMP}{C_M} \qquad (2)$$

H represents hit latency, same to that in AMAT. C_H and C_M represent hit concurrency and miss concurrency respectively. pMR is different from conventional MR, which is redefined as the number of pure misses divided by the number of accesses [10]. $pAMP$ is the average pure miss cycles per pure miss access.

According to Eq. 2, C_H and C_M are required to calculate C-AMAT. The method for calculating the average C_H and C_M is provided in [10], where two detectors, namely hit concurrency detector and miss concurrency detector, are added to the original hardware structure. These two detectors both consist of detecting logic and registers. The detecting logic in hit concurrency detector monitors whether there are cache tag query activities and registers are used to count total hit cycles and record hit phases. Total number of registers required can be calculated in the following way: each hit phase needs two registers (can be also called a register pair, one records the starting cycle and the other records the ending cycle), once the cycles in each hit phase (cycles fall in between starting cycle and ending cycle) are added to total hit cycles, the corresponding register pair can be freed and reused for next hit phase, therefore, it is unnecessary for allocating a new register pair for each hit phase. The number of register pairs can be selected as the maximum number of hit accesses coexist during the same cycle, which is an empirical value, we set it 20 in this paper. Besides, one long-bit sized register (e.g. 64-bit register) is needed to count total hit cycles.

The detecting logic in miss concurrency detector monitors whether there are new requests arriving at MSHR (Missing Status Holding Register) and registers are used to count total pure miss cycles and record miss phases. The method for calculating total number of registers required in miss concurrency detector is similar to that in hit concurrency detector, except that the number of register pairs can be selected as the maximum number of miss accesses coexist during the same cycle, which equals to the number of MSHR entries times the number of targets in a MSHR entry. Based on the above analysis, we can estimate the hardware resources for calculating the average C_H and C_M, which incur high hardware overhead for C-AMAT.

Different memory systems (also called research targets in this paper) can be divided into different factors. In this paper, factor refers to a component of a target memory system or part of memory accesses in certain memory hierarchy. For example, if L1 cache is the target memory system, L1 instruction cache and L1 data cache can be its factors; if L2 cache (unified cache) is the research target, instruction accesses and data accesses can be its factors. Similarly, we regard the C-AMAT of the target memory system as the overall C-AMAT and regard the C-AMAT of a component or part of memory accesses as factor's C-AMAT. The overall C-AMAT generally has higher evaluation accuracy than factor's C-AMAT for its comprehensiveness. However, calculating the overall C-AMAT also means higher hardware overhead, which is shown in Fig. 1.

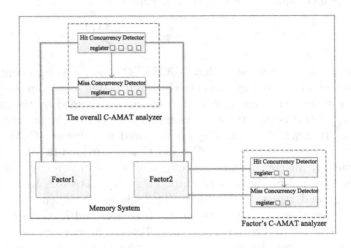

Fig. 1. Structures for measuring C_H and C_M of the overall C-AMAT and factor's C-AMAT

We can see from Fig. 1 that the memory system is divided into two factors. To calculate factor2's C-AMAT, the detecting logic (gray lines in this figure) needs only to be added to factor2 (detects corresponding signal) and some registers are required to record memory access phases. However, to calculate the overall C-AMAT, detecting logic needs to be added to both factor1 and factor2, besides, more registers are required. We take L1 cache as an example, whose default configurations are show in Table 1. The L1 cache consists of instruction cache and data cache, which can be regarded as its two factors. To calculate data cache's C-AMAT, hit detecting logic and miss detecting logic should be added to data cache. Actually, the wiring from various detecting signals is more complicated in real chip design. In addition, according to the above analysis, 20 register pairs are needed to record hit access phases, 160 register pairs (8 MSHR entries times 20 targets per entry) are required to record miss access phases, 2 registers count total hit cycles and total pure miss cycles respectively. Therefore, 181 register pairs are required in total, assume each register is 64-bit, this will incur 2.8 KB storage cost. As instruction cache has the same configurations with data cache, calculating the overall C-AMAT doubles the detecting logic as well as number of register pairs, which means higher hardware overhead.

Based on the observation, we propose FC-AMAT. The key idea of FC-AMAT is using factor's-first C-AMAT to evaluate effects of optimizations applied to a memory system if the factor's C-AMAT meets certain requirement. By using the factor's C-AMAT, FC-AMAT reduces the hardware overhead (include detecting logic and storage cost), meanwhile, it guarantees an acceptable evaluation accuracy by checking whether the factor's C-AMAT meets the requirement. We can select the appropriate factor's C-AMAT in the following way:

(1) If an optimization is applied to a factor of the memory system, we can use the optimized factor's C-AMAT if it meets the requirement;
(2) If an optimization is applied to the whole memory system, we can look for a leading factor which has more influence on the overall memory system and choose its C-AMAT if it meets the requirement;
(3) If we cannot find the ideal factor's C-AMAT or the factor's C-AMAT does not meet the requirement, the overall C-AMAT is selected.

As memory systems have become a key factor of the overall performance, the memory performance should influence and correlate to the overall performance [12], an appropriate metric should be chosen to reflect this correlation relation. We use correlation coefficient [7] to describe the variation similarity between C-AMAT (represents the memory performance) and IPC (represents the overall performance), which we regard as the evaluation accuracy of C-AMAT in this paper. The correlation coefficient is a value between -1 and 1. The higher the absolute of correlation coefficient is, the closer the relation between the two variables is [7]. The mathematical definition of correlation coefficient is shown as follows:

$$r_{xy} = \frac{\sum XY - \frac{(\sum X)(\sum Y)}{n}}{\sqrt{[(\sum X^2 - \frac{(\sum X)^2}{n})(\sum Y^2 - \frac{(\sum Y)^2}{n})]}} \qquad (3)$$

where, array X and Y are sampling points for two variables, n represents number of sampling points.

If the correlation coefficient is larger than 0, there is a positive relation between the two variables, in other words, if one variable increases, the other also increases. Otherwise, if it is less than 0, there is a negative relation between the two variables, that means if one variable increases, the other decreases. Generally speaking, it is believed that the two variables have a strong relation if the absolute value is greater than 0.8, and have a dominant relation if the absolute value is greater than 0.9, otherwise if less than 0.5, the relation is weak [11].

Based on the above analysis, we propose the reference standard of requirement. Since there is a strong relation between the two variables if the absolute value is greater than 0.8, we regard 0.8 as the reference standard, which means if the evaluation accuracy of factor's C-AMAT is greater than or equal to 0.8, we think it meets the requirement, otherwise, the overall C-AMAT is used to evaluate the performance of a memory system.

3   Methodology

We adopted a detailed out-of-order superscalar CPU model in the GEM5 simulator [2] whose default configurations are shown in Table 1. Each experimental configuration is based on the default and only one parameter is changed in the simulation. The detailed experimental configurations are shown in Table 2. Each configuration is simulated in single core mode.

Table 1. Default processor and cache configuration parameters

Parameters	Values
Processor	1 core, 4 GHz, 4-issue width
Function units	6 IntALU: 1 cycle; 1 IntMul: 3 cycles; 2 FPAdd: 2 cycles; 1 FPCmp: 2 cycles; 1 FPMul: 4 cycles; 1 FPDiv: 12 cycles; 1 FPCvt: 2 cycles
ROB and LSQ size	ROB 64, LQ 48, SQ 24
L1 caches	32KB inst/ 32KB data, 2-way, 64B line, 4-cycle hit latency inst/ 4-cycle data, ICache 8 MSHR entry, 20 targets per entry DCache 8 MSHR entry, 20 targets per entry
L2 cache	512KB, 16-way, 64B line, 24-cycle hit latency 16 MSHR entry, 12 targets per entry
DRAM latency/width	240-cycle access latency/64bits

There are three groups of configurations. The first group includes C1–C13 and they are basic L1 cache (include instruction cache and data cache) configurations, which only change cache size and associativity. These configurations can be further divided into three subgroups. The first subgroup consists of C1–C5, in which L1 cache configurations (size and associativity) are changed. C6–C9 comprise the second subgroup, in which L1 instruction cache configurations are changed. The third subgroup is composed of C10–C13, which changes L1 data cache configurations. The second group, including C14–C17, are basic L2 cache configurations which also change cache size and associativity. The third group, which consists of C18–C20, changes memory access parallelism by changing the number of MSRH entries. These are advanced cache configurations, which take the effect of non-blocking cache into consideration. By changing memory system configurations, it is possible to observe the overall/factor's C-AMAT and IPC variation trend.

The simulations were conducted with 29 benchmarks from SPEC CPU2006 suite [8], 2 benchmarks in the set were omitted because of compatibility issues with the simulator. The benchmarks were complied using GCC 4.3.2 with -O2 optimization and the suite-provided reference input sizes were adopted. For these

Table 2. A series of detailed configurations

ID	Description	Changed parameter
1	L1: 32 KB, 2way; L2: 512 KB, 16way	Default config.
2	L1: 32 KB, 4way; L2: 512 KB, 16way	L1 cache assoc.
3	L1: 32 KB, 8way; L2: 512 KB, 16way	L1 cache assoc.
4	L1: 16 KB, 2way; L2: 512 KB, 16way	L1 cache size
5	L1: 64 KB, 2way; L2: 512 KB, 16way	L1 cache size
6	L1: I$32 KB, 4way; D$32 KB, 2way; L2: 512 KB,16way	Only ICache assoc.
7	L1: I$32 KB, 8way; D$32 KB, 2way; L2: 512 KB,16way	Only ICache assoc.
8	L1: I$16 KB, 2way; D$32 KB, 2way; L2: 512 KB,16way	Only ICache size
9	L1: I$64 KB, 2way; D$32 KB, 2way; L2: 512 KB,16way	Only ICache size
10	L1: I$32 KB, 2way; D$32 KB, 4way; L2: 512 KB,16way	Only DCache assoc.
11	L1: I$32 KB, 2way; D$32 KB, 8way; L2: 512 KB,16way	Only DCache assoc.
12	L1: I$32 KB, 2way; D$16 KB, 2way; L2: 512 KB,16way	Only DCache size
13	L1: I$32 KB, 2way; D$64 KB, 2way; L2: 512 KB,16way	Only DCache size
14	L1: 32 KB, 2way; L2: 256 KB, 16way	L2 size
15	L1: 32 KB, 2way; L2: 1024 KB, 16way	L2 size
16	L1: 32 KB, 2way; L2: 512 KB, 8way	L2 assoc.
17	L1: 32 KB, 2way; L2: 512 KB, 32way	L2 assoc.
18	L1: 32 KB, 2way, MSHR 1; L2: 512 KB, 16way	MSHR entry
19	L1: 32 KB, 2way, MSHR 2; L2: 512 KB, 16way	MSHR entry
20	L1: 32 KB, 2way, MSHR 4; L2: 512 KB, 16way	MSHR entry

simulations, we first warmed up the simulations for 10 million instructions, then collected statistics based on the following 100 million instructions.

4   Results

We conducted experiments based on three groups of configurations. In each group, we run simulations for 29 benchmarks. Note that those benchmarks whose IPC remain unchanged or change in a very small range across different configurations were omitted. Because their C-AMAT may not remain unchanged or change by the same extent as IPC, in this case, their correlation coefficients may be very low or even zero, which is meaningless. For each group, we calculated the evaluation accuracy of the overall C-AMAT and the factor's C-AMAT. For all selected benchmarks, we calculated the average evaluation accuracy of these benchmarks. Then the average values were compared to the standard to check whether the factor's C-AMAT meets the requirement. In addition, the hardware overhead (include detecting logic and registers) for calculating C-AMAT was also compared.

4.1   Basic L1 Cache Configurations

We regard L1 cache as the research target, instruction cache and data cache are two factors, and cache configuration changes can be seen as optimizations applied to them. Therefore, the overall C-AMAT is the C-AMAT of L1 cache, and the factor's C-AMAT includes C-AMAT of instruction cache and data cache. In the following figures, EA represents evaluation accuracy, EA_L1 represents the evaluation accuracy of the overall C-AMAT, while EA_I and EA_D represent the evaluation accuracy of the factor's C-AMAT.

Basic L1 Instruction Cache Configurations. Only L1 instruction cache configurations are changed in this subgroup and instruction cache is regarded as the optimized factor. Based on the rules of FC-AMAT, the C-AMAT of instruction cache is expected to be selected and checked first. The average evaluation accuracy of instruction cache's C-AMAT are -0.991 and -0.995 for changing size and changing associativity respectively, with the absolute value larger than 0.8, its C-AMAT meets the requirement. As a comparison, we also calculate the evaluation accuracy of overall C-AMAT and data cache's C-AMAT. The detailed results are shown in Fig. 2.

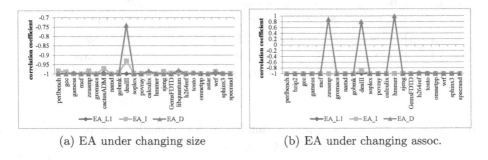

    (a) EA under changing size   (b) EA under changing assoc.

Fig. 2. The results of changing L1 instruction cache configurations

It can be seen that the C-AMAT of instruction cache has similar evaluation accuracy with the overall C-AMAT for most selected benchmarks, which is much higher than that of data cache's C-AMAT for some benchmarks. The average evaluation accuracy of the overall C-AMAT are -0.999 and -1 respectively, we can see that the evaluation accuracy gap between the overall C-AMAT and instruction cache's C-AMAT is negligible. In terms of hardware overhead, calculating the overall C-AMAT needs two sets of detecting logic, one for detecting instruction access events, the other for detecting data access events. However, calculating instruction's C-AMAT needs only one set of detecting logic. As for storage cost, calculating instruction cache's C-AMAT needs 181 register pairs (see the example in Sect. 2). However, as instruction cache has the same configurations with data cache, calculating the overall C-AMAT doubles the number of register pairs. Therefore, selecting instruction's C-AMAT can simplify the detecting logic and reduce the storage cost by 50%.

Basic L1 Data Cache Configurations. Only L1 data cache configurations are changed in this subgroup, thus data cache is the optimized factor and its C-AMAT should be checked first. Its average evaluation accuracy are -0.999 and -0.987 for changing size and changing associativity respectively. According to rules of FC-AMAT, data cache's C-AMAT meets the requirement. The detailed results are shown in Fig. 3.

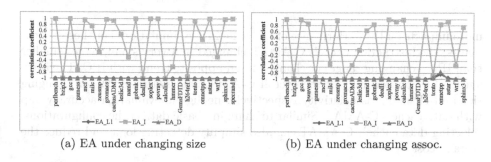

(a) EA under changing size   (b) EA under changing assoc.

Fig. 3. The results of changing L1 data cache configurations

We can see that the data cache's C-AMAT has almost the same evaluation accuracy with the overall C-AMAT for most benchmarks, much higher than that of instruction cache for most benchmarks. This is because the configurations of instruction cache remained unchanged during simulations and its C-AMAT varied in a very small range, which failed to match the changing trend of IPC. The average evaluation accuracy of the overall C-AMAT are -0.999 and -0.989 respectively and the evaluation accuracy gap between the overall C-AMAT and data cache's C-AMAT is negligible. Similar to changing basic instruction cache configurations, selecting data cache's C-AMAT can also simplify the detecting logic and reduce the storage cost by 50%.

Basic L1 Cache Configurations. In this subgroup, both instruction cache and data cache configurations are changed and they are both optimized factors. In this case, a leading factor's C-AMAT should be checked first. The average evaluation accuracy of data cache's C-AMAT are -0.991 and -0.995 for changing size and changing associativity respectively, much higher than that of instruction cache's C-AMAT, which are -0.836 and -0.695 respectively. Therefore, data cache is the leading factor and its C-AMAT should be selected. The results are shown in Fig. 4.

It shows that data cache's C-AMAT has higher evaluation accuracy than that of instruction cache for some benchmarks, demonstrating that data cache has

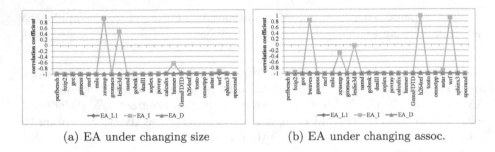

　　　(a) EA under changing size　　　　　　(b) EA under changing assoc.

Fig. 4. The results of changing L1 cache configurations

more impacts on the performance of L1 cache in the simulation. For these benchmarks, the instruction cache's C-AMAT changed in a very small range (smaller than IPC's changing range) or changed in an apposite trend with IPC. The average evaluation accuracy of the overall C-AMAT are both −0.999 for changing size and changing associativity respectively, negligible evaluation accuracy gap with data cache's C-AMAT. Similar to changing basic data cache configurations, selecting data cache's C-AMAT can also simplify detecting logic and reduce the storage cost by 50%.

4.2　Basic L2 Cache Configuration

This group contains configurations that change L2 cache size and associativity. As L2 cache is a unified cache, the optimizations affect both instructions and data accesses. We divide the accesses to L2 cache into two factors, instructions and data accesses. As the number of data accesses to L2 cache is greater than that of instructions in the simulation, data access is the leading factor and it is expected to be selected and checked first. The average evaluation accuracy of data access's C-AMAT are −0.99 and −0.966 for changing size and changing associativity respectively. Therefore, data access's C-AMAT meets the requirement and it can be selected. The results are shown in Fig. 5.

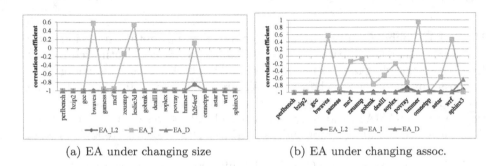

　　　(a) EA under changing size　　　　　　(b) EA under changing assoc.

Fig. 5. The results of changing L2 cache configurations

It can be seen that data access's C-AMAT has similar evaluation accuracy with L2 cache's C-AMAT for most benchmarks, much higher than that of instruction's C-AMAT for some benchmarks. For these benchmarks, C-AMAT of instructions remained relative stable or just changed in a small range, which mismatched with the changing trend of IPC. The evaluation accuracy of L2 cache's C-AMAT are −0.99 and −0.98 respectively, compared to that of data access's C-AMAT, the evaluation accuracy gap is negligible. In terms of hardware overhead, calculating data access's C-AMAT uses the same detecting logic with calculating the L2 cache's C-AMAT, however, as instruction access phases are not required to be recorded, we can use fewer register pairs. According to the ratio of instructions to data accesses (including hit and miss accesses), we can use about 90% of original storage cost for calculating data access's C-AMAT.

4.3 Advanced Cache Configurations

We change the number of MSHR entries for both instruction and data cache in this group, therefore, instruction and data cache are both optimized factors. The average evaluation accuracy of data cache's C-AMAT is −0.987, much higher than that of instruction cache's C-AMAT and the overall C-AMAT, which are 0.26 and −0.649 respectively. Note that the evaluation accuracy of instruction cache's C-AMAT is a positive value, demonstrating that instruction's cache C-AMAT evaluates the memory system performance inaccurately. Therefore, data cache's C-AMAT should be selected. The results are shown in Fig. 6.

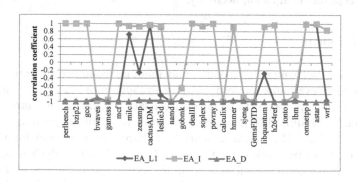

Fig. 6. The results of changing MSHR entries

We can see that the evaluation accuracy of data cache's C-AMAT is even higher than that of the overall C-AMAT for some benchmarks, such as milc, zeusmp, cactusADM, libquantum and astar. This is because the hit rate of instruction cache is very high and few instruction misses were handled by MSHR. Therefore, the instruction cache's C-AMAT is insensitive to the number of MSHR entries, which can be seen from Fig. 6. As L1 cache includes both instruction cache and data cache, its C-AMAT changed in a smaller range than that of data cache's C-AMAT, which did not correlate well with IPC for these benchmarks. Similar to changing basic L1 cache configurations, using data cache's C-AMAT can simplify the detecting logic and reduce the storage cost by 50%.

5   Related Work

Traditional memory metrics, such as MR, AMP and AMAT discussed in Sect. 1, mainly focus on certain component or evaluate the performance based on sequential single-access activity, which is inaccurate for evaluating memory systems with concurrent accesses. X.H. Sun *et al.* proposed C-AMAT [10]. It takes both memory locality and memory concurrency into consideration, thus, can evaluate modern memory systems more accurately. D.W. Wang *et al.* introduced another memory metric called APC (Access Per Cycle) [12], which is defined as the total number of memory accesses divided by the total memory access cycles. Mathematically, C-AMAT is the reciprocal of APC. The advantage of C-AMAT lies in its effectiveness for evaluating memory system designs and APC's attraction as a metric is its simplicity. Based on C-AMAT, Y.H. Liu *et al.* proposed a model called LPM (Layered Performance Matching) [5]. The key idea of LPM is adjusting hardware configurations dynamically in each layer of a memory hierarchy to match the requests of the layer directly above it. In addition, Y.H. Liu *et al.* reevaluated data stall time using C-AMAT [6]. Our work is based on C-AMAT, however, by selecting the factor's C-AMAT rather the overall C-AMAT, it reduces the hardware overhead (including detecting logic and storage cost), with an acceptable evaluation accuracy.

6   Conclusion

C-AMAT takes both memory locality and memory concurrency into consideration, therefore, evaluates modern memory systems more accurately and comprehensively. However, additional hardware resources, including detecting logic and registers are required to measure the parameters (hit concurrency and miss concurrency) of C-AMAT, which incur high hardware overhead for this metric. Based on this observation, we propose FC-AMAT, an analysis model based on C-AMAT. FC-AMAT divides a memory system into factors according to actual research demands and uses factor's-first C-AMAT rather than the overall C-AMAT to evaluate effects of optimizations applied to a memory system if the factor's C-AMAT meets certain requirement. By selecting factor's C-AMAT, FC-AMAT can reduce the hardware overhead for measuring its parameters, meanwhile, it guarantees an acceptable evaluation accuracy through a rigorous check. Simulations with varied cache configurations were conducted to verify the usefulness of FC-AMAT. Experimental results show that FC-AMAT can simplify the detecting logic and reduce the storage cost for recording memory access phases, without sacrificing obvious evaluation accuracy, demonstrating the effectiveness of FC-AMAT.

Acknowledgments. This work is supported in part by National Natural Science Foundation of China under Grant No.: 61433019, 61472435, 61572508 and 61672526.

References

1. Agarwal, A., Royn, K., Vijaykumar, T.N.: Exploring high bandwidth pipelined cache architecture for scaled technology. In: Proceedings of Design, Automation and Test in Europe Conference and Exhibition (DATE 2003), pp. 778–783. IEEE Computer Society Press, Los Alamitos (2003)
2. Binkert, N., Beckmann, B., Black, G., Reinhardt, S.K., et al.: The gem5 simulator. ACM SIGARCH Comput. Architect. News **39**(2), 1–7 (2011)
3. Hennessy, J.L., Patterson, D.A.: Computer Architecture: A Quantitative Approach, 4th edn. Morgan Kaufmann Publishers Inc., San Francisco (2006)
4. Kroft, D.: Lockup-free instruction fetch/prefetch cache organization. In: Proceedings of the 8th Annual Symposium on Computer Architecture (ISCA 1981), pp. 81–87. IEEE Computer Society Press, Los Alamitos (1981)
5. Liu, Y.H., Sun, X.H.: LPM: concurrency-driven layered performance matching. In: Proceedings of the 44th International Conference on Parallel Processing (ICPP 2015), pp. 879–888 (2015)
6. Liu, Y., Sun, X.: Reevaluating data stall time with the consideration of data access concurrency. J. Comput. Sci. Technol. **30**(2), 227–245 (2015)
7. Rummel, R.: Understanding correlation (2011). http://www.hawaii.edu/powerkills/UC.HTM
8. Spradling, C.D.: SPEC CPU2006 benchmark tools. ACM SIGARCH Comput. Archit. News **35**(1), 130–134 (2007)
9. Sun, X.H., Ni, L.M.: Another view on parallel speedup. In: Proceedings of the ACM/IEEE Conference on Supercomputing (SC 1990), pp. 324–333. IEEE Computer Society Press, Los Alamitos (1990)
10. Sun, X.H., Wang, D.: Concurrent average memory access time. Computers **47**(5), 74–80 (2014)
11. Sun, X., Wang, D.: APC: a performance metric of memory systems. ACM SIGMETRIVS Perform. Eval. Rev. **40**(2), 125–130 (2012)
12. Wang, D., Sun, X.: APC: a novel memory metric and measurement methodology for modern memory system. IEEE Trans. Comput. **63**(7), 1626–1639 (2011)
13. Wulf, W.A., McKee, S.A.: Hitting the memory wall: implications of the obvious. ACM SIGARCH Comput. Archit. News **23**(1), 20–24 (1995)

An Experimental Comparison of Two Approaches for Diagnosability Analysis of Discrete Event Systems - A Railway Case-Study

Abderraouf Boussif$^{(\boxtimes)}$ and Mohamed Ghazel$^{(\boxtimes)}$

IFSTTAR, Cosys/Estas, 59650 Villeneuve d'Ascq, France
{abderraouf.boussif,mohamed.ghazel}@ifsttar.fr

Abstract. In this paper, two approaches for diagnosability analysis of discrete event systems are discussed and experimentally evaluated. The considered approaches are the *diagnoser-based approach* proposed in [1,2] and the *model-checking reformulation approach* proposed in [3,4]. Experiments are performed on a level crossing benchmark, using the software tools integrating the considered approaches. These two approaches show different features in terms of state-space building and procedure for analyzing diagnosability. Based on the obtained results through the benchmark, a comparative discussion is provided particularly regarding the generated state-spaces and the time consumption for analyzing diagnosability.

Keywords: Discrete event systems · Diagnosability analysis · Fault diagnosis · Model-checking

1 Introduction

Fault diagnosis is an important task in large complex systems and has received a lot of attention in industry and academia during the two last decades [5]. Fault diagnosis involves (*i*) detecting when a fault has occurred, (*ii*) isolating the true fault from many possible fault candidates, and (*iii*) identifying the true damage to the system. In the context of discrete event systems (DES), fault diagnosis is often discussed through two main issues: online diagnosis and diagnosability analysis [6,7]. Online diagnosis consists in inferring the occurrence of predetermined faults from the online observed behavior of the system, where diagnosability refers to the ability to infer within a finite delay, from the observable part of the system behavior, about the occurrence of faults [6].

The pioneering work dealing with these issues has been proposed in [1,6] in the framework of regular languages and automata theories, where a formal definition of diagnosability was introduced. Such a work provided a necessary and sufficient condition for diagnosability as well as a systematic technique, based on the construction of a deterministic automaton called diagnoser, with

K. Barkaoui et al. (Eds.): VECoS 2017, LNCS 10466, pp. 92–107, 2017.
DOI: 10.1007/978-3-319-66176-6_7

the aim of verifying diagnosability and perform the online diagnosis. In [2,8,9], some improvements of this approach have been proposed regarding the diagnoser construction and the diagnosability verification algorithm. Currently, such approaches are known as 'diagnoser-based approaches' since the diagnosability verification is based on the diagnoser construction.

Another class of approaches, called 'twin-plant/verifier-based' approaches, were introduced in [10–12] in order to improve the computing complexity of analyzing diagnosability. The basis idea behind these approaches is to build an intermediate automaton called twin-plant (or verifier), by performing a parallel composition of the system model with itself. The diagnosability issue can then be addressed by analyzing every pair of executions that share the same observation. Such a task is performed using polynomial-time algorithms. Nevertheless, these approaches deal only with diagnosability analysis and do not consider online diagnosis. Recently, authors in [3,4,13,14] attempted to bring forward an effective framework for the diagnosability analysis by proposing some reformulations of the twin-plant/verifier-based approaches as model-checking problems. Thus, checking diagnosability can be reduced to a reachability analysis problem in the twin-plant structure and then be tackled by means of model-checking tools.

In this paper, two approaches for fault diagnosis of discrete-event systems (DES) are evaluated. The case study using the railway level crossing benchmark is carried out to compare features, advantages and limits of these approaches, namely the diagnoser-based approach in [1,2] and the model-checking reformulation approach in [3,4]. It is worth noticing that we have particularly chosen these two approaches since they correspond respectively to the recent improved versions of the *diagnoser-based* and the *twin-plant/verifier* approaches.

The paper is structured as follows: in Sect. 2, we briefly introduce some notations pertaining to DES modeling and diagnosability analysis. In Sect. 3, an overview of the two approaches is given with a comparative discussion regarding the main features of the approaches. In Sect. 4, we evaluate the approaches through a level crossing benchmark and we discuss the obtained results. Finally, some concluding remarks are given is Sect. 5.

2 Preliminaries

2.1 The System Model

The system to be diagnosed is modeled as a finite state automaton $G = \langle X, \Sigma, \delta, x_0 \rangle$, where X is a finite set of states, Σ is a finite set of events, $\delta : X \times \Sigma \rightarrow 2^X$ is the partial transition function, and $x_0 \in X$ is the initial state. A triple $\langle x, \sigma, x' \rangle \in X \times \Sigma \times X$ is called a *transition* if $x' \in \delta(x, \sigma)$. The model G accounts for the normal and faulty behavior of the system, which can be described by the prefix-closed language $L \subseteq \Sigma^*$ generated by G, where Σ^* denotes the *Kleene-closure* of set Σ. Some events in Σ are observable, i.e., their occurrence can be observed, while the others are unobservable. Thus, set Σ can be partitioned as $\Sigma = \Sigma_o \uplus \Sigma_u$, where Σ_o denotes the set of observable events and Σ_u the set of unobservable events. In the context of fault diagnosis, faults are basically represented using unobservable events ($\Sigma_f \subseteq \Sigma_u$).

An event trace $s = \sigma_1\sigma_2\ldots\sigma_n$, with $\sigma_i \in \Sigma$, is said to be *associated* with state trace $\pi = (x_1, x_2, \ldots, x_{n+1})$ if $\forall\, 0 < i \leq n, x_{i+1} \in \delta(x_i, \sigma_i)$. The partial transition function δ can be extended to sequences of events, i.e., one can write $x_{n+1} \in \delta(x_1, s)$. We write s_i to denote the ith event in s. We denote by L/s the post-language of L upon s, i.e., $L/s := \{t \in \Sigma^* \,|\, s.t \in L\}$. We write $s \leq s'$ to denote that s is a prefix of s'. Also, $\psi(\Sigma_f)$ denotes the set of event-traces in L that end with a faulty event in Σ_f. That is, $\psi(\Sigma_f) := \{s.\sigma_f \in L : \sigma_f \in \Sigma_f\}$. Let us consider $\sigma \in \Sigma$ and $s \in \Sigma^*$. We write $\sigma \in s$ to denote that $\exists\, 1 \leq i \leq |s| : s_i = \sigma$. With a slight abuse of notation, we write $\Sigma_f \in s$ to denote that $\exists\, \sigma_f \in \Sigma_f$ such that $\sigma_f \in s$.

To capture the observed behavior of the model, we define the projection mapping $P : \Sigma^* \to \Sigma_o^*$. In the usual manner, $P(\sigma) = \sigma$ for $\sigma \in \Sigma_o$; $P(\sigma) = \epsilon$ for $\sigma \in \Sigma_u$, and $P(s.\sigma) = P(s)P(\sigma)$, where $s \in \Sigma^*$, $\sigma \in \Sigma$. The inverse projection operation P_L^{-1} is defined by $P_L^{-1}(y) = \{s \in L(G) : P(s) = y\}$.

2.2 Definition of Diagnosability

Diagnosability is a qualitative property which refers to the ability to infer accurately, from partially observed executions, about the faulty behavior within a finite delay after a possible occurrence of a fault in a system model. Such a property is widely studied in fault diagnosis of DESs.

The original definition of diagnosability was introduced in the seminal work of Sampath et al. [6] under the assumptions that faults are permanent (i.e., once a fault occurs, the system remains irreparably faulty), the language generated by a system model G is live, and no cycles composed only of unobservable events exist in G. The formal definition of diagnosability is recalled as follows.

Definition 1 *(diagnosability* [6]*). A prefix-closed and live language L is said to be diagnosable, with respect to projection mapping P and class of faults Σ_f, if the following holds:*

$$(\exists n \in \mathbb{N})\, [\forall s \in \psi(\Sigma_f)]\, (\forall t \in L/s)\, [|t| \geq n \Rightarrow D]$$

where D is: $\omega \in P_L^{-1}[P(s.t)] \Rightarrow \Sigma_f \in \omega$.   ◇

This definition means the following: Let s be any sequence generated by G that ends with a fault event in Σ_f, and let t be any sufficiently long continuation of s. Condition D then requires that every sequence ω belonging to language L, which produces the same observable event-trace as $s.t$ ($P(\omega) = P(s.t)$), must hold a fault event from Σ_f.

Example 1. Let us consider finite state automaton (FSA) G in Fig. 1 (adapted from [6]) as a running example. The set of observable events is $\Sigma_o = \{a, b, d, t\}$ and the set of unobservable events is $\Sigma_u = \{u, f\}$ with $f \in \Sigma_f$. G is non-diagnosable model since there exist two infinite event-traces (i.e., $fa(bud)^*$ and $a(bud)^*$) which share the same observable infinite event-trace $a(bd)^*$ such that one event-trace is fault-free and the other one is faulty.

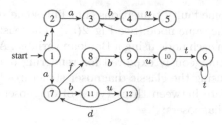

Fig. 1. System model G of Example 1

3 The Considered Approaches

In this section, we first present the approaches considered, namely the *diagnoser-based approach* and the *model-checking reformulation approach*, and then we discuss their main features.

3.1 The Diagnoser-based Approach [1, 2]

The so-called diagnoser-based approach has been firstly introduced in [6] and then improved in [1, 2]. In this paper, we are interesting in the approach discussed in [2].

In order to present the approach, we firstly introduce the following notations:

- $Enable_{\Sigma}(x) = \{\sigma \in \Sigma | \delta(x, \sigma) \neq \emptyset\}$, is the set of events in Σ that are enabled from state x. The generalization to a subset of states $X' \subseteq X$ and a subset of events $\Sigma' \subseteq \Sigma$, is $Enable_{\Sigma'}(X') = \{\sigma \in \Sigma' | \exists x \in X' : \delta(x, \sigma) \neq \emptyset\}$ which denotes the set of enabled events in Σ' from the set of states X', i.e., $Enable_{\Sigma'}(X') = \bigcup_{x \in X'} Enable_{\Sigma'}(x)$.
- $Img(X, \sigma) = \bigcup_{x \in X'} \delta(x, \sigma)$ with $\sigma \in \Sigma$, is the generalization of the transition relation to a subset of states $X' \subseteq X$. The generalization of the transition relation δ to a subset of states $X' \subseteq X$ and a subset of events $\Sigma' \subseteq \Sigma$ is $Img(X', \Sigma') = \bigcup_{x \in X'} \bigcup_{\sigma \in \Sigma'} \delta(x, \sigma)$.
- $Reach_{\Sigma'}(x) = \{x\} \cup \{x' \in X | \exists t \in \Sigma'^{*}, x' \in \delta(x, t)\}$ is the set of states reached by the occurrence of a sequence of events in Σ' from x (will be used particularly for the unobservable reachability). The generalization of this notion for a set of states is $Reach_{\Sigma'}(X') = \bigcup_{x \in X'} Reach_{\Sigma'}(x)$.

The Structure of the Diagnoser Node. Each diagnoser node is partitioned into two distinct subsets of system states:

1. **the set of normal states** (denoted by $\mathcal{X}_N$), which is the subset of states in the node that are reachable from fault-free event-traces;
2. **the set of faulty states** (denoted by $\mathcal{X}_F$), which is the subset of states in the node that are reachable from faulty event-traces.

There may exist some faulty transitions that link some states in $\mathcal{X}_N$ to some others in $\mathcal{X}_F$ within the same node (See Fig. 2(a)). The existence of such transitions is encoded within each node using a Boolean variable. Actually, such a node structure can be advantageously explored for rendering diagnosability analysis more efficiently than using the classic diagnoser structures [1, 6, 8].

One can differentiate between three types of diagnoser nodes, in the same way as in the classic diagnosers:

- **N-certain node**: is a node of which the set of faulty states is empty ($\mathcal{X}_F = \emptyset$);
- **F-certain node**: is a node of which the set of normal states is empty ($\mathcal{X}_N = \emptyset$);
- **F-uncertain node**: is a diagnoser node of which neither the normal set, nor the faulty set, is empty i.e., $\mathcal{X}_N \neq \emptyset$ and $\mathcal{X}_F \neq \emptyset$.

To simplify the notation, we use $a.\mathcal{X}_N$ (resp. $a.\mathcal{X}_F$) to indicate the set of normal states $\mathcal{X}_N$ (resp. set of faulty states $\mathcal{X}_F$) of a given diagnoser node a.

Definition 2 (the diagnoser). *Let $G = \langle X, \Sigma, \delta, x_0 \rangle$ be an FSA to be diagnosed. The diagnoser associated with G is a deterministic FSA $\mathcal{D} = \langle \Gamma, \Sigma_o, \delta_\mathcal{D}, \Gamma_0 \rangle$, where:*

1. *Γ is a finite set of diagnoser nodes;*
2. *Γ_0 is the initial diagnoser node with:*
    (a) $\Gamma_0.\mathcal{X}_N = Reach_{\Sigma_u \backslash \Sigma_f}(x_0)$;
    (b) $\Gamma_0.\mathcal{X}_F = Reach_{\Sigma_u}(Img(\Gamma_0.\mathcal{X}_N, \Sigma_f))$.
3. *$\delta_\mathcal{D} : \Gamma \times \Sigma_o \to \Gamma$ is the transition relation, defined as follows: $\forall a, a' \in \Gamma$, $\sigma \in \Sigma_o : a' = \delta_\mathcal{D}(a, \sigma) \Leftrightarrow a'.\mathcal{X}_N = Reach_{\Sigma_u \backslash \Sigma_f}(Img(a.\mathcal{X}_N, \sigma)) \wedge a'.\mathcal{X}_F = Reach_{\Sigma_u}(Img(a'.\mathcal{X}_N, \Sigma_f) \cup Img(a.\mathcal{X}_F, \sigma))$.* ◇

To summarize, the diagnoser $\mathcal{D}$ is constructed as follows: let the current node be a, and σ is an observable event. The target diagnoser node a' is computed following the rules below:

1. If $\sigma \in Enable(a.\mathcal{X}_N) \cap Enable(a.\mathcal{X}_F)$ then:
    - $a'.\mathcal{X}_N = Reach_{\Sigma_u \backslash \Sigma_f}(Img(a.\mathcal{X}_N, \sigma))$.
    - $a'.\mathcal{X}_F = Reach_{\Sigma_u}(Img(a'.\mathcal{X}_N, \Sigma_f) \cup Img(a.\mathcal{X}_F, \sigma))$.
2. If $\sigma \in Enable(a.\mathcal{X}_N) \backslash Enable(a.\mathcal{X}_F)$ then:
    - $a'.\mathcal{X}_N = Reach_{\Sigma_u \backslash \Sigma_f}(Img(a.\mathcal{X}_N, \sigma))$.
    - $a'.\mathcal{X}_F = Reach_{\Sigma_u}(Img(a'.\mathcal{X}_N, \Sigma_f))$.
3. If $\sigma \in Enable(a.\mathcal{X}_F) \backslash Enable(a.\mathcal{X}_N)$ then:
    - $a'.\mathcal{X}_N = \emptyset$.
    - $a'.\mathcal{X}_F = Reach_{\Sigma_u}(Img(a.\mathcal{X}_F, \sigma))$. ◇

As the diagnoser is constructed on the fly and since all the successors of an F-certain diagnoser node are also F-certain, one does not need to construct them (i.e., the subsequent F-certain nodes) because it is unnecessary from the diagnosis point of view. Indeed, as regards diagnosability analysis, only the analysis of F-uncertain cycles is necessary and since faults are permanent, one can be certain that no such cycle can be generated following an F-certain node.

Example 2. In order to better illustrate the diagnoser construction procedure, let us again consider FSA G in Fig. 1. *Then, its corresponding diagnoser is depicted in* Fig. 2(b). *The initial node* (a_0) *is composed of the initial state of G (state 1) and state 2 reachable from state 1 by the occurrence of faulty event f. One can also notice that there exists an F-uncertain cycle composed of nodes* (a_1) *and* (a_2) *by executing the observable event sequence* $a(bd)^*$. *Diagnoser node* (a_3) *is reached after the occurrence of event t and it contains only a set of faulty states* $(a_3.\mathcal{X}_N = \emptyset)$.

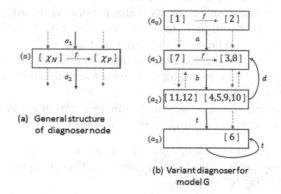

(a) General structure
of diagnoser node

(b) Variant diagnoser for
model G

Fig. 2. The diagnoser node and the diagnoser of model G

Diagnosability Analysis. The necessary and sufficient condition for diagnosability is formulated on the basis of the diagnoser structure and a systematic procedure for checking such a condition on the fly and directly upon the diagnoser is developed in [2].

Proposition 1. *Let* $c\ell = a_1, a_2, \ldots, a_n$ *be an F-uncertain cycle*[1] *in* $\mathcal{D}$, *with* $\delta_{\mathcal{D}}(a_i, \sigma_i) = a_{(i+1) \bmod n}$ *for* $1 \leq i \leq n$. *Then, there exists at least one fault-free cycle in FSA G that shares the same observation* $(\sigma_1, \sigma_2, \ldots, \sigma_n)^*$.   ◇

This result is interesting for checking *F-indeterminate* cycles[2]. It is, in fact, sufficient to check that an *F-uncertain* cycle in the diagnoser corresponds to a faulty cycle in the original model (or the intermediate model), without checking the existence of the faulty-free cycle (the reader is referred to [1,2,6] for more details about these notions).

---

[1] **An F-uncertain cycle** is a cycle in the diagnoser which is composed of only *F*-uncertain nodes.

[2] **An F-indeterminate cycle** in the diagnoser is an *F*-uncertain cycle for which some cycles, which share the same observable projection, exist in the system model such that: (1) at least one cycle involves only normal states and (2) at least one cycle involves only faulty states.

The necessary and sufficient condition for diagnosability is established on the basis of the notion of 'indicating sequence', which is associated with the F-uncertain cycles.

Definition 3 (cl-indicating sequence). Let $cl = a_1, a_2, \ldots, a_n$ be an F-uncertain cycle in $\mathcal{D}$, with $\delta_{\mathcal{D}}(a_i, \sigma_i) = a_{(i+1) \bmod n}$ for $1 \leq i \leq n$. cl-indicating sequence $\rho^{cl} = \mathcal{S}_1, \mathcal{S}_2, \ldots$, is an infinite sequence of sets of states, such that:
- $\mathcal{S}_1 = a_1.\mathcal{X}_F$;
- $\forall i > 1 : \mathcal{S}_i = Reach_{T_u}(Img(\mathcal{S}_{i-1}, \sigma_{(i-1) \bmod n}))$;   ◇

In fact, the cl-indicating sequence tracks the subsets of faulty states in each node of cl without considering the faulty states generated through the occurrence of some faulty transitions outgoing from the normal set of states in the traversed nodes (except for $\mathcal{S}_1$ which holds all the faulty states of $a_1.\mathcal{X}_F$, i.e., $\mathcal{S}_1 = a_1.\mathcal{X}_F$).

Actually, the cl-indicating sequence is introduced with the aim of tracking the actual faulty cycles corresponding to a given F-uncertain cycle, if such cycles exist in the original model.

Hereafter, we state the necessary and sufficient condition for diagnosability on the basis of the notion of cl-indicating sequence.

Theorem 1. For an F-uncertain cycle $cl = a_1, a_2, \ldots, a_n$ in $\mathcal{D}$, and $\rho^{cl} = \mathcal{S}_1, \mathcal{S}_2, \ldots$ its corresponding cl-indicating sequence. Then, cl is an F-indeterminate cycle if and only if: $\forall i \in \mathbb{N}^* : \mathcal{S}_i \neq \emptyset$.   ◇

We recall that a system model G is diagnosable if and only if its corresponding diagnoser does not contain F-indeterminate cycles [6].

For the actual verification of diagnosability, a systematic procedure is derived directly from Theorem 1 and can be performed as follows:

During the on the fly construction of the diagnoser, when an F-uncertain cycle cl is found in $\mathcal{D}$, then:

1. generate the successive elements of cl-indicating sequence ρ^{cl} (starting from $\mathcal{S}_1$), and for each element $\mathcal{S}_i$ check the following conditions:
   (a) if $\mathcal{S}_i = \emptyset$, then cycle cl is not an F-indeterminate cycle and therefore the procedure is stopped;
   (b) else, if $\mathcal{S}_i \neq \emptyset$ and $\exists k \in \mathbb{N} : i = 1 + kn$ (with $n = |cl|$), then:
      i. if $\mathcal{S}_i = \mathcal{S}_{(i-n)}$, then cycle cl is an F-indeterminate cycle and stop the procedure;
      ii. else continue.

This procedure is repeated on each non-explored F-uncertain cycle generated on the fly in $\mathcal{D}$.

Example 3. Let us take once again diagnoser $\mathcal{D}$ of model G depicted in Fig. 2(b). An F-uncertain cycle $cl = a_1, a_2$ exists in $\mathcal{D}$. Thus, let us pick the cl-indicating sequence $\rho = S_1, S_2, S_3, S_4$. One can observe that $S_4 = S_{2=4-2} = \{4, 5\} \neq \emptyset$, which means that, according to Theorem 1, the F-uncertain cycle cl is also an F-indeterminate cycle. Thus, G is non-diagnosable.

3.2   The Model-Checking Reformulation Approach [3,4]

This approach for analyzing diagnosability is carried out by combining the twin-plant construction method [11], and some reformulation on LTL/CTL model-checking [3,4].

Firstly, we recall the twin-plant structure, the necessary and sufficient condition for diagnosability, and then the reformulation of diagnosability issue as a model-checking problem (Fig. 3).

In order to define the twin-plant, let us introduce the so-called '*generator*' $G' = \langle X_o, \Sigma_o, \delta_{G'}, x_0 \rangle$ which is a non-deterministic automaton derived directly for the system model G, with $X_o = \{x_0\} \cup \{x \in X | \exists x' \in X, \exists \sigma \in \Sigma_o : x \in \delta(x', \sigma)\}$ is the finite set of reached states, $x_0 \in X$ is the initial state, Σ_o is the set of observable events, and $\delta_{G'} \subseteq X_o \times \Sigma_o \times X_o$ is the transition relation, defined as follows: $\langle x, \sigma, x' \rangle \in \delta_{G'}$ if $\exists s \in \Sigma^* : x' \in \delta(x, s)$ subjected to $s = \sigma_1 \sigma_2 \ldots \sigma_n = \sigma$: $\sigma_i \in \Sigma_u (i = 1, 2, \ldots, n - 1)$ and $\sigma_n \in \Sigma_o$. It is worth recalling that when, the generator is combined with the tagging function that associates to each state a tag ('N' for normal states and 'F' for faulty ones), then it is called a pre-diagnoser or an augmented generator [1,6].

Twin-Plant Construction. The twin-plant simply consists of two synchronized copies of (augmented) generator G' of system model G, i.e., the parallel system event-traces are synchronized on the observable events. Thus, any event-trace in the twin-plant corresponds to a pair of event-traces in the system model that share the same observation.

Definition 4 *(Twin-plant). A twin-plant of a system model G is an FSA $\mathcal{P} = \langle \mathcal{Q}, \Sigma_o, \Gamma, q_0 \rangle$, where,*

- $\mathcal{Q} \subseteq \{(x, x') \mid x, x' \in X_o \}$ *is the set of states.*
- Σ_o *the set of the (observable) events.*
- $\Gamma \subseteq \mathcal{Q} \times \Sigma_o \times \mathcal{Q}$ *is the partial transition relation s.t. $(q, \sigma, q') \in \Gamma$, with $q = (x_1, x_2)$, and $q' = (x_1', x_2')$ if and only if $(x_1, \sigma, x_1'), (x_2, \sigma, x_2') \in \delta_o$.*
- $q_0 = (x_0 \times x_0) \in \mathcal{Q}$ *is the initial state.*

Each twin-plant state $q = \{(x_1, l_1), (x_2, l_2)\}$ is a pair of the system states with $x_i \in X_o$ and $l_i \in \{N, F\}$. The initial diagnoser state $q = \{(x_o, N), (x_o, N)\}$. If

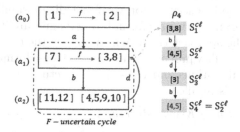

Fig. 3. Generation of $c\ell$-indicating sequences for analyzing diagnosability

$l_i = N$ (resp. $l_i = F$) for $i = 1, 2$, the twin-plant state q is said to be N-certain (resp. F-certain). Otherwise, state q is an F-*ambiguous* state.

We define an F-confused cycle (called also an infinite critical path) in the twin-plant as a cycle which is composed exclusively of F-*ambiguous* states. Authors in [11] have developed a necessary and sufficient condition for diagnosability on the basis of the twin-plant structure as follows:

Theorem 2 *(Necessary and sufficient condition). An FSA G is diagnosable with respect to projection mapping P and class of faults Σ_f if and only if no F-confused cycle exists in its corresponding twin-plant $\mathcal{P}$.*   ◇

Example 4. Let us take again automaton G of Fig. 1. Figure 4 *depicted its corresponding twin-plant $\mathcal{P}$. It is worth noticing that only the live part of $\mathcal{P}$ is constructed. One can observe that $\mathcal{P}$ contains some F-confused cycles (drawn in orange color). Therefore, according to* Theorem 2, *G is non-diagnosable.*

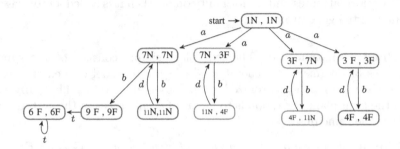

Fig. 4. Twin plant $\mathcal{P}$ of model G (Color figure online)

Diagnosability as a Model-Checking Problem. The model-checking [15] is an automatic formal verification technique that is widely applied to the design of complex dynamic systems (communication protocols, hardware design, etc.). It allows for verifying whether the behavior of a system (modeled by a Kripke structure) satisfies a given property (expressed as a temporal logic formula, such as LTL or CTL) or not using efficient algorithms based on an exhaustive exploration of the system behavior.

In order to use model-checking for verifying diagnosability, authors in [3] proposed a practical framework for reformulating diagnosability issue as a model-checking problem. The approach consists in modeling the twin-plant as a Kripke structure, the diagnosability property as a temporal logic formula, and then using the model-checking algorithms and tools for the actual verification. Hereafter, such a reformulations is recalled.

(a) The twin-plant as a Kripke structure:

In simple terms, a Kripke structure is a non-deterministic state/transition model with atomic propositions assigned to the states (or the actions). Each state of the Kripke structure represents some possible configuration of the system, while a labeling function associates with each state the properties holding in it.

In order to formulate a twin-plant as a Kripke structure, one can simply encode states (of the two copies of the system model) and the observed events of the twin-plant in the state-space of the Kripke structure, i.e., a state in the Kripke structure which corresponds to a state of twin-plant is defined as a vector (x_1, x_2, σ, ϕ), where x_1, x_2 are the states of the system copies and σ is a feasible (observable) event from both x_1 and x_2, and ϕ is an atomic proposition associated with each state, and which takes one proposition from $\{N, F\} \times \{N, F\}$.

(b) The diagnosability condition as a temporal logic formula:

As mentioned above, the diagnosability property can be verified by looking for F-confused cycles in a twin-plant. Moreover, the existence of such cycles can be expressed as a model-checking problem using LTL/CTL specifications.

In order to formulate the diagnosability problem as Model-Checking one, we first express the notion of F-confused cycle using a CTL specification.

The CTL formula which characterizes each state of an F-confused cycle is:

$$\phi \ : \ EG(\textbf{Amb})$$

'Amb' is an atomic proposition associated to each *F-ambiguous* state in the twin-plant. This specification can be read as follows: *"from the current state, all the successor states are F-ambiguous states"*.

Now, the diagnosability issue can be expressed as a model-checking problem as follows:

$$K_\mathcal{P}, S_\mathcal{P} \models \neg \ EF \ EG(\textbf{Amb})$$

where $K_\mathcal{P}$ is the Kripke structure corresponding to the twin-plant $\mathcal{P}$ of G, and $S_\mathcal{P}$ is the initial state in $K_\mathcal{P}$.

3.3 The Main Features of the Considered Approaches

The *diagnoser-based* approach is based on the construction of the diagnoser, which is a *deterministic automaton* derived directly from the system model [1,9]. Such a technique allows for analyzing diagnosability offline and (if the model is diagnosable) performing the online diagnosis task. However, the combinatorial explosion problem is inherent to this approach since the state-space of the diagnoser is, in the worst case, exponential w.r.t. the size of the system model state-space [6].

The main feature of the *model-checking reformulation* approach is the idea of combining the twin-plant construction method [11] with the model-checking reformulation [3,4] for the actual verification of diagnosability. Since the twin-plant construction can be performed using a polynomial-time algorithm [11], the diagnosability property can be checked within a reduced computing complexity regarding the diagnoser-based approach. Nevertheless, this approach allows only for analyzing diagnosability and do not consider online diagnosis (due to the *non-deterministic* nature of the twin-plant).

Regarding the software tools integrating the approaches, the diagnoser-based approach is implemented in DIAG-Tool [2], which is a command-line software developed in C# programming language. DIAG-Tool takes as inputs: (*i*) the system models in *'fsm'* format, and (*ii*) a text file which specifies the sets of observable, non-observable and faulty events. Using these ingredients, DIAG-Tool builds on the fly the diagnoser and simultaneously analyzes the diagnosability. When the model is non-diagnosable, DIAG-Tool outputs the generated part of the diagnoser as well as a witnessed diagnoser event-trace that violated the diagnosability property (the first encountered event-trace). When the model is stated to be diagnosable. DIAG-tool generates the part of the diagnoser that is sufficient to perform the online diagnosis.

Regarding the model-checking reformulation approach, a wide range of powerful and optimized model-checking tools can be used for implementing the technique and analyzing diagnosability. In [3,4], the used tool for analyzing diagnosability is the symbolic model-checker NuSMV [16] (*which is widely used for formal verification in both academia and industry*). The model-checker NuSMV is originated from the re-engineering, re-implementation and extension of CMU SMV tool. Its main advantage is the integration of model-checking techniques based on propositional satisfiability analysis(SAT), which is currently enjoying a substantial success in several industrial fields.

In Table 1, we summarize the main features of the two approaches.

Table 1. Features of the considered approaches

Features	Diagnoser-based approach	Model-checking reformulation
Intermediate model	Deterministic	Non-deterministic
Complexity	Exponential	Polynomial
Diagnosability analysis	Yes	Yes
Online diagnosis	Yes	No
Verification algorithms	Ad-hoc algorithms	Model-checking algorithms
Tools	DIAG-Tool	Model-checkers (NuSMV)

4   The Railway Case-Study

In this section, we apply the two techniques to perform the diagnosability analysis of a railway level crossing benchmark [17]. Firstly, we introduce the considered benchmark and then we discuss the experimental results.

4.1   Railway Level Crossing Benchmark

The considered benchmark consists of a level crossing (LC) system which is an intersection where a railway line intersects with a road or path at the same level. The system is mainly constituted of railway traffic, barriers subsystems and a local controller, which is responsible for activating/deactivating the sound alarms, the road lights and the barriers.

The railway level crossing benchmark was developed in [17] for analyzing various diagnosis issues. The associated Labeled Petri net (LPN) model has been shown to be live and bounded (see Fig. 5). Moreover, while the size of the model grows linearly as the number of railway tracks increases, the associated state-space grows exponentially. Hence, for the sake of scalability analysis, the number of tracks in the benchmark can be increased iteratively as necessary.

The operational logic of a multi-track LC considers the railway traffic on each track:

- the LC is closed to road traffic when at least one train is in the crossing zone;
- the LC is reopened to road traffic only if no train is in the crossing zone.

For diagnosis purposes, a single $(n = 1)$ and multi $(n > 1)$-track LC benchmark with two classes of faults are considered using n (n is the number of tracks)

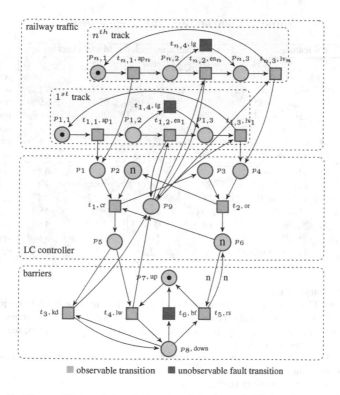

Fig. 5. The multi-track level crossing benchmark (Color figure online)

railway traffic blocks, an LC controller block and a barrier block, as shown in Fig. 5.

The two fault classes which may occur are denoted by red colored transitions in the LPN model (Fig. 5). The first one, named T_{F_1}, related to a train-sensing defect is modeled by unobservable transition $(t_{i,4}, ig)$ and indicates that the train may enter the LC zone before the barriers are lowered. The second failure, named T_{F_2}, modeled by unobservable transition (t_6, bf) indicates a defect of the barriers that results in a premature rising. Either of these two faults can induce incorrect operation of the LC control and possibly train-car collisions.

As the LC system is modeled by an LPN, we first generate its reachability graph with the help of TINA Tool [18] and then perform the two techniques based on the generated reachability graph. In order to assess the scalability, we increase the number of railway track n progressively.

4.2 Experimentation

The experiments were performed on 64-bit PC (CPU: Intel Core i5, 2.5 GHz, Processor with 4 core and 6 GB RAM). We fix 4 h as a maximum analysis duration above which we consider that the tool failed to return a result. The experimental results are summarized in Table 2.

Table 2. Comparative experimental results

	PN features				Diagnoser approach		Model-checking app.			
n	$\lvert P\rvert$	$\lvert T\rvert$	$\lvert\mathcal{N}\rvert$	$\lvert\mathcal{A}\rvert$	$\lvert\mathcal{D}\rvert$	$e_d(s)$	$\lvert S\rvert$	$e_s(s)$	Diag	
1	12	10	20	43	10	0.0	21	0.1	yes	
2	15	14	142	500	13	0.0	216	0.1	no	
3	18	18	832	4085	15	0.0	6246	5.9	no	
4	21	22	4314	27142	28	0.0	68811	424.9	no	T_{f_1}
5	24	26	20556	157551	34	0.5	*	o.t.	no	
6	27	30	92070	831384	36	2.3	*	o.t.	no	
7	30	34	393336	4086585	38	11.8	*	o.t.	no	
1	12	10	20	43	10	0.0	25	0.1	yes	
2	15	14	142	500	83	0.0	484	0.2	yes	
3	18	18	832	4085	483	0.0	5322	7.4	yes	
4	21	22	4314	27142	2434	1.0	49569	395.9	yes	T_{f_2}
5	24	26	20556	157551	11304	31.8	*	o.t.	yes	
6	27	30	92070	831384	56136	1560	*	o.t.	yes	
7	30	34	393336	4086585	*	o.t.	*	o.t.	yes	

*: No result obtained in 4 hours.   o.t.: Out of time

- n: the number of tracks;
- $\lvert P\rvert$ and $\lvert T\rvert$ are, respectively, the number of places and transitions in the Petri net models;
- $\lvert\mathcal{A}\rvert$ and $\lvert\mathcal{N}\rvert$ are, respectively, the number states and arcs in the reachability graph;
- $\lvert\mathcal{D}\rvert$ and $e_d(s)$ are, respectively, the numbers of states in the diagnoser and the required simulation time (in seconds);
- $\lvert S\rvert$ and $e_s(s)$ are, respectively, the numbers of states of the Kripke structure and the required simulation time (in seconds);
- 'Diag' is the diagnosability verdict.

In what follows, we highlight the main observations that can be derived from the obtained results. First, we give some comments regarding the LC models.

• The size of the reachability graph corresponding the LC models (generated by TINA tool [18]) grows very quickly (exponentially) as the number of tracks n increases. This is due to the fact that places p_2 and p_6 can hold as many as n tokens, because of which so many markings exist. Such an exponential evolution of the reachability graph allows for assessing the scalability of the diagnosis approaches.

• Regarding the diagnosability analysis of the LC models, both approaches tested output the same verdicts, namely, while the barriers' failure (T_{F_2}) is diagnosable, the sensor failure (T_{F_1}) is not (except for $n = 1$). A discussion regarding the critical scenarios (transition sequences in the LPN models) which help to understand the diagnosability verdict, can be found in [17, 19].

Regarding the results obtained, the following remarks can be underlined:

• In the case of non-diagnosable models, i.e., when the sensor failure (T_{F_1}) is considered, one can observe that DIAG-tool efficiently analyzes the diagnosability by only constructing the relevant part of the diagnosers, which reduces the memory/time consumption. Actually, while NuSMV blocks from $n = 4$, DIAG-Tool provides the diagnosability verdict in a few seconds even for large values of n. This is due to the on-the-fly analysis which allows for performing the diagnosability analysis based on a partial building of the diagnoser. In other terms, the state-space generation as well as the verification process are stopped as soon as an F-indeterminate cycle is met. This is an interesting feature especially when we deal with such large models. It is worth noticing that NuSMV does not use on-the-fly algorithms for the actual verification. However, by using other model-checkers which perform the on-the-fly analysis, we may obtain similar results to that of DIAG-Tool.

• In the case of diagnosable models, i.e., when the barriers' failure (T_{F_2}) is considered, the diagnoser approach implementing an on the fly procedure potentially needs to construct a larger part of the diagnoser state-space. Consequently, the verification process checks all the F-uncertain cycles that exist in the diagnosers to decide about the diagnosability of the models. In this case, the obtained results clearly reflect the exponential feature of the diagnoser-based approaches. Actually, this is unavoidable when working with diagnoser-based approaches, since it is due to the deterministic nature of the diagnoser.

• Regarding the generated state-spaces, the results show that the diagnoser approach is more efficient and generates less state-space than the model-checking reformulation approach *for the considered benchmark*. This does not violate the claim that the twin-plant approach is more efficient in terms of time complexity (polynomial complexity for the twin approach versus exponential for the diagnoser approach), since the theoretical complexity is computed while considering the worst case.

As a concluding remark, one can underline that from the practical point of view, the efficiency of these two (classes of) approaches developed for analyzing diagnosability greatly depends on the model structure and the sensor mapping configuration, namely the number of observable/unobservable events, the number of strongly connected components, the number of fault events, etc. Therefore, although these aforementioned techniques show different complexity range from a theoretical point of view, in practice (for a given model), it is difficult to decide which the most efficient technique is. Consequently, both approaches remain interesting to investigate and improve.

5   Conclusion

This paper compares two approaches for analyzing diagnosability of discrete event systems, namely a recent version of the diagnoser-based approach and the model-checking reformulation approach. A railway level crossing benchmark, which shows both diagnosable and non-diagnosable faults, is chosen as an experimental benchmark. Two software tools associated with the considered approaches are used for the actual verification. The approaches are evaluated particularly in terms of the generated state-space of advanced models and the required time for constructing such models and analyzing diagnosability.

Acknowledgement. The authors acknowledge the support of the ELSAT2020 project. ELSAT2020 is co-financed by the European Union with the European Regional development Fund, the French state and the Hauts-de-France Region Council.

References

1. Cassandras, C.G., Lafortune, S.: Introduction to Discrete Event Systems. Springer, Heidelberg (2008)
2. Boussif, A.: Contributions to fault diagnosis of discrete event systems. Ph.D. Thesis - University of Lille 1 (2016)
3. Cimatti, A., Pecheur, C., Cavada, R.: Formal verification of diagnosability via symbolic model checking. In: International Conference on Artificial Intelligence, pp. 363–369 (2003)
4. Boussif, A., Ghazel, M.: Diagnosability analysis of input/output discrete event system using model checking. In: The 5th IFAC International Workshop on Dependable Control of Discrete Systems (DCDS), pp. 71–78 (2015)
5. Zaytoon, J., Lafortune, S.: Overview of fault diagnosis methods for discrete event systems. Ann. Rev. Control **37**(2), 308–320 (2013)
6. Sampath, M., Sengupta, R., Lafortune, S.: Diagnosability of discrete event systems. IEEE Trans. Autom. Control **40**(9), 1555–1575 (1995)
7. Lin, F.: Diagnosability of discrete event systems and its applications. Discr. Event Dynamic Syst. **4**(2), 197–212 (1994)
8. Hashtrudi Zad, S., Kwong, R.H., Wonham, W.M.: Fault diagnosis in discrete event systems: framework and model reduction. IEEE Trans. Autom. Control **48**(7), 1199–1212 (2003)
9. Boussif, A., Ghazel, M., Klai, K.: Combining enumerative and symbolic techniques for diagnosis of discrete event systems. In: Verification and Evaluation of Computer and Communication Systems, pp. 1–15 (2015)

10. Yoo, T.-S., Lafortune, S.: Polynomial-time verification of diagnosability of partially observed discrete event systems. IEEE Trans. Autom. Control **47**(9), 1491–1495 (2002)
11. Jiang, S., Huang, Z., Chandra, V., Kumar, R.: A polynomial algorithm for testing diagnosability of discrete event systems. IEEE Trans. Autom. Control **46**(8), 1318–1321 (2001)
12. Moreira, M.V., Jesus, T.C., Basilio, J.C.: Polynomial time verification of decentralized diagnosability of discrete event systems. IEEE Trans. Autom. Control **56**(7), 1679–1684 (2011)
13. Boussif, A., Ghazel, M.: Using model-checking techniques for diagnosability analysis of intermittent faults-a railway case-study. In: Verification and Evaluation of Computer and Communication Systems, pp. 93–104 (2016)
14. Bourgne, G., Dague, P., Nouioua, F., Rapin, N.: Diagnosability of input output symbolic transition systems. In: 1st International Conference on Advances in System Testing and Validation Lifecycle, pp. 147–154 (2009)
15. Clarke, E.M., Grumberg, O., Peled, D.: Model Checking. The MIT Press, Cambridge (1999)
16. Bozzano, M., Cavada, R., Cimatti, A., Dorigatti, M., Griggio, A., Mariotti, A., et al.: nuXmv: 1.0 user manual (2014)
17. Ghazel, M., Liu, B.: A customizable railway benchmark to deal with fault diagnosis issues in DES. In: 13th International Workshop on Discrete Event Systems, pp. 177–182 (2016)
18. Berthomieu, B., Ribet, P.-O., Vernadat, M.: The tool TINA: construction of abstract state spaces for Petri nets and time Petri nets. Int. J. Prod. Res. **42**(14), 2741–2756 (2007)
19. Liu, B., Ghazel, M., Toguyeni, A.: Model-based diagnosis of multi-track level crossing plants. IEEE Trans. Intell. Transp. Syst. **17**(2), 546–556 (2016)

Mobility Load Balancing over Intra-frequency Heterogeneous Networks Using Handover Adaptation

Hana Jouini[1,2]([✉]), Mohamed Escheikh[1], Kamel Barkaoui[1,2],
and Tahar Ezzedine[1]

[1] Communications Systems Laboratory (SysCom),
National Enginneering School of Tunis (ENIT),
University of Tunis El Manar (UTM), BP 37, 1002 Tunis Le Belvédère, Tunisia
{hana.jouini,mohamed.escheikh,tahar.ezzedine}@enit.rnu.tn
[2] Conservatoire National des Arts et Métiers,
Ecole SITI - Département Informatique Lab. Cedric Vespa,
2, Rue Conté, 75141 Paris Cedex 03, France
kamel.barkaoui@cnam.fr

Abstract. Heterogeneous Networks (HetNet) present a straightforward and effective key factor for enhancing performance of next generation cellular networks. Since outdoor macro-cells are often likely to be affected by heavy loaded situations, a major issue in HetNet planning is to ensure that small-cells actually serve enough user equipments (UE). A scenario to consider is the traffic offloading from macro-cells to small-cells. The concept of Mobility Load Balancing (MLB) which had arisen with the 3rd Generation Partnership Project (3GPP) Release 8 [1,2] to maximize the whole capacity of the system by optimally distributing traffic among neighbouring cells, may play a key role in such a situation. In this paper, we present a review of MLB algorithms proposed in the literature and designed for HetNets by classifying these algorithms based on the UE state (i.e. UE in idle or connected mode). In fact the adopted MLB technique is closely related to the mode of the UE (idle or connected mode). We also present a technique for MLB based on optimizing handover (HO) by adapting hysteresis values based on cells' loads.

Keywords: HetNet · Mobility load balancing · Connected mode · Hysteresis · Handover

1 Introduction

Giving the exponentially increasing number of mobile broadband, data subscribers and highly bandwidth demanding applications, operators had recourse to advance physical layer technologies such as Orthogonal Frequency Division Multiple Access (OFDMA), multi-antenna techniques or more efficient modulation/coding schemes, when deploying 4G cellular networks and especially Long

© Springer International Publishing AG 2017
K. Barkaoui et al. (Eds.): VECoS 2017, LNCS 10466, pp. 108–123, 2017.
DOI: 10.1007/978-3-319-66176-6_8

Term Evolution (LTE) systems. However, it seems that capacity demand increasing is faster than spectral efficiency improvement. Then the above mentioned solutions alone are insufficient in particular at hotspot areas and cell edges where network performance can significantly degrade. One solution maybe to add more macro-cells or multiplying the number of sectors/antennas per macro-cell. Such a solution is difficult to consider given the high cost of macro-cells deployment especially in urban zones [3]. While HetNet seems to be an attractive way to deal with system capacity/coverage limitations, operators started integrating small-cells with their macro-cell networks. A new LTE network topology had arisen and will strongly influence next generations of cellular networks. Traditional HetNets deal with the interworking of wireless local area networks such as wifi and cellular networks [4]. Whereas a HetNet in 3GPP definition is a network containing cell sites with different characteristics such as different values of transmission power (Tx power) or radio frequency (RF) coverage areas. The result is a HetNet with large coverage macro-cell layer combined with small-cell deployments producing increased bitrates per unit area. A typical HetNet may gather macro-cell, picocell and femtocell layers. A femtocell may be a closed subscriber group (CSG) cell allowing only its UE members to access it. Picocells are typically managed together with macro-cells by operators. In general, they are open access. Excellent contributions have been provided in [5–7] to better understand HetNets. Authors in [5] discuss theoretical models including coverage and throughput analysis, signal-to-interference-plus-noise ratio (SINR) distribution, cell association and cellular spatial models for understanding the requirements of future HetNet against current cellular topologies. A theoretical framework for two-tier cellular networks based on random spatial models was developed to investigate network performance when using enhanced technologies such as enhanced Inter-Cell Interference Coordination (eICIC) or Cell Range Extension (CRE, a.k.a. Cell Range Expansion). Concerning HetNet new features, the work in [6] compares between traditional networks and heterogeneous ones by discussing aspects such as KPI performance metrics, mobility and interference management, cell association or network topology. A potential 5G cellular architecture based on HetNet deployment is proposed in [7] where authors discuss some promising key technologies that can be adopted in 5G systems.

In the context of HetNet, cell offloading generally means the transfer (i.e. offload) of extra traffic from macro- to small-layer to improve macro-cells capacity. As a large amount of indoor traffic can be offloaded from macro- to small-layer, fewer macro-cells will be needed for indoor coverage. The reduction of macro-cell sites will result in a huge CAPEX (i.e. significant saving in macro-cell deployments) and OPEX (i.e. significant saving in backhauling) reductions for operators. Since Load Balancing[1] (LB) refers to techniques that enable the balance of traffic between hot spot cells and low loaded cells, offloading may be studied under the general heading of LB. In 3GPP LTE systems the MLB is closely related to the

---

[1] Throughout this scope we use the terms Load Balancing and mobility load balancing interchangeably.

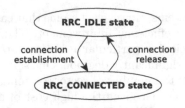

Fig. 1. UE RRC connection states in 3GPP LTE systems

UE connection mode (i.e. UE in idle or connected mode) (Fig. 1). In fact, MLB may be performed at any instance of the radio resource control (RRC) UE state machine. This includes offloading UEs while being in idle or connected states. MLB in idle state is performed by means of cell selection and reselection procedures. The main motivation for offloading idle UEs is to mitigate signalling overhead from potential load driven HO executions. After switching to the connected mode, a situation where the camping cell does not have enough resources to serve the newly arrived UE may occur. To resolve such a situation, implementing a connected mode MLB scheme seems to be the most effective solution. In this context, cells can quickly react to inter-layer load variations and take the proper offloading decision either by updating mobility parameters or executing forced HOs. The challenge for connected MLB schemes is to maintain HO executions at an acceptable level, as they cost in terms of signalling. In this paper we will investigate MLB in HetNets, first by presenting a literature review on existing techniques and then by implementing and simulating MLB schemes under realistic network scenarios of a two-tier HetNet deployment. The rest of this paper is organized as follows: in Sect. 2 we focus our attention on the study of MLB for HetNets in both UE idle and connected states. In Sect. 3 we give a brief insight on the HO procedure in 3GPP LTE systems and then we formulate the problem of MLB by defining the cell load measurement. In Sect. 4 we detail the proposed MLB schemes while in Sect. 5 we present simulation results and conclude our work in Sect. 6.

2   Literature Review of MLB in HetNets

2.1   MLB in Idle Mode: Load-Aware User Association

The problem of User Association[2] (UA) for network MLB has attracted much attention in the recent years. In fact, an efficient method to balance the traffic between macro- and small-layers seems to be optimizing the cell selection scheme. Radio Access Technology (RAT) selection has been extensively studied in earlier works (see [8] for a survey). It has been shown that an efficient cell association scheme for HetNets should jointly consider two objectives; balancing the load

---

[2] Throughout this dissertation, we use the terms user association, cell association and cell selection interchangeably.

among different layers while minimizing the inter-cell interference [9]. From that point of view many recent works cope with MLB issue by proposing UA schemes. These latter are generally considered as a binary NP-hard matching problems [10], that aim to minimize inter- and intra-layer load disparity in HetNets. In this context a classical cell selection approach where UEs camp in the cell with the best downlink (DL) signal strength is unsuitable. Since HetNets combine both macro-cells with high Tx power and small-cells with low Tx power. The concept of CRE proposed by 3GPP [11] is a popular solution that has been studied in many works. Authors in [16] propose a CRE based approach for UA. The technique consists on minimising a-fairness objective function using distributed learning algorithms in near-potential games with load and outage constraints. Authors in [32] investigate an inter-RAT offloading using biased received power, where the optimal bias resulting in the highest SINR and the highest rate coverage were determined using numerical evaluation techniques. Authors in [12] propose to perform cell selection based on a hybrid scheme where a centralized entity sends load information to idle UEs which perform UA based on a global utility to maximize Quality of Service (QoS) by achieving optimum values of throughput and call blocking probability. Ye et al. propose in [13] a distributed load-aware UA scheme defined as a logarithmic maximisation problem and aims to maximize UE data rate. First, authors relax the deterministic UA to a fractional association by allowing UEs to associate more than one cell at the same time (i.e. fractional UA). Then the primal combinatorial optimization problem is converted into a convex optimization problem. By exploiting the convexity of the problem, a distributed UA algorithm was developed with the assistance of dual decomposition and the gradient descent method. A similar approach was adopted in [14] where authors aim to optimize UA decision by utilizing a logarithmic utility function based on weighted proportional fairness as objective but without relaxing the deterministic UA constraint in order to approach a realistic system modelling. Authors in [15] address the UA problem for HetNets from an optimization perspective under the proportional fairness criterion. Based on pricing strategy, UEs are associated with a cell according to the value of a utility minus a price. Authors in [17] propose to utilize the concept of topology potential for measuring the desirability of different cells to UEs in UA issue. Then the problem is resolute as a utility proportional fairness optimization function. A virtually distributed UA algorithm is proposed in [18] for software-defined Radio Access Network (RAN) architecture where the UA scheme is implemented in a centralized manner at the RAN controller (RANC).

2.2   MLB in Connected Mode

In 3GPP LTE systems connected mode refers to the state where a connection is established between the cell and the UE according to the RRC protocol specifications. When UEs are in RRC connected state, the mobility management is implemented by means of HO executions. Many works investigate the MLB issue while UEs are in connected state. Authors in [19] propose to balance the load by dividing the traffic of each UE among the different layers forming the

HetNet. In fact, [19] presents the heterogeneity as an overlapping of cell layers with divergent characteristics in terms of frequency bands, RAT and backhaul support. The problem is treated as a weighted base LB where the traffic of an UE is divided into subflows, each of which is transmitted via a different layer. MLB is investigated jointly with interference mitigation in [20] where authors exploit massive multiple-input multiple-output (MIMO) technology as one of the key factors of 5G systems. Since MLB is closely related to the manner how we schedule UEs among different cells, authors in [20] design a DL macro-cell scheduler which offload macro UEs to small-cell layer. Authors in [21] consider a relaxed problem formulation where each UE can be associated with multiple cells and show that this problem can be solved by convex optimization. For a weight-based MLB scheme, the performance of this latter is highly depended on the specific weight, which was heuristically obtained in [21]. Based on the concept of auction in game theory, authors in [22] propose a two-stage LB scheme for offloading UEs to small-cell layer. The proposed algorithm allows a small-cell that has received a HO request message from an UE to calculate the received signal strength indicator (RSSI) of its neighbouring small-cells which is used to identify if there are other small-cells that are more suitable for the UE. Authors in [23] propose to improve the energy efficiency of the LTE network by inter-working with low energy consuming WiFi networks. The basic idea is to try to hand over UEs with low signal quality in LTE as many as possible to WiFi layer which has enough resources to accommodate more users. Authors in [24] apply the technique of design of experiments (DOE) to dynamically optimize small-CRE according to the load of neighbouring macro-cells. Authors in [25] propose a LB scheme in which each small-cell locally performs a load balanced scheduling to equalise the performance of its connected UEs that are scheduled in subframes overlapping and non-overlapping with macro-cell ABS. Authors in [26] investigate and analyse the behaviour of a novel distributed MLB scheme where the cell individual offset (CIO) is updated for each cell depending on calculation of its composite available capacity (CAC) [27]. In the next two sections, we first formulate the general problem of MLB in connected mode by defining HO procedure as specified in LTE 3GPP systems. After the definition of cell load is given and the concept of available capacity is introduced, the MLB scheme is decided.

3   Problem Formulation and System Model

The HO procedure enables one cell to hand over an UE to another cell while maintaining the RAN services at the new cell. In 3GPP LTE systems intra-frequency HO is triggered based on A3 event [29]. The entering condition to be satisfied for A3 event can be formulated as follows:

$$M_j + CSOff > M_i + Hys_{i \rightarrow j} \tag{1}$$

where M_i and M_j are the UE measurement corresponding to the serving cell i and the neighbouring cell j respectively. $CSOff$ is a parameter depending on the measurement biasing (i.e. $CSOff$ calculation depends on whether we have intra- or inter-layer HO) and $Hys_{i \rightarrow j}$ is the HO offset from cell i to j (a.k.a. hysteresis). If the serving cell i is overloaded, one way to offload the excess traffic to its neighbours is by decreasing $Hys_{i \rightarrow j}$ value. To alleviate the traffic in the congested cell, we adopt two scenarios:

- Inter-layer HO biasing: a principle issue in HetNet is the traffic balancing between the macro-layer, more sensitive to overloaded situations, and the small-layer. Inter-layer HO biasing concerns the biasing of HO threshold between a congested macro-cell and its neighbouring from the small-tier (i.e. small-cells).
- Intra-layer HO biasing: since loads in different cells from the same macro-layer are frequently unequal [28], a scenario to consider when balancing the network traffic concerns the biasing of HO threshold between a congested macro-cell and its neighbours from the same tier (i.e. macro-cells).

The proposed MLB scheme relies on the performing of intra- and inter-layer HO biasing to guarantee a best interoperability, scalability and reliability of the traffic offloading. In this paper we consider the DL transmission of a two-tier 3GPP LTE HetNet with multiple macro-cells and small-cells as shown in Fig. 3. Each eNB consists of three macro-cells (i.e. sectors) and a small-cell represents a femtocell configured in open access mode. Femtocells are composed by one small-cell. In HetNet, the total bandwidth in a cell is determined by the network's frequency planning. To facilitate the implementation of intra-frequency MLB algorithm, a full frequency reuse scheme is considered (we assume a frequency reuse of one). This means that no frequency partitioning is performed between cells which is considered as a realistic scenario for LTE systems. We adopt a regular deployment for modelling the macro-cell layer where eNBs are deployed in an hexagonal layout. All UEs and small-cells are scattered into each macro-cell in a random manner. We denote C the set of cells including macro-cells and small-cells, and represent the set of scheduled UEs as U. We assume that the number of connected UEs in the network is constant along the simulation duration. C_i represents the cell i. $C_{i,j}$ denotes a neighbouring cell C_j of a cell C_i. The amount of Physical Resource Blocks (PRBs) quantifying time-frequency resources of a cell is denoted R (We assume that all cells have the same amount of PRBs). $U_i(t)$ is the set of UEs scheduled in C_i at time t and $U_{i,k}(t)$ indicates an UE k scheduled in C_i at time t. $R_{i,k}(t)$ is the amount of consumed PRBs by $U_{i,k}(t)$ at time t. The load $\rho_i(t)$ of C_i at time t can be calculated as follows:

$$\rho_i(t) = \frac{\sum_{k \in U_i(t)} R_{i,k}(t)}{R} \tag{2}$$

To detect an overloaded situation, each cell periodically monitors information about its own load conditions and exchange load information with its neighbouring cells. LTE systems define the X2 interface between neighbouring eNBs which allows cells to be aware about network load condition [27]. Load information is transmitted over the X2 interface in the form of Composite Available Capacity

(CAC) parameter. Formally, CAC expresses the amount of load that a particular cell is willing to accept subject to several factors such as resource utilization, QoS requirements, backhaul capacity and the load of control channels. We define CACD as the CAC in DL. Let $CACD_i$ be the overall available resource level that a cell i can offer for MLB purposes in DL. Then it can be expressed as:

$$CACD_i(t) = 1 - \rho_i(t) \tag{3}$$

Depending on $CACD$ value, each cell may estimate its load condition and decide whether to enable the MLB algorithm if it experiences an overloaded situation or to keep it disabled.

4   MLB Based HO Biasing

The MLB algorithm developed to balance the load among neighbouring cells relies on the principles described in [28]. The proposed MLB scheme is based on calculating new HO thresholds based on the load of each cell as illustrated in Fig. 2.

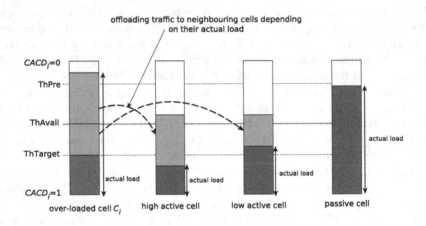

Fig. 2. Illustration of the proposed offloading scheme

We introduce three thresholds, with values between 0 to 1, that would serve to estimate cell load status:

- $ThPre$: If $CACD_i$ decreases below this threshold, C_i is declared as an overloaded cell and should enable the MLB algorithm to balance its load by updating HO threshold values according to the MLB scheme.
- $ThTarget$: If $CACD_i$ of an overloaded cell C_i that activated the MLB algorithm increases over this threshold, C_i should deactivate the MLB algorithm and restore default HO threshold values.

– *ThAvail*: it serves to estimate the degree of neighbouring cells' capability to receive offloaded traffic.

These thresholds are operator-configurable parameters and are transmitted as an input to the MLB algorithm. E.g. if we set *ThPre* to 0 the MLB scheme is only executed when the concerned cell is fully-loaded and has zero available resources. If *ThTarget* is set to 1, the MLB scheme will be disabled only if the cell is totally empty. Operators may tune thresholds according to their specific objectives. Low *ThAvail* values mean that more cells will participate to MLB if it's enabled by a neighbouring cell. To maximize the number of active cells, *ThAvail* should be set to 0. High *ThPre* values may be chosen if operators want to promote network performance in terms of QoS. This means that the network will be very sensitive to overloaded situations and will aim to avoid call blocking/dropping situations by optimising load distribution among different network tiers. Low *ThTarget* values mean that the operator aims to minimise signalling traffic between cells by minimising HO executions due to LB, while high values will reduce the risk of ping-pong HO.

Cells periodically perform load measurements and estimate their own CACD. If a cell C_i is overloaded (i.e. $CACD_i \leqslant ThPre$) it should offload some of its attached UEs to neighbouring cells. As shown in Fig. 2 and Table 1, neighbouring cells are classified into three categories given their own load conditions and based on the aforementioned thresholds; High active cells correspond to nodes whose available capacity is higher than *ThTarget* threshold and are willing to accept more traffic. On the contrary, those with a *CACD* value equal or under *ThAvail* are denoted as passive and constitute cells declared incapable to participate to MLB procedure. Ultimately, cells operating within the $[ThAvail, ThTarget]$ *CACD* range are characterized as low active ones as they may participate in MLB procedures with little rate of resources. Formally, all MLB procedures are triggered by overloaded macro-cells. Therefore, upon overload declaration, the cell has to estimate an hysteresis decrement so that excess traffic is offloaded to adjacent cells. In addition, it informs its active neighbours over the X2 interface to the new hysteresis modification subject to their own cell load conditions. Both active and passive cells need to estimate their *CACD*. Once $CACD_j(t)$ is estimated, it is basically mapped to an $\alpha-$modification. We propose three versions of the MLB algorithm depending on how we calculate new hysteresis values:

Table 1. Neighbouring cells classification

Neighbouring cell load condition	Neighbouring cell status
$CACD_j > ThTarget$	High active
$ThAvail < CACD_j \leqslant ThTarget$	Low active
$CACD_j \leqslant ThAvail$	passive

1. version 1: slow MLB

$$\alpha_{i \to j} = \begin{cases} 1 \ if \ CACD_j \leq ThTarget \\ 0 \ if \ CACD_j > ThTarget \end{cases} \tag{4}$$

2. version 2: fast MLB

$$\alpha_{i \to j} = \begin{cases} 1 \ if \ CACD_j \leq ThAvail \\ 0 \ if \ CACD_j > ThAvail \end{cases} \tag{5}$$

3. version 3: smooth MLB

$$\alpha_{i \to j} = \begin{cases} 1 & if \ CACD_j \leq ThAvail \\ 1 - \frac{ThAvail - CACD_j}{ThAvail - ThTarget} & if \ ThAvail < CACD_j \leq ThTarget \\ 0 & if \ CACD_j > ThTarget \end{cases} \tag{6}$$

The new hysteresis value between C_i and $C_{i,j}$ (i.e. $NewHys_{i \to j}$) is adjusted as follows:

$$NewHys_{i \to j} = \alpha_{i \to j} \times Hys_{i \to j} \tag{7}$$

5 Simulation Assumptions and Results

System level simulations using the discrete-event network simulator ns-3 [31] are considered in this paper. We consider the dual stripe model proposed by 3GPP to illustrate realistic scenarios of dense-urban Home eNBs (HeNB[3]) deployment [30]. Simulations implement an intra-frequency network where both macro-cells and small-cells are deployed at 2 GHz sharing 5 MHz of bandwidth. Figure 3 illustrates the multi-cell network considered in the 3GPP dual stripe model. The

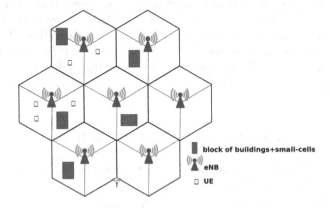

Fig. 3. Network topology

---

[3] Also known as femtocell.

simulated network is composed by 7 eNBs (21 cells) regularly deployed in hexagonal layout where the distance between two eNBs is assumed equals to 500 m. 4 blocks (apartment buildings) are randomly dropped among the network. Each block represents two stripes of apartments, each stripe has 2 by 10 apartments (Fig. 4). We simulate a street between the two stripes of apartments with width of 10 m. Each small-cell block has one floor. Each block has 1 small-cell. The number of connected macro-UEs is gradually increased to show the effect of high traffic generation areas (hotspots) on the network performance.

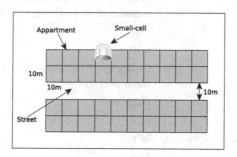

Fig. 4. block of small-cells lyaout

A fixed number of home UEs is considered (i.e. $nbHomeUE = 16$). Table 2 summarizes the main parameters of the simulated scenarios. Thresholds values are fixed as follows:

- $ThPre = 0.2$: In fact $ThPre$ refers to the point from which a cell may enable the MLB scheme. $ThPre = 0.2$ means that when 80% of the cell resources are occupied and only 20% are still available the cell is considered as overloaded, which may be a realistic assumption if no QoS is required.
- $ThTarget = 0.8$: It refers to the point that, when reached, the cell may disable the MLB scheme. A reason to set $ThTarget$ to such a high value is to avoid ping-pong HO due to MLB while offloading UEs to neighbouring cells.
- $ThAvail = 0.5$: operators can control the number of neighbouring cells that may participate to LB by tuning $ThAvail$.

To evaluate the trade-off between capacity enhancements provided by LB and a potential mobility performance degradation, the following cases are considered:

- Fixed hysteresis: No hysteresis adjustments are performed. A fixed handover hysteresis of 3 dB is assumed for all cell pairs; hence, $Hys_{m \to m} = Hys_{m \to s} = 3db$ (i.e. $Hys_{m \to m}$ is the hysteresis value for HO between macro-cells and $Hys_{m \to s}$ is the hysteresis value fro HO from a macro-cell to a neighbouring small-cell)
- Slow MLB algorithm: Hysteresis range is calculated based on Eq. 4 for both $Hys_{m \to m}$ and $Hys_{m \to s}$.

Table 2. Simulation parameters

Parameter	Value
Macro-tier cellular layout	7 eNBs (21 cells) in hexagonal layout
Number of smallcells	16
Inter-eNBs distance	500 m
Macro-cell Tx power	46 db
small-cell Tx power	20 db
Path loss model	both outdoor and indoor communication are considered in pathloss calculation
Carrier frequency	2 Ghz
System bandwidth	5 Mhz
Traffic model	Guaranteed Bit Rate (GBR) conversational voice over IP
UE distribution	random
Macro UE densities	$\{0.1, 0.2, 0.3, 0.4, 0.5, 0.6, 0.7, 0.8, 0.9, 1\} \times 10^{-4}$
UE measurement reporting interval	50 ms
Simulation duration	50 s
MLB parameters tuning	
Hysteresis default value	3.0 db
Hysteresis margin with MLB	[0..3 db]
ThPre	0.2
ThTarget	0.8
ThAvail	0.5

- Fast MLB algorithm: The hysteresis range is calculated based on Eq. 5 for both $Hys_{m \to m}$ and $Hys_{m \to s}$.
- smooth MLB algorithm: In this case, $Hys_{m \to m}$ and $Hys_{m \to s}$ are dynamically adjusted based on Eq. 6 and within the range of [0 db, 3 db] dB.

Cell load observations are performed periodically every second. Figure 5 illustrates the global network throughput for all simulated schemes with different UEs densities. When using a MLB algorithm, the global throughput is ameliorates across different network cells, especially for high traffic simulations. As observed, the MLB impact on network performance depends closely on UEs density. For relatively low UEs densities (i.e. $[10^{-5}, 5 \times 10^{-5}]$) MLB integration has low impact on the network performance. Since in such case a heavy-loaded situation may not occur during the simulation, MLB algorithm will very probably not be enabled. For higher densities (i.e. $[6 \times 10^{-5}, 10^{-4}]$), some macro-cells will fall under a heavy-loaded situation. Then by offloading extra traffic from those macro-cells to its macro neighbours and to the small-cell layer the network global throughput is significantly ameliorated.

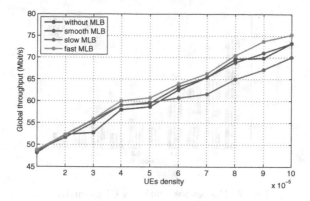

Fig. 5. Global network throughput vs UEs density

To highlight the impact of deploying small-cell layer alongside the macro-cell layer, we present the macro-layer's cells throughput for each simulated scheme and for a UE density of 5×10^{-5} (Fig. 6). We notice that the throughput disparity between macro-cells is more severe for simulations without a MLB scheme; while cells 15 and 18 experience high throughput values which may result in high call blocking/dropping rates, cells 6, 17 and 20 present low throughput leading to a resource waste. This disparity is mitigated when integrating a MLB algorithm, especially for fast and smooth MLB schemes. Figure 7 represents the Packet Loss Ratio (PLR) evolution with respect to UEs density with and without activation of the MLB algorithms. Results show that smooth MLB scheme presents the lower values of PLR. This phenomenon may be explained by the particularity of smooth

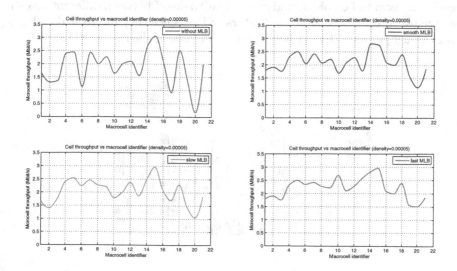

Fig. 6. Macro-cells throughput vs macro-cell's identifier

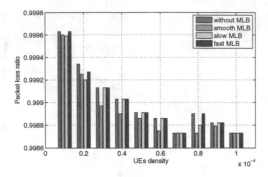

Fig. 7. Packet loss ratio vs UEs density

MLB scheme that tune hysteresis values in a non-aggressive and progressive manner with a more meticulous respect to neighbours' load conditions comparing to fast and slow MLB schemes (see Eqs. 4, 5 and 6). Figure 8 highlights Jain's Fairness Index (JFI) versus UEs density. We observe that JFI values are improved for relatively high densities in a similar manner when activating MLB algorithms. For lower densities, no improvement in the fairness between macro-cells is generated and the simulated MLB schemes present in some cases (i.e. 0.1×10^{-4} and 0.2×10^{-4}) a degradation in JFI values. Figure 9 illustrates the evolution of the number of successful HOs according to UEs density with and without MLB algorithms activation. The number of successful HOs is almost unchanged when activating one of the MLB algorithm or when deactivating MLB schemes. This may be considered as a significant gain, since a MLB scheme promotes enabling more HOs in order to attenuate load disparity between cells. Then the implemented MLB algorithms seem to be able to find convenient trade-off between different investigated network key performance indicators (KPIs) since they improve global network throughput and PLR without strongly increasing the rate of HO signalling.

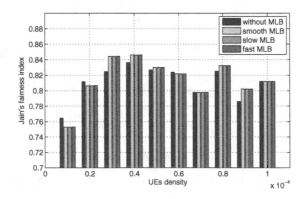

Fig. 8. Jain's fairness index vs UEs density

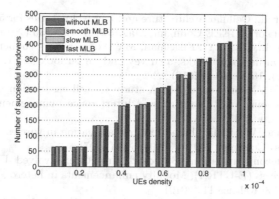

Fig. 9. Number of successful HOs vs UEs density

6   Conclusion

With the emerging trend of heterogeneity and cells? dense deployment among new generations of cellular networks dealing to a massive deployment of small-cells, inter- and intra-traffic balancing management is more complicated to model. In this paper we propose an implementation, using ns-3, of a MLB algorithm based adaptive HO for downlink LTE SON HetNets. Intensive simulations for MLB scheme under realistic network scenarios of a two-tier HetNet deployment were considered. Numerical results show that enhancements provided by the proposed MLB schemes are closely dependent on network UEs density and are illustrated in this paper through different KPIs. These improvements concern particularly PLR reduction, JFI and network global throughput without HO overhead. For future works, more effort should be made to evaluate the impact of MLB thresholds (i.e. $ThAvail$, $ThPre$ and $ThTarget$) on MLB algorithms' performance.

References

1. European Telecommunications Standards Institute: LTE; Evolved Universal Terrestrial Radio Access Network (E-UTRAN); Architecture description. 3GPP TS 36.401 version 8.6.0 Release 8 (2009)
2. European Telecommunications Standards Institute: LTE; Evolved Universal Terrestrial Radio Access Network (E-UTRAN); Architecture description. 3GPP TS 36.401 version 12.2.0 Release 12 (2015)
3. Hwang, I., Song, B., Soliman, S.S.: A holistic view on hyper-dense heterogeneous and small cell networks. IEEE Commun. Mag. **51**, 20–27 (2013)
4. Mehmeti, F., Spyropoulos, T.: Performance analysis of mobile data offloading in heterogeneous networks. IEEE Trans. Mobile Comput. **16**(2), 482–497 (2016)
5. Ghosh, A., et al.: Heterogeneous cellular networks: from theory to practice. IEEE Commun. Mag. **50**(6), 54–64 (2012)
6. Andrews, J.G.: Seven ways that HetNets are a cellular paradigm shift. IEEE Commun. Mag. **51**(3), 136–144 (2012)

7. Wang, C.X., et al.: Cellular architecture and key technologies for 5G wireless communication networks. IEEE Commun. Mag. **52**(2), 122–130 (2014)
8. Liu, D., Wang, L., Chen, Y., Elkashlan, M., Wong, K.K., Schober, R., Hanzo, L.: User association in 5G networks: a survey and an outlook. IEEE Commun. Surv. Tutorials **18**(2), 1018–1044 (2016)
9. Chinipardaz, M., Noorhosseini, M.: A study on cell association in heterogeneous networks with joint load balancing and interference management. Telecommun. Syst. **66**(1), 1–20 (2017)
10. Kuo, W.H., Liao, W.: Utility-based resource allocation in wireless networks. IEEE Trans. Wireless Commun. **6**(10), 3600–3606 (2007)
11. European Telecommunications Standards Institute: Evolved Universal Terrestrial Radio Access (E-UTRA); Mobility enhancements in heterogeneous networks. 3GPP TS 36.839 Release 11 (2012)
12. Elayoubi, S.E., Altman, E., Haddad, M., Altman, Z.: A hybrid decision approach for the association problem in heterogeneous networks. In: 10th Proceedings IEEE INFOCOM, San Diego, CA, USA, pp. 1–5 (2010)
13. Ye, Q., Rong, B., Chen, Y., Al-Shalash, M., Caramanis, C., Andrews, J.G.: User association for load balancing in heterogeneous cellular networks. IEEE Trans. Wireless Commun. **12**(6), 2706–2716 (2013)
14. Chen, Y., Li, J., Lin, Z., Mao, G., Vucetic, B.: User association with unequal user priorities in heterogeneous cellular networks. IEEE Trans. Veh. Technol. **65**(9), 7374–7388 (2016)
15. Shen, K., Yu, W.: Distributed pricing-based user association for downlink heterogeneous cellular networks. IEEE J. Sel. Areas Commun. **32**(6), 1100–1113 (2014)
16. Ali, M.S., Coucheney, P., Coupechoux, M.: Load balancing in heterogeneous networks based on distributed learning in near-potential games. IEEE Trans. Wireless Commun. **15**(7), 5046–5059 (2016)
17. Zhang, T., Xu, H., Liu, D., Beaulieu, N.C., Zhu, Y.: User association for energy-load tradeoffs in HetNets with renewable energy supply. IEEE Commun. Lett. **19**(12), 2214–2217 (2015)
18. Han, T., Ansari, N.: A traffic load balancing framework for software-defined radio access networks powered by hybrid energy sources. IEEE/ACM Trans. Networking (TON) **24**(2), 1038–1051 (2016)
19. Son, H., Lee, S., Kim, S.C., Shin, Y.S.: Soft load balancing over heterogeneous wireless networks. IEEE Trans. Veh. Technol. **57**(4), 2632–2638 (2008)
20. Vu, T.K., Bennis, M., Samarakoon, S., Debbah, M., Latva-aho, M.: Joint Load Balancing and Interference Mitigation in 5G Heterogeneous Networks. arXiv preprint arXiv:1611.04821 (2016)
21. Li, J., Bjorson, E., Svensson, T., Eriksson, T., Debbah, M.: Joint precoding and load balancing optimization for energy-efficient heterogeneous networks. IEEE Trans. Wireless Commun. **14**(10), 5810–5822 (2015)
22. Tseng, C.C., Wang, H.C., Ting, K.C., Wang, C.C., Kuo, F.C.: Fast game-based handoff mechanism with load balancing for LTE/LTE-A heterogeneous networks. J. Netw. Comput. Appl. **85**, 106–115 (2017)
23. Zhou, F., Feng, L., Yu, P., Li, W.: Energy-efficiency driven load balancing strategy in LTE-WiFi interworking heterogeneous networks. In: Wireless Communications and Networking Conference Workshops (WCNCW), 10th Proceedings of IEEE INFOCOM, New Orleans, LA, USA, pp. 276–281 (2015)
24. Siomina, I., Yuan, D.: Load balancing in heterogeneous LTE: range optimization via cell offset and load-coupling characterization. In: IEEE International Conference on Communications (ICC), Ottawa, ON, Canada, pp. 1357–1361 (2012)

25. Lopez-Perez, D., Claussen, H.: Duty cycles and load balancing in HetNets with eICIC almost blank subframes. In: 24th IEEE International Symposium on Personal, Indoor and Mobile Radio Communications (PIMRC Workshops), London, UK, pp. 173–178 (2013)
26. Fotiadis, P., Polignano, M., Laselva, D., Vejlgaard, B., Mogensen, P., Irmer, R., Scully, N.: Multi-layer mobility load balancing in a heterogeneous LTE network. In: IEEE Vehicular Technology Conference (VTC Fall), Quebec City, QC, Canada, pp. 1–5 (2012)
27. European Telecommunications Standards Institute: LTE; Evolved Universal Terrestrial Radio Access Network (E-UTRAN); X2 Application Protocol (X2AP). 3GPP TS 36.423 version 12.3.0 Release 12 (2014)
28. Jouini, H., Escheikh, M., Barkaoui, K., Ezzedine, T.: Mobility load balancing based adaptive handover in downlink LTE self-organizing networks. Int. J. Wireless Mobile Comput. (IJWMN) 8(4), 89–105 (2016)
29. European Telecommunications Standards Institute: Radio Resource Control (RRC); Protocol specification. 3GPP TS 36.331 version 11.5.0 Release 11 (2013)
30. Alcatel-Lucent, picoChip Designs and Vodafone: Simulation assumptions and parameters for FDD HeNB RF requirements (2009)
31. Network Simulator 3. https://www.nsnam.org/
32. Singh, S., Dhillon, H.S., Andrews, J.G.: Offloading in heterogeneous networks: modeling, analysis, and design insights. IEEE Trans. Wireless Commun. 12(5), 2484–2497 (2013)

A Toolset for Mobile Systems Testing

Pierre André$^{(\boxtimes)}$, Nicolas Rivière, and Hélène Waeselynck

LAAS-CNRS, Université de Toulouse, CNRS, UPS, Toulouse, France
{pierre.andre,nicolas.riviere,helene.waeselynck}@laas.fr

Abstract. Validation of mobile applications needs taking account of context (such network topology) and interactions between mobile nodes. Scenario-based approaches are well-suited to describe the behavior and interactions to observe in distributed systems. The difficulty to control accurately the execution context of such applications has led us to use passive testing. This paper presents a toolset which supports specification and verification of scenarios. A UML-based formal language, called TERMOS, has been implemented for specifying scenarios in mobile computing systems. These scenarios capture the key properties which are automatically checked on the traces, considering both the spatial configuration of nodes and their communication. We give an overview of the language design choices, its semantics and the implementation of the tool chain. The approach is demonstrated on a case study.

Keywords: Mobile computing systems · Scenario-based testing · UML sequence diagrams · UML profile · Trace analysis

1 Introduction

Mobile computing systems involve devices (smartphone, laptop, intelligent car) that move within some physical areas, while being connected to networks by means of wireless links (Bluetooth, IEEE 802.11, LTE). Compared to "traditional" distributed systems, such systems run in an extremely dynamic context. The movement of devices yields an evolving topology of connection. Links with other mobile devices or with infrastructure nodes may be established or destroyed depending on the location. Moreover, mobile nodes may dynamically appear and disappear as devices are switched on and off, run out of power or go to standby mode.

Our work is aimed at developing a framework and a toolset to support the testing of such systems based on a passive approach. Passive testing (see e.g., [5]) is the process of detecting errors by passively observing the execution trace of a running system. In our case, the properties to be checked are specified using graphical interaction scenarios. A scenario captures a key property of a mobile application, depicting mandatory or forbidden behavior, to be checked on the traces. For mobile computing systems, a property has to be checked according to the topology of the mobile nodes involved in the scenario. A scenario should have both (i) a spatial view, depicting the dynamically changing topology of nodes as

© Springer International Publishing AG 2017
K. Barkaoui et al. (Eds.): VECoS 2017, LNCS 10466, pp. 124–138, 2017.
DOI: 10.1007/978-3-319-66176-6_9

a sequence of graphs, and (ii) an event view representing the communications between nodes.

Graphical scenario languages (e.g., Message Sequence Charts [11], UML Sequence Diagrams [19]) allow the visual representation of interactions in distributed systems. Typical use cases, forbidden behaviors, test cases and many more aspects can be depicted. The need to automate analysis of test traces led us to design a scenario language with a formal semantics [10]. This graphical language is a formal UML-based language called TERMOS (Test Requirement Language for Mobile Settings) [21]. It depicts scenarios including the node context.

The global concept followed for testing mobile computing applications needs two main elements: an execution platform and software tools to process the recorded data. The execution platform is composed of three components: a context controller (to manage mobility of nodes), a network controller (to manage communication) and an execution environment support to run the system under test (SUT). The SUT is run in a simulated environment, using a synthetic workload. The platform controls the context, to observe and to record execution traces data during the testing campaigns.

Nevertheless, software tools are needed for checking a large amount of traces against scenarios. In order to support the verification, we designed a test framework. There are three main activities: the specification of scenarios, the capture of traces via the execution platform, and the analysis of traces.

In a previous work [3], we demonstrated our approach with a first prototype which integrated the TERMOS language and algorithms in an open-source UML environment. Since then, significant improvements and extensions have been achieved:

1. the different pieces of our toolset have been developed and fully integrated,
2. the specification of the language has been extended to take account of predicates,
3. several checks have been implemented during specification and analysis,
4. a man-machine interface has been created for an accurate analysis of test verdicts.

This paper aims at giving an overview of a full demonstrator for the approach, from the graphical editing of requirement scenarios to their automated use for checking test traces.

The structure of the paper is the following:

- Section 2 gives an overview of the test framework.
- Section 3 presents the choices and development done for the specification of graphical scenarios for mobile settings.
- Section 4 explains the principle of the trace analysis.
- Section 5 concludes with results provided by the application of the test method to a case study.

2   Toolset Overview

The goal of our work is the validation of mobile computing systems. Our work focuses on the use of scenarios to analyze execution traces of mobile computing systems. It is essential to take account the network topology and the interactions between mobile nodes. To achieve this analysis, we need to run the application within an execution platform. It can be either a platform producing real traces from real physical devices or a simulation platform. For a better reproducibility of the test campaigns, the system under test (SUT) is run in a simulated environment, using a synthetic workload. The SUT may involve both fixed nodes and mobile devices. The movement of the latter ones is managed according to some mobility model, a context manager being in charge of producing location-based data. The network simulator can simulate delays or communication errors on wireless or wired links. Execution traces are collected, including both communication messages and location-based data from which the system spatial configurations can be retrieved.

We want to check whether the test trace exhibits some behavior patterns described by scenarios. The properties are specified using graphical interaction scenarios which represent test requirements or test purposes. The TERMOS language has been developed to capture the three classes of scenarios exemplified by Fig. 1. *Positive requirements* capture key invariant properties of the following form: whenever a given interaction happens in the trace, then a specific interaction always follows. *Negative requirements* describe forbidden behaviors that should never occur in the trace. Any observed violation of a requirement must be reported. *Test purposes* describe behaviors to be covered by testing, that is, we would like these behaviors to occur at least once in the trace. If the interaction appears in the trace, the test purpose is reported as covered.

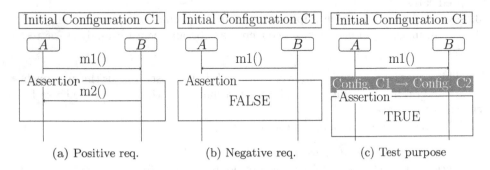

| (a) Positive req. | (b) Negative req. | (c) Test purpose |

Fig. 1. Requirement and test purpose scenarios (event views)

We interpret TERMOS scenarios as generic behavior patterns that may be matched by various subsets of the system during the test run. In Fig. 1, the node ids A and B are symbolic ones. For example, the positive requirement (Fig. 1a) is interpreted as:

Whenever two nodes exhibit spatial configuration *C1*, and the node matching *A* sends message *m1()* to the node matching *B*, then the node matching *B* must answer with message *m2()*.

At some point of a test run, we may have two simultaneous instances of *C1*, one with system nodes x and y matching *A* and *B*, and one with x and z. At some later point, system node x may play the role of *B* in yet another instance of *C1*.

Given a scenario, the analysis of a test trace thus involves two steps:

1. Determine which physical nodes of the trace exhibit the (sequence of) configuration(s) of the scenario, and when they do so.
2. Analyze the order of events in the identified configurations using an automaton.

Assuming that system configuration graphs can be built from the contextual test data, step 1 can be formulated as a graph matching problem. We explained in [2, 18] how subgraph isomorphism can be used to search for all instances of the scenario configurations in a trace. Then, in step 2, the order of communication and configuration change events are analyzed using an automaton for all found spatial matches.

To automate the execution of the test and the processing of the traces, a test framework has been implemented. We made the choice to distribute the different steps in three main activities, as shown in Fig. 2, each performing a specific task in the testing of mobile applications: the specification of scenarios, the capture of traces via the execution platform, and the analysis of traces.

The overall principles of the toolset are the following. The trace capture provides execution traces where location-based data and communication messages are time stamped. Requirement scenarios are specified manually within a UML-workshop. A scenario is transformed, after checks, into an automaton and a pattern containing a sequence of topologies. Finally, trace analysis is processed in fours steps with specific tools we have developed, and is concluded with a verdict (pass, fail, inconclusive).

3 Scenario Specification

The scenario specification, the right green block in Fig. 2, consists of three steps: **scenario modeling, scenario format checks** and **scenario transformation**.

In the first step, requirements are captured using our scenario based language, which includes the mobility related extensions. Our language TERMOS is a specialization of UML Sequence Diagrams [19]. Its genesis can be found in our work [17, 21]. Like in usual sequence diagrams, lifelines are drawn for the nodes and the partial orders of their communications are shown. We first noticed that the spatial configurations of nodes should be a first class concept. As a result, a scenario should have both (i) a spatial view, depicting the dynamically changing topology of nodes as a sequence of graphs, and (ii) an event view representing the

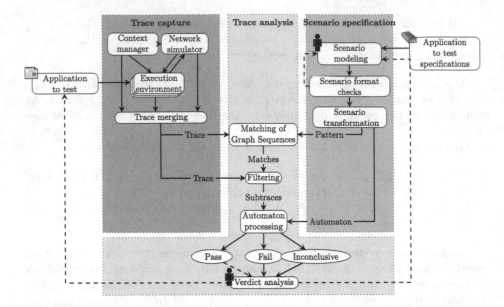

Fig. 2. Test framework architecture (Color figure online)

communications between nodes. The syntax of the language includes elements for representing spatial configurations, changes in the communication structure, broadcast messages and predicates. These are called non standard elements in the following.

Next, the scenario to be verified automatically must meet a number of constraints. In this way, a verification stage for the well-formedness of the scenario has been set up. It aims at ensuring the correct syntactic form of the scenario, and the determinism of verdicts with the use of an unambiguous semantics. There are three categories of specific constraints for the language: *UML* syntactic restrictions, consistency between event views and spatial views, and specific elements of the language.

After all format checks passed successfully, it is possible to process the transformation of the graphical scenario in a suitable format for the trace analysis. The scenario is then decomposed in two files: a graph sequence representing the sequence of spatial configurations, and an automaton representing all event order paths available for this scenario.

Our language has been implemented within a *UML* workshop. For this implementation, we have chosen *Eclipse Papyrus* workshop for its extension capabilities through the use of *UML* profiles and the development of *Eclipse* plugins.

3.1   Scenario Modeling

UML Profile for Non-standard Elements. A scenario in a mobile setting contains two connected views. These views were integrated into Papyrus with the use of a UML profile in order to represent of non-standard UML elements and some syntactic restrictions to sequence diagrams. The first two views are relevant to the mobile setting, while the syntactic restrictions are relevant to the use of TERMOS for checking execution traces. With this profile, we proposed three extensions: representation of a spatial view, consideration for spatial configuration change events in sequence diagrams, representation of broadcast communication events.

The sequence diagram illustrated Fig. 3 depicts a piece of TERMOS scenario. The upper note "Initial Configuration: C1" reports that our scenario starts with a topology called *C1*. There is a life line in the diagram for each node of the spatial configuration. The spatial configuration change "CHANGE (C2)" impacts all the nodes, this is why this event is common to each life line. The "hello" broadcast message is sent by node *n2* and received by every node at communication range. This sequence diagram implies that nodes *n1*, *n3* and *n4* are connected with *n2*.

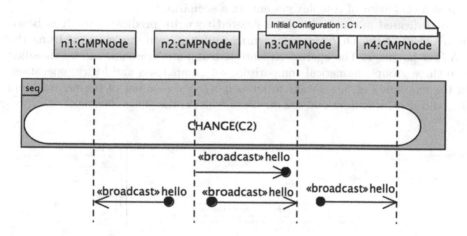

Fig. 3. TERMOS example

Local broadcast is used as a basic step for the discovery layer in mobile-based applications (group discovery for group membership services, route discovery in routing protocols, etc.). In order to represent a broadcast message in the neighborhood, we used a stereotype ≪broadcast≫ associated with an integer attribute to link several events together, as in Fig. 4. This stereotype can be applied to lost/found *hello* message events as represented in Fig. 3.

A Grammar for the Predicates. In order to provide a richer description of scenarios, we extended the specification language to take account of predicates [1]. The scenario in Fig. 5 contains two expressions to evaluate in the Assert block.

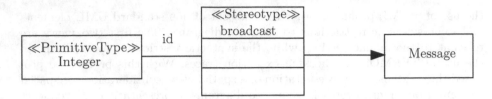

Fig. 4. UML profile for broadcast

$$(m1.members\ includes\ n1)\ and\ (m1.members = m2.members)$$

Variables used in this expression may have various origins, e.g. variables from nodes as node identifier or node attributes, or message attributes from the event view. For example $n1$ is a node identifier from the spatial view. Variable like $m1.members$ comes from the content of the first message. The ability to use variables from either spatial and event view of a scenario is very useful to represent behavior of complex systems in a scenario.

A dedicated grammar has been created to write predicates [1]. It is based on a subset of the *OCL* language syntax and has been implemented using the *ANTLR* language. The operations feasible using our grammar can be classified into three groups: numerical comparison, set comparison and logical operation. In the example Fig. 5, we want to know if $n1$ is a member of the $m1.members$ list, and if $m1.members$ and $m2.members$ contain the same elements.

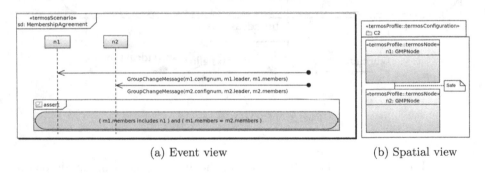

(a) Event view   (b) Spatial view

Fig. 5. Scenario example using predicates

3.2   Scenario Format Checks

Before processing the verification steps of scenarios on an execution trace, it is necessary to verify that the scenario complies with the constraints of our language. The objectives of this stage are: to ensure the correct syntactic form of scenarios, and to ensure the determinism of verdicts using an unambiguous semantics.

Some checks are run before the scenario is transformed into an automaton. The scenario modification is guided by a feedback provided to the user with all possible details. The goal is to have an error free scenario for the next steps. The constraints introduced by our language may be classified into three categories.

UML Syntax Restrictions. To adapt the sequence diagrams representation of interactions within mobile systems, some UML elements have been deleted and some constraints have been introduced [16]. For example, the following operators where deleted: *Strict, Loop, Ignore, Neg, Break* and *Critical.* In terms of constraints, some operators are considered as global events. The *Assert* operator in Fig. 5 must cover all the lifelines of the scenario and be the last element of the sequence diagram.

Consistency Constraints Between Event View and Spatial View. As our scenarios are composed of two views, we must ensure consistency between them. For example, the nodes present in an event view must be present in the spatial view.

Specific Elements of the Language. The link between the spatial view and the event view of the scenario is managed by a global event called *Configuration Change.* An example of this specific element of the language is represented in Fig. 3 by the event *CHANGE (C2).* Another specific element is the broadcast communication event. Here we need to link several receive message events with one unique send event.

3.3 Scenarios Processing

Before running trace analysis, a scenario transformation is mandatory to generate input patterns for trace analysis. This step occurs after all format checks have been passed successfully. As mentioned in Fig. 2, the scenario transformation process produces two behavior patterns. An event order analysis of the scenario is run to produce them. The configuration changes in the scenario are analyzed to build a sequence of graphs that depicts the needed sequence of network topology. An automaton is also built with all possible event sequences that may represent the scenario [1,21].

Some checks have to be executed once the complete automaton is produced. This is the case when a scenario includes some predicates. For each predicate, it is necessary to check that all the variables required for its assessment are available. Considering the example in Fig. 5, the predicate in the Assert block uses variables *m1.members* and *m2.members* from the two preceding messages. All the branches that led to a state where a predicate is assessed must contain a valuation of the variables.

4 Trace Analysis

The trace analysis part (the central yellow block in Fig. 2) consists of severals steps: **matching of graph sequences, trace filtering, automaton processing and verdict analysis.**

4.1 Principles

There is a gap between the abstract spatial configurations defined in the requirement scenarios and the concrete ones observed in the trace. It is necessary to decide which node from the execution environment can play the roles depicted in the scenarios. Based on their types and connections, the abstract nodes have to be mapped to the concrete ones found in the trace. However, usually there are several possible matchings. Moreover, the matching should take into account not only one configuration, but also the changes in a sequence of configurations like *C1* followed by *C2* in Fig. 3. To address this issue, we developed a method and a tool, called GraphSeq [2,21], which reasons on a series of abstract and concrete configuration graphs, and return the set of possible matches and valuations.

Considering the example of the Fig. 5, there is only one spatial view containing two nodes $n1$ and $n2$ which are closed enough to exchange messages. For each occurrence of the pattern identified by GraphSeq, a match is returned. A match identifies a subset of concrete nodes that exhibits the searched sequence of patterns and its duration. It contains the valuation of each existing variable in the pattern. For each match, a sub-trace is generated. A sub-trace contains only configuration changes identified by GraphSeq, and communication messages sent or received by the identified nodes during the time window.

All sub-traces are evaluated with respect to the requirements using the automaton. Each event in the sub-trace triggers a transition in the automaton until the check reaches a final state or the end of the sub-trace. Each state of the automaton is linked to a verdict. Finally, a pass, fail or inconclusive verdict is assigned to a *(trace, requirement, matching)* combination according to the reached state.

During the analysis of the execution trace, a new check has to be performed. Indeed, the use of predicates may lead to some cases of non-determinism. To detect them, from the current state, we are seeking if more than one transition can be fired.

Each sub-trace can lead to several verdicts. Indeed, in the automaton some transitions are labelled as initial ones. That means they can trigger a new validation of the automaton from the fired event.

The Fig. 6 is an ordered event sequence extracted from a trace we want to check against the scenario of Fig. 5. GrapSeq has valuated node $n1$ with real node A from the trace and respectively $n2$ with B. The sequence diagram that depicts the event view of Fig. 5 shows that we expect two unordered messages, one for each node. Each message (from ❶ to ❺) has been identified as an initial transition. Then, the sets of messages ❶-❹, ❷-❹, ❸-❹, ❹-❺ lead to the predicate assessment and then to a verdict pass or fail. Considering the set ❺, containing only one message, it is impossible to assess the predicate and leads to an inconclusive verdict. On the other hand the occurence of ❻ does not lead to a verdict because it occurs after a configuration change. ❻ is represented here in order to explain how our tool works. However it cannot occur in a sub-trace because it will be filtered by the time window founds by GraphSeq in the previous steps of analysis.

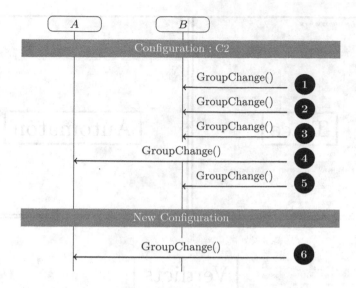

Fig. 6. Multiple verdicts from one trace

4.2 Verdict Analysis

The automaton execution stage leads mostly to a set of verdicts that it is difficult to analyze manually. We have implemented a verdict analysis tool based on a man-machine interface allowing an accurate analysis of test verdicts. The interface of this tool shown Fig. 7 is composed of three areas. The first one contains all verdicts of the current execution. It may contain a large number of verdicts because an automaton check can be run on all the sub-traces identified in the first step of the trace analysis. In this part of the interface, the user is able to select and analyze in details a verdict through the analysis of the automaton transition triggered to reach the verdict. The trigerred transitions are displayed in the automaton area. For each transition, the event that triggered it is highlighted in the trace area. It is also possible to display the content of the message for manual analysis.

With this analysis interface, the user has a better feedback to understand more easily the behavior of the system and take the necessary actions to correct it. Actions can be changed in the source code of the application under test or the scenario may be rewriten in the right way. These actions are represented in Fig. 2 by the feedback from **Verdict analysis** to **Application to test** and **Scenario modeling**.

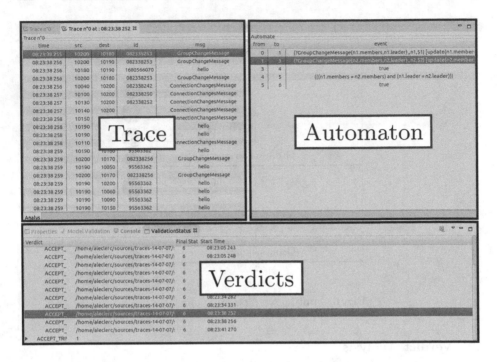

Fig. 7. Verdict analysis interface

5   Results

Our test framework was validated with a case study. To be used, our method requires two elements: detailed specifications in order to design test cases and functional implementation for the collection of execution traces. The application we have verified is a group membership protocol called GMP whose specifications are detailed in [9]. Its implementation was provided by the authors.

The main functionality of the GMP is to maintain a consistent view of who is in the group. The studied implementation dynamically merges and splits groups of nodes according to a notion of safe distance. The safe distance is determined to give enough time for two nodes in the same group for: (i) moving away from each other at their maximum speed, (ii) splitting up the group before loosing network connection between them. Using this notion, a link between two nodes can have three labels: *safe distance, communication range, disconnected* and *any* (wildcard for any of the three labels).

The GMP works with two main operations, *GroupSplit* and *GroupMerge*. We used specifications of the protocol fully described in [9] to write tests scenarios and check key properties of this protocol.

One example of property was described using our language in Fig. 5. This scenario depicts a property called *Membership Agreement*. It aims at ensuring that two nodes connected together with a *safe* link have to be in the same group.

To collect traces of execution, we have instrumented the application under test. This instrumentation consists, on each mobile node, to simulate a location device acting as a GPS and to record all communications events with the outside world. To observe how the protocol works, several nodes must be running at the same time. To manage the simulation and coordinate nodes movements between them, a mobility simulator was used.

We tested our scenarios considering the traces collected during the execution of the GMP using 16 nodes during 15 min. This execution produced a global trace containing 900 configuration graphs and more than 500,000 sent or received message events. Firstly, as shown in Fig. 2, for each scenario, we searched for spatial patterns and generated subtraces. This step found 3,116 spatial matches and generated one subtrace for each of them. Next, we check the automaton on each subtrace. The automaton may be checked more than once per subtrace because we look for *initial* events in the subtrace, and run the automaton starting at each initial event detected. This step led to 36,460 executions of the automaton, distributed as follows:

- **16 186** executions reached the final state of the automaton. In other words, the verdict of the execution is *accept*.
- **20 240** executions have not reached the assert block of the scenario. In this scenario, this is due to the lack of one of the two *GroupChange* messages.
- **34** executions stopped inside the assert block. These cases revealed violation of the property.

Table 1. Summary of scenarios validation for a trace of more than 500,000 events.

Tested scenario	Matches		Accept		Reject
	Spatial	Event	Stringent	Trivial	
Local monotonicity	16	3,608	3,478	16	114
Self inclusion	16	3,608	3,606	0	2
Membership change justification	16	3,608	3,495	16	97
Membership agreement	3,116	36,460	16,186	20,240	34
Wrong split*	8768	53702	0	53098	604
Concurrent merge*	2450	2487	0	2336	151
Concurrent split	162	569	52	387	130

Complete results about tested scenarios are presented Table 1. With these results displayed in the verdict analysis interface presented in the previous section, the user is able to analyse each verdict and detect which events caused it.

All the *GMP* properties were described using *TERMOS* language, and verified on traces from the SUT presented above. Each property was violated at least once. The results show the usefulness of our tool which can detect properties violation easily on execution traces. The user only needs to describe properties using our UML editor, run analysis on execution traces and analyse the results given by our tool.

6 Related Works

We did not find any testing framework or tools like our toolset. The closest work we can find is a methodology for testing autonomous systems based on graphical scenarios [15].

Other works have investigated how to incorporate mobility into UML scenarios [4,7,13]. However, the focus was more on logical mobility (mobile computation) than on physical one (mobile computing). It induces a view of mobility that consists of entering and exiting administrative domains, the domains being hierarchically organized. This view is adequate to express the migration of agents, but physical mobility requires further investigation, e.g., to account for dynamic ad-hoc networking. Also, there is not always a formal semantics attached to the notations.

Having a formal semantics is crucial for our objective of automated analysis of traces. We had a thorough look at existing semantics for UML Sequence Diagrams that led to the one presented in [10]. More details on UML-semantics can be found in a survey [16]. We also looked at other scenario languages distinguishing potential and mandatory behavior. The most influential work for the TERMOS semantics was work on Live Sequence Charts (LSC) [6,12], as well as work adapting LSC concepts into UML Sequence Diagrams [8,14].

GraphSeq implements an algorithm to match sequences of configurations: the sequence of symbolic configurations of the scenario, and the sequence of concrete configurations traversed during SUT execution. To the best of our knowledge, this is an original contribution. The comparison of sequences of graphs has been much less studied than the comparison of two graphs. The closest work we found is for the analysis of video images. In [20], the authors search for sequences of patterns (called pictorial queries) into a sequence of concrete graphs extracted from video images. Some differences with us are that their patterns do not involve label variables, and that there is at most one possibility for matching a pattern node with an image object.

7 Conclusion

This paper presented a tooling support for TERMOS, a UML-based scenario language for the testing of mobile computing systems. Its formal semantics allows an automated analysis of test traces. A grammar for predicates has been created to accommodate richer descriptions of scenarios. Several checks during the verification process from the depiction of requirements scenarios to trace analysis have been implemented to ensure the correctness of our method. A man-machine interface was integrated to help the user to analyze the test verdict. The full integration of our main tools, GraphSeq and TERMOS, led us to develop a complete tool chain for the automated checking of test traces. The integration has been done in a UML workshop called Papyrus.

In order to validate our test framework, we led experiments on a group membership protocol. During this experimentation, we have proven the efficiency of our tools using them on traces of several hundred of thousands events. Detailed information on the testing tools and the tested scenarios of the GMP case study are available at https://www.laas.fr/projects/TERMOS. The tool will be made available online for the scientific community.

References

1. Andre, P.: Test of ubiquitous systems with explicit consideration of mobility. Ph.d. [in french], UPS Toulouse. https://tel.archives-ouvertes.fr/tel-01261593
2. André, P., Rivière, N., Waeselynck, H.: GraphSeq revisited: more efficient search for patterns in mobility traces. In: Vieira, M., Cunha, J.C. (eds.) EWDC 2013. LNCS, vol. 7869, pp. 88–95. Springer, Heidelberg (2013). doi:10.1007/978-3-642-38789-0_8
3. Andre, P., Waeselynck, H., Riviere, N.: A UML-based environment for test scenarios in mobile settings. In: International Conference on Computer, Information, and Telecommunication Systems (CITS 2013). IEEE (2013)
4. Baumeister, H., Koch, N., Kosiuczenko, P., Stevens, P., Wirsing, M.: UML for global computing. In: Priami, C. (ed.) GC 2003. LNCS, vol. 2874, pp. 1–24. Springer, Heidelberg (2003). doi:10.1007/978-3-540-40042-4_1
5. Cavalli, A., Maag, S., de Oca, E.M.: A passive conformance testing approach for a MANET routing protocol. In: Proceedings of the 2009 ACM Symposium on Applied Computing (SAC 2009), pp. 207–211, NY, USA (2009). http://doi.acm.org/10.1145/1529282.1529326
6. Damm, W., Harel, D.: LSCs: breathing life into message sequence charts. Formal Methods Syst. Des. **19**(1), 45–80 (2001)
7. Grassi, V., Mirandola, R., Sabetta, A.: A UML profile to model mobile systems. In: Baar, T., Strohmeier, A., Moreira, A., Mellor, S.J. (eds.) UML 2004. LNCS, vol. 3273, pp. 128–142. Springer, Heidelberg (2004). doi:10.1007/978-3-540-30187-5_10
8. Harel, D., Maoz, S.: Assert and negate revisited: modal semantics for UML sequence diagrams. Softw. Syst. Model. **7**(2), 237–252 (2008)
9. Huang, Q., Julien, C., Roman, G.: Relying on safe distance to achieve strong partitionable group membership in ad hoc networks. IEEE Trans. Mobile Comput. **3**(2), 192–205 (2004)
10. Huszerl, G., Waeselynck, H., Egel, Z., Kovi, A., Micskei, Z., Nguyen, M.D., Pinter, G., Riviere, N.: Refined design and testing framework, methodology and application results, HIDENETS project deliverable D5.3 (2008). http://www.hidenets.aau.dk/
11. International Telecommunication Union: Message Sequence Chart (MSC), recommendation Z.120 (2011). http://www.itu.int/rec/T-REC-Z.120
12. Klose, J.: Live Sequence Charts: A Graphical Formalism for the Specification of Communication Behavior. Ph.D. thesis, Carl von Ossietzky Universitat Oldenburg (2003)
13. Kusek, M., Jezic, G.: Extending UML sequence diagrams to model agent mobility. In: Padgham, L., Zambonelli, F. (eds.) AOSE 2006. LNCS, vol. 4405, pp. 51–63. Springer, Heidelberg (2007). doi:10.1007/978-3-540-70945-9_4
14. Küster-Filipe, J.: Modelling concurrent interactions. Theor. Comput. Sci. **351**(2), 203–220 (2006)

15. Micskei, Z., Szatmári, Z., Oláh, J., Majzik, I.: A concept for testing robustness and safety of the context-aware behaviour of autonomous systems. In: Jezic, G., Kusek, M., Nguyen, N.-T., Howlett, R.J., Jain, L.C. (eds.) KES-AMSTA 2012. LNCS, vol. 7327, pp. 504–513. Springer, Heidelberg (2012). doi:10.1007/978-3-642-30947-2_55
16. Micskei, Z., Waeselynck, H.: The many meanings of UML 2 sequence diagrams: a survey. Softw. Syst. Model. **10**(4), 489–514 (2011)
17. Nguyen, M.D., Waeselynck, H., Riviere, N.: Testing mobile computing applications: toward a scenario language and tools. In: Proceedings of the 2008 International Workshop on Dynamic Analysis (WODA 2008), pp. 29–35. ACM (2008)
18. Nguyen, M.D., Waeselynck, H., Riviere, N.: GraphSeq: a graph matching tool for the extraction of mobility patterns. In: 3rd International Conference on Software Testing, Verification and Validation (ICST), pp. 195–204, April 2010
19. Object Management Group: Unified Modeling Language (UML) 2.4.1 Superstructure Specification, formal/2011-08-06 (2011)
20. Shearer, K., Venkatesh, S., Bunke, H.: Video sequence matching via decision tree path following. Pattern Recognit. Lett. **22**(5), 479–492 (2001)
21. Waeselynck, H., Micskei, Z., Rivière, N., Hamvas, Á., Nitu, I.: TERMOS: a formal language for scenarios in mobile computing systems. In: Sénac, P., Ott, M., Seneviratne, A. (eds.) MobiQuitous 2010. LNICSSITE, vol. 73, pp. 285–296. Springer, Heidelberg (2012). doi:10.1007/978-3-642-29154-8_24

Intertwined Global Optimization Based Reachability Analysis

Ibtissem Seghaier$^{(\boxtimes)}$ and Sofiène Tahar

Department of Electrical and Computer Engineering,
Concordia University, Montréal, QC, Canada
{seghaier,tahar}@ece.concordia.ca

Abstract. This paper proposes a semi-formal reachability analysis technique based on global optimization for hybrid systems. In order to model the hybrid system dynamics with parameter and noise disturbance, a system of stochastic recurrence equations formalism is proposed. Then, a reachability analysis approach is adopted to compute the reachable sets under an interval of initial conditions and in light of system parameters variability. The novelty of our approach is in approximating the reachable bounds in an intertwined forward/backward manner. The backward corrections refine the obtained reachable bounds in the forward scheme and so reduce the high reachability over-bounding due to the wrapping effect. Finally, a Monte Carlo hypothesis testing based technique is performed on the resultant reachable bounds to uncover the hybrid system failure with regard to a certain specification. These failures are quantified in terms of parametric yield rate which reflects the sensitivity of the hybrid system to variations in its parameters. We demonstrate the effectiveness of our proposed verification methodology by applying it on a mixed analog and digital electronics building block commonly used in communications systems.

Keywords: Hybrid systems · System of stochastic recurrence equations · Intertwined forward-backward reachability analysis

1 Introduction

Continuous and discrete systems behaviors have been extensively analyzed separetly by control theory and formal verification communities, respectively. However, the verification of their composition in the same system, termed as hybrid system, has gained a lot of attention lately [1]. Indeed, hybrid systems are basic blocks in embedded control systems that involve interaction between digital systems and the physical world via analog plants (e.g., sensors and actuators) [2]. The complex infinite possible behaviors that a hybrid system exhibits rend the verification of such systems both challenging and critical, especially for safety critical applications such as avionics, automotive engine, and medical systems [3]. Verification becomes particularly challenging with hybrid models that account

© Springer International Publishing AG 2017
K. Barkaoui et al. (Eds.): VECoS 2017, LNCS 10466, pp. 139–154, 2017.
DOI: 10.1007/978-3-319-66176-6_10

for real system imperfections such as system parameter variations due to fabrication impurities along with input fluctuations. Monte Carlo simulation is a cornerstone and perhaps the most common practice in the verification of hybrid systems [4]. However, it is not sufficient to carry out multiple simulations when the system is actually required to match its specifications for all possible initial conditions and process parameters. Instead, reachability analysis techniques which refer to computing the set of all possible system behaviors emanating from an initial reachable set are adopted to prove that they satisfy a desired specification. Current reachability analysis techniques can be broadly classified into three main categories. Namely, SMT-solving [5], theorem proving [6] and flowpipe computation-based techniques [7]. Most of these reachability analysis techniques can only handle hybrid systems with linear continuous dynamics but a few are readily scalable to systems with nonlinear dynamics. In addition, because reachalbility analysis is in general undecidable, over-approximation is required to ensure the decidability of the reachability problem. This leads to verification errors in the computed reachable set that accumulates and even blows up with the reachable set evolution over time. This problem, known as *wrapping effect*, becomes a great concern for an accurate verification of hybrid systems. Hence, an efficient verification of these systems dictates two key requirements: (1) a uniform modeling formalism that fully reflects the relations as well as the interactions of the discrete and continuous parts of the system. With the uniformity, the model should also provide accuracy by realistically replicating noise, parameters and initial conditions variation; and (2) an accurate reachability analysis scheme that can handle nonlinear continuous hybrid systems and assess the effect of parameter variations while reducing the wrapping effect.

In this paper, we present a novel methodology for modeling and verification of continuous and hybrid systems under parameter and initial conditions uncertainties using a system of stochastic recurrence equations formalism. We propose an intertwined forward/backward reachability analysis technique based on global optimization that is capable of reducing the wrapping effect. The key insights is that for the purpose of nonlinear hybrid system verification, the reachable sets are tracked precisely by a backward reachability correction approach and the system failure rate is estimated using a hypothesis testing based approach.

The rest of this paper is organized as follows: in Sect. 2, we introduce some preliminary definitions of hybrid system modeling, including Latin Hypercube sampling and hypothesis testing techniques. Section 3 then discusses our proposed methodology for hybrid systems modeling and verification. In Sect. 4, we demonstrate the effectiveness of our methodology by applying it on a common analog and mixed signal design used in communication systems. Finally, conclusions and future work are given in Sect. 5.

2   Preliminaries

In this section, we define the terminology that will be used for hybrid systems modeling. We also present some background on the Latin Hypercube Sampling technique, and statistical hypothesis testing along with their definitions.

2.1   Hybrid System Modeling: System of Stochastic Recurrence Equations

Hybrid systems contain two different types of components: those with continuous dynamics and those with discrete dynamics. Despite their heterogeneous nature, a careful time domain discretization allows a unified description of all the hybrid systems components. Due to the statistical behavior that hybrid systems exhibit in the presence of uncertainties (such as noise and parameter variability), we are interested in modeling hybrid systems as a System of Stochastic Recurrence Equations (SSRE) [8], which is a formalism that allows to capture the statistical properties of the system in a unified discrete-time description. Moreover, the temporal properties of these hybrid components and their interactions can be expressed as SSRE. In what follows, we explain the SSRE notations and detail the conversion process of system equations and properties to SSREs. A system of recurrence equations is a set of relations between consecutive elements of a sequence. The notion of recurrence equations to describe discrete systems using the normal form: *generalized If-formula* was first proposed by Al-Sammane [9]. In addition, a stochastic recurrence equation can be generated for the case of continuous systems using the discrete version of their Stochastic Differential Equation (SDEs) [10]. In the following, we briefly present the SSRE theory. An SSRE is a set of SREs with stochastic processes. Let us consider the following Itô process $\{X_t, 0 \leq t \leq T\}$ SDE [11]:

$$dX_t(\omega) = f(X_t(\omega))dt + \sigma(X_t(\omega))dW_t(\omega) \tag{1}$$

where the stochastic variable W_t is a Brownian motion [12] (see Definition 1), the initial condition $(X_{t_0} = X_0)$ and the diffusion coefficient σ are deterministic variables.

Definition 1. *(Brownian Motion)   A scalar standard Brownian process, or standard Winer process over [0, T] is a random variable W_t that depends continuously on $t \in [0, T]$ and satisfies the following conditions:*

Condition 1. $W(0) = 0$ *with probability 1.*

Condition 2. *For $0 \leq s < t \leq T$ the random variable given by the increment $W_t - W_s$ is normally distributed with mean zero and variance $(t - s)$ $(W_t - W_s \sim \sqrt{t - s}\mathcal{N}(0, 1))$.*

Condition 3. *For $0 \leq s < t < u < v \leq T$ the increments $W_t - W_s$ and $W_v - W_u$ are independent.*

By integrating Eq. (1) between s and $s + \Delta s$, we will have:

$$dX_{s+\Delta s}(\omega) = X_s(\omega) + \int_s^{s+\Delta s} f(X_{s+\Delta s}(\omega))dt + \int_s^{s+\Delta s} f\sigma(X_{s+\Delta s}(\omega))dW_{s+\Delta s}(\omega) \tag{2}$$

The Euler scheme [13] consists in approximating the integral Eq. (2) by the following iterative scheme:

$$\bar{X}_{s+\Delta s}(\omega) = \bar{X}_s(\omega) + f(\bar{X}_s(\omega))\Delta s + \sigma(W_{s+\Delta s}(\omega) - W_s(\omega)) \tag{3}$$

Definition 2. *(Generalized If-formula) The generalized **If-formula** is a class of symbolic expressions that extend recurrence equations to describe discrete systems. Let i and n be natural numbers. Let $\mathbb{K}$ be a numerical domain in ($\mathbb{N}, \mathbb{Z}, \mathbb{Q}, \mathbb{R}$ or $\mathbb{B}$), an **If-formula** is one of the following:*

- *A variable $X_i(n)$ or a constant C that takes values in $\mathbb{K}$*
- *Any arithmetic operation $\diamond \in \{+, -, \times, \div\}$ between variables $X_i(n)$ that take values in $\mathbb{K}$*
- *A logical formula: any expression constructed using a set of variables $X_i(n) \in \mathbb{K}$ and logical operators: $not, and, or, xor, nor, \ldots,$ etc.*
- *A comparison formula: any expression constructed using a set of variables $X_i(n) \in \mathbb{K}$ and comparison operators $\triangle \in \{\neq, =, <, \leq, >, \geq\}$*
- *An expression $If(X, Y, Z)$, where X is a logical formula or a comparison formula and Y, Z are any generalized **If-formula**.*

Here, $If(X, Y, Z) : \mathbb{B} \times K \times K \longrightarrow \mathbb{K}$ satisfies the axioms:

1. *If(true, X ,Y) = X*
2. *If(false, X ,Y) = Y*

Definition 3. *(SSRE) Consider a set of variables $X_i(n) \in \mathbb{K}$, $i \in V = 1, \ldots, k, \omega \in, \mathbb{R}$, an SSRE is a system of the form:*

$$X_i(\omega) = f_i(X_j(\omega)\gamma)), (j, \gamma) \in \varepsilon_i, \forall \omega \in \mathbb{R} \qquad (4)$$

where $fi(X_j(\omega)\gamma))$ is a generalized **If-formula** of the recurrence stochastic differential equation given in Eq. (3). The set ε_i is a finite non empty subset of $1, \ldots, k \times \mathbb{N}$. The integer γ denotes the delay.

2.2 Latin Hypercube Sampling

To study parameter variation effects on the behavior of hybrid systems, an optimal exploration of the variation domain of the parameter values is very important in order to achieve a good accuracy and avoid non-informative verification runs. Traditional sampling techniques (e.g., Pseudo Random Sampling (PRS), Fractional Factorial, Central Composite, etc.) only arrange parameter values at some specific corners in the parameter space and can not handle multivariate stochastic parameters especially in terms of correlation. Consequently, when performing verification, it cannot mimic the system behavior in a global system parameter space. We first look at PRS as applied in the estimation of system failure in order to justify the use of Latin Hypercube Sampling (LHS). It has been demonstrated that the LHS technique gives samples that could reflect the integral distribution more effectively with a reduced samples variance [14]. Figure 1 illustrates the differences while using Monte Carlo PRS and Gaussian Monte Carlo LHS of a random normal parameter of transistor width for 1000 trials.

In the sequel, we explain the Latin Hypercube Sampling (LHS) main steps to generate a sample size N from n hybrid system parameter variables $\xi = [\xi_1, \xi_2, \ldots, \xi_n]$ with the probability distribution function $f_\xi(.)$.

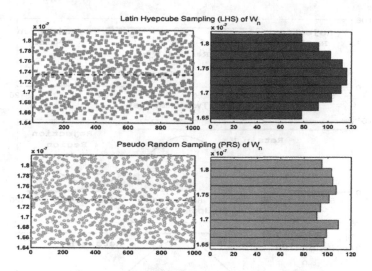

Fig. 1. Sampling differences between Monte Carlo PRS and LHS

First, the approach involves the partitioning of the range of each system parameter variable into N non overlapping intervals on the basis of equally probability size $\frac{1}{N}$. One value from each interval is randomly selected w.r.t. the conditional probability density in the variation interval defined by the technology library. The N values thus obtained for ξ_1, are paired in a random manner with the N values of ξ_2. These N pairs are combined in a random manner with the N values of ξ_3 to form N triplets, and so on, until a set of $N \times n$-tuples is formed. The choice of this sampling technique can be justified by its variance sampling reduction, which results in a better sampling coverage and consequently a better verification coverage [15].

2.3 Hypothesis Testing

Hypothesis testing [16] uses statistics to make decisions about the acceptance or the rejection of some statements based on the data from random samples. In this technique, the property of interest is formulated as a null hypothesis (H_0) which is tested against an alternative hypothesis (H_1). If we reject H_0, then the decision to accept H_1 is made.

Definition 4. *Given the property $\mathcal{P}$ within the ambit of a null hypothesis H_0, a significance level α, and a test statistic T, hypothesis testing is the process of verifying whether a system $\mathcal{S}$ satisfies H_0 with a probability greater than or equal to α (i.e., $\mathcal{S} \models Pr(T) \geq \alpha$).*

As depicted in Fig. 2, Hypothesis testing can be a one side test (upper test or lower tes) or two sided. In the case of a two sided test for example, we can verify if a variable X is within a bounded region $[x_1, x_2]$ as follows:

$$H_0 : P(x_1 < X < x_2) = P(X < x_2) - P(X < x_1) = 1 - \alpha \tag{5}$$

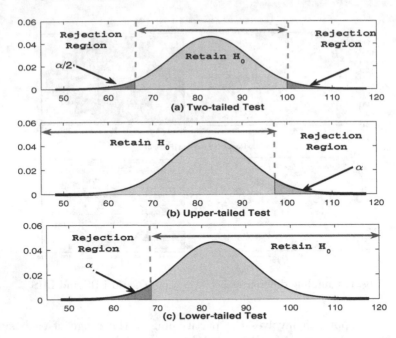

Fig. 2. Hypothesis testing concept

Following are the central steps to carry out hypothesis testing:

1. Elucidate the property to be verified and formulate it as H_0 and H_1.
2. Specify the appropriate level of significance α and determine the type of the test, namely, upper test, lower test or two sided test.
3. Select the appropriate test statistic.
4. Compute the critical region or p-value of the test statistic.
5. Compute the test statistic of the observed value for the original data.
6. Make the decision of accepting or rejecting the null hypothesis H_0. If the computed test statistic falls in the critical region, then the null hypothesis is rejected, otherwise H_0 is accepted.

The performance criteria of this approach is related to two types of errors as shown in Table 1:

Table 1. System verification classification

	Passed	Failed
Good System	✓	Type I error
Failed System	Type II error	✓

Type I error (α) or false positive, the null hypothesis H_0 is true but the decision based on the testing process erroneously rejected it. In other words, it represents the probability of accepting H_0 when H_1 holds.

Type II error (β) or false negative, the null hypothesis H_0 is false but the testing process concludes that it should be accepted. In other words, it corresponds to the probability of accepting H_1 when H_0 holds.

3   Proposed Methodology

An overview of the proposed methodology for intertwined forward/backward reachability analysis is shown in Fig. 3. Given a nonlinear hybrid system description, SSREs that express its stochastic behavior under noise perturbation are generated. The proposed SSRE formalism features a sound treatment of noise. It actually allows a consistent consideration of the noise effect to which the system is incurred during the reachability analysis process. More details about the system uncertainties modeling can be found in [17]. Then, parameter values from a certain distribution of the parameter space are derived using the efficient LHS technique. Next, reachability bounds of the hybrid system for a continuous set of initial conditions, and under the derived system parameters are generated using a novel intertwined forward/backward reachability analysis technique. The reachability computed using SSRE system model with parameters selected by the LHS procedure and for initial conditions that are defined within intervals (n-cubes) is based on the global optimization theory. The SSRE is not solved for every initial condition value but it employs the reachability analysis algorithm to optimize the search for the global extremum.

The output of this step is a refined reachability set generated from the backward reachability correction that includes all possible actual behaviors (trajectories) of the system. The main advantage of the proposed verification scheme is its generality and scalability. In fact, it does not make any assumption about the nature of the hybrid system dynamics: it works for any hybrid system with linear and nonlinear behavior. Next, appropriate null and alternative hypotheses are formulated from a certain SSRE specification of the hybrid system under verification. For each selected system parameters in the reachability iteration, Hypothesis Testing based Monte Carlo (MC) technique is conducted to estimate the system parametric failure which refers to failures caused by the deviation between manufactured system parameter values and intended parameter values. Each time the null hypothesis H_0, which represents the desired system property, is rejected, we draw a conclusion that the system fails to comply with its property and so we increment the number of system failures $N_{failure}$. Finally, the system yield rate is computed based on the probability of failure $P_{Failure}$ as follows:

$$P_{Failure} = \frac{Nb.\ of\ Rejected\ H_0}{Total\ Nb.\ of\ MC\ Trials}$$
$$Yield = 1 - P_{Failure}$$

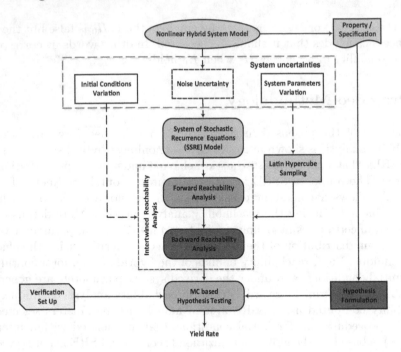

Fig. 3. Proposed verification methodology

3.1 Forward-Backward Reachability Analysis

Definition 5. *(Reachability Analysis) Reachable set (or bounds) is the collection of all possible trajectories or states of the hybrid system dynamical behavior originated from an interval of initial conditions. Mathematically, this can be defined as follows:*

$$X_{Reachable\_set} = \{x \in \mathbb{R}^{N_x} \mid \underline{X_L} \leq x \leq \overline{X_U}\} \tag{6}$$

where $\underline{X_L}$ is the lower reachable bound of the reachable set (or region) and $\overline{X_U}$ is the upper bound of the reachable set.

The proposed intertwined reachability analysis approach is shown in Fig. 4. The definition of reverse time dynamics of the SSRE model allows the forward/backward reachability exchange. The detailed implementation of the intertwined reachability analysis approach is summarized in Algorithm 1. Hybrid dynamical systems: An introduction to control and verification. Given an interval system of stochastic differential equations (an SSRE whose initial conditions are intervals), the algorithm defines the region of uncertainty of the system as an hypercube (n-cube) at time t_0 (Lines 3 and 18). Hence, the reachability analysis problem at a given simulation time point t^* for each system output (or state space) is equivalent to finding the maximum and minimum bounds of the SSRE model. In the proposed algorithm, the reachability analysis problem is so cast

---

Algorithm 1. Intertwined Forward/Backward Reachability Analysis

---

Require: $SSRE$: Hybrid System Model, X_0 : Interval of Initial Conditions, P : System parameters,
$\quad N_x$: Number of state variables, t_0 : Initial time, t_f : Final time

1: **for** $t_1^* \leftarrow t_0$ to t_f **do**
2: $\quad$ **for** $j \leftarrow 1$ to N_x **do**
3: $\quad\quad X_{ext}(t_1^*) = Generate(X_0)$ $\qquad\qquad\qquad$ ▷ external surface of the uncertainty region
4: $\quad\quad X_{max}(t_1^*, j) = -\infty$
5: $\quad\quad X_{min}(t_1^*, j) = \infty$
6: $\quad\quad$ **for** $each$ $state$ $variable$ $X_{ext}(j) \in X_{ext}$ **do**
7: $\quad\quad\quad Const = UpdateConstar(j, SSRE, P, X_{ext})$
8: $\quad\quad\quad Grad = UpdateGrad(j, t_1^*, SSRE, P, X_{ext}))$
9: $\quad\quad\quad [X_{max}(t_1^*), X_{min}(t_1^*)] = Global\_Opt(SSRE, j, t_0, t_1^*, P, X_{ext}), Grad, Constr)$
10: $\quad\quad$ **end for**
11: $\quad\quad B_{L_{Forward}}(t_1^*) \leftarrow X_{min}(t_1^*)$
12: $\quad\quad B_{U_{Forward}}(t_1^*) \leftarrow X_{max}(t_1^*)$
13: $\quad\quad update\_forward(t_1^*, \Delta_t)$
14: $\quad$ **end for**
15: **end for**
16: **for** $t_2^* \leftarrow t_f$ to t_0 **do**
17: $\quad$ **for** $j \leftarrow 1$ to N_x **do**
18: $\quad\quad X_{ext}(t_2^*) = Generate(B_{L_{Forward}}(t_2^*), B_{U_{Forward}}(t^*))$ $\qquad$ ▷ external surface of the
$\quad$ approximate reachability bounds
19: $\quad\quad X_{max}(t_2^*, j) = B_{U_{Forward}}(t_2^*, j)$
20: $\quad\quad X_{min}(t_2^*, j) = B_{L_{Forward}}(t_2^*, j)$
21: $\quad\quad$ **for** $each$ $state$ $variable$ $X_{ext}(j) \in X_{ext}$ **do**
22: $\quad\quad\quad Const = UpdateConstar_B(j, SSRE, P, X_{ext})$
23: $\quad\quad\quad Grad = UpdateGrad_B(j, t_2^*, SSRE, P, X_{ext}))$
24: $\quad\quad\quad [X_{max}(t_2^*), X_{min}(t_2^*)] = Global\_Opt_B(SSRE, j, t_f, t_2^*, P, X_{ext}), Grad, Constr)$
25: $\quad\quad$ **end for**
26: $\quad\quad B_{L_{corrected}}(t_2^*) \leftarrow X_{min}(t_2^*)$
27: $\quad\quad B_{U_{corrected}}(t_2^*) \leftarrow X_{max}(t_2^*)$
28: $\quad\quad update\_backward(t_2^*, \Delta_t)$
29: $\quad$ **end for**
30: **end for**

---

into a constrained multivariable nonlinear global optimisation problem. It was proven that under continuity condition, it is sufficient to compute the evolution of the external surface of the uncertainty region [18]. This means that to calculate the reachable bounds, it is sufficient to compute the trajectories emanating from the external surface of the region of the uncertainty region.

The extreme functions (Max and Min) at a specific time t^* of the system equations $SSRE(t^*, j, X_{ext}), \forall j = 1, \ldots, N_x$, which bound the system behavior, are first computed using the forward reachability analysis. We used the MATLAB Optimization solver [19] based on trust regions (Lines 1 to 15) to get these extreme functions of $SSRE(t^*, j, X_{ext}), \forall j = 1, \ldots, N_x$ by fixing the time variable to t^* and constraining the system behavior to evolve over the external uncertainty region (Line 7). The computed optimization point is then passed to the SSRE model, which uses X_{ext} as initial conditions and generates a partial derivatives (gradient) values that are used to control the stability of the reachability analysis (Line 8). The algorithm terminates if the optimisation method considers $SSRE(t^*, j, X_{ext}), \forall j = 1, \ldots, N_x$ as an extremum;

Otherwise the gradient values are used to select new points from the external uncertainty region X_{ext} and the above described steps are repeated. Athough this step guarantees the completeness of the reachability set, the upper and lower

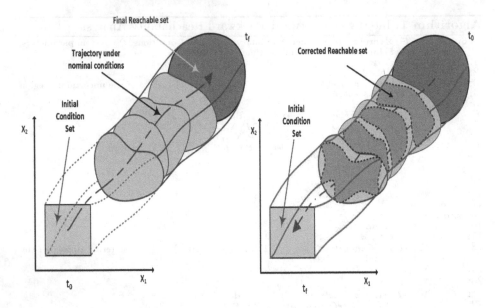

Fig. 4. Intertwined reachability analysis concept

obtained reachable sets are highly overbounded due to the *wrapping effect*. One way to tighten the reachability space is to conduct a backward reachability (Lines 16 to 30). Starting from the final computed set (Line 18), the backward optimization algorithm is now performed on the hybrid system SSRE reversed in time in order to compute backwards the reachability bounds and consequently correct the overbounded forward reachability set.

4   Application: PLL Frequency Synthesizer

In this section, we validate our proposed intertwined forward reachability analysis with backward correction methodology on a Phase Locked Loop (PLL) mixed signal design. More details about PLL case study as well as the results of another application are reported in [17]. All computation and hybrid system models were integrated in MATLAB environment and were run on a 64-bit Windows 7 machine with 2.8 GHz processor and 24 GB memory. The hypothesis testing is conducted for a level of significance $\alpha = 5\%$.

The PLL based frequency synthesizer is a basic and essential block of modern communication systems. It is basically a feedback circuit that tries to reduce the phase error between the input and the reference signals. In this case study, we consider a simple frequency synthesizer, that generates an output signal whose frequency is N times the frequency of the reference signal. We consider for this application a *Sine wave* reference signal with a frequency of ω_0, the PLL output is a *Cosine wave* signal with frequency $N \times \omega_0$.

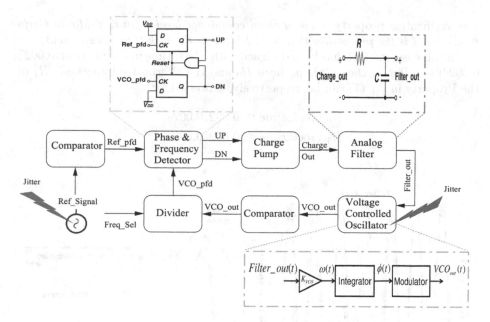

Fig. 5. PLL design block diagram

Figure 5 shows a block based description of a second order PLL based frequency synthesizer. It consists of a reference oscillator, a Charge Pump (CP), a Low Pass Filter (LPF), and a Voltage Controlled Oscillator (VCO). In order to model this PLL using SSREs notation, we need to model each block separately and then link them according to the PLL architecture in Fig. 5. The noise considered in this case study is the random temporal variation of the phase (a.k.a jitter) in the reference oscillator and the VCO block. It is well-known that jitter is the most dominant and critical noise metric in PLL because large jitter can modulate the oscillator signal both in frequency and amplitude. These modulation effects can cause a deviation in the phase from targeted locking range and hence results in a design failure. The efficient verification of PLL for a certain design specification has always been a challenge for circuit designers. We apply the proposed methodology to verify the locking property of a second order PLL design shown in Fig. 5. The lock time property is a safety property that expresses how fast the frequency synthesizer switches from one frequency to another. The verification of this property is achieved by checking that the PLL reaches the proper DC value within the lock time parameter range which is $\in [0.002, 0.0024]$ seconds.

This property is defined within the ambit of an SSRE model in Eq. (7), where the SSRE concatenation operator ($\wedge$) indicates that the two Boolean expressions hold simultanuously.

$$Property\_PLL = If(Filter\_out(Lock\_time_{min} + n) \in DC\_level\_range \wedge \quad (7)$$
$$Filter\_out(Lock\_time_{max} - n) \in DC\_level\_range, true, false)$$

The verification property is *For a given confidence level α, and N Monte Carlo trials, what is the probability that the PLL meets the lock-time requirement?*.

In this case, the PLL has been designed with a lock-time in the range of [0.002 , 0.0024] sec. Hence, the null hypothesis H_0 and the alternative hypothesis H_1 of the Property in Eq. (7) can be, respectively, expressed as:

$$H_0 : lock\_time \in [0.002, 0.0024]$$
$$H_1 : lock\_time \notin [0.002, 0.0024]$$

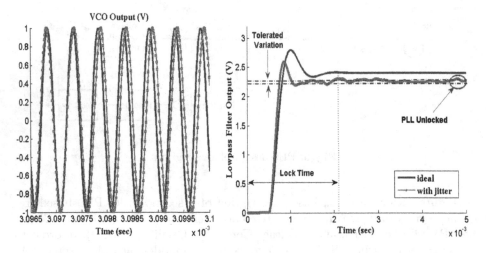

Fig. 6. PLL Output with and without phase noise (Color figure online)

Figure 6 depicts a comparison between the locking property of the PLL design whose parameter values are listed in Table 2 with and without jitter. A comparison of the same reachability algorithm without backward refinement [20] for the PLL design is given in [17]. It can be remarked that in the case of jittery PLL (red dotted line), the low pass filter outputs do not stabilize to the tolerated DC level and keep fluctuating outside the tolerated range. As a result, the PLL locking property is violated and the verification fails. Therefore, the verification of the PLL with consideration of jitter is very important when performing reachability analysis. Now, we validate our proposed intertwined forward/backward reachability technique on the jittery PLL design for an entire range of initial conditions and with consideration of parameter variations. The derived forward and backward reachable bounds are shown in Fig. 7, in which the forward reachability bound is painted in red and the backward reachability bound in green. In the forward iteration, the reachable set is highly over-approximating the PLL behavior. By performing the backward correction, we were able to tighten up this over-approximation and trace back the circuit dynamics down to the initial condition. The results of the PLL yield estimation using a variant of statistical Monte Carlo

Table 2. PLL frequency synthesizer parameters

Name	Value	Unit
RC	0.0001	s
α	$exp(\frac{-10^8}{0.0001})$	-
V_c	5	V
ω_0	$\pi \times 10^6$	rad.Hz
ω_{vco}	$2\pi \times 10^6$	rad.Hz
K_{vco}	$\frac{2\omega_{vco}}{V_c}$	rad.Hz
DC_{level}	2.5	V

technique [21] called Monte Carlo-Jackknife (MC-JK) and our proposed inter-twined reachability technique are summarized in Table 3. It is worth mentioning that our technique converges in one iteration only while Monte Carlo technique requires thousands of runs. From Table 3, it can be noticed that our proposed method finds a lower yield percentage compared to the statistical Monte Carlo scheme in [21]. This can be explained by the fact that our verification approach can weed out PLL locking failures that were not covered in [21].

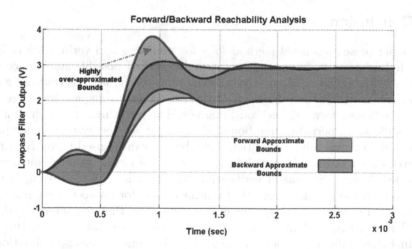

Fig. 7. Intertwined forward/backward reachability analysis of PLL under jitter (Color figure online)

In addition, the presence of combined jitter, initial conditions and process variations (Columns $8-10$) have substantially decreased the PLL yield, meaning the PLL presents more probability of lock failure.

The presence of jitter alone has shown a lower yield rate. This can be justified by the high sensitivity of the VCO block to jitter. The failure of the PLL is not

Table 3. Verification results for the PLL Lock-Time property

N=	Phase noise only			Parameter variation only			Phase noise & P.V		
	[21]	Our method	RE	[21]	Our method	RE	[21]	Our method	RE
	Yield (%)	Yield (%)	(%)	Yield (%)	Yield (%)	(%)	Yield (%)	Yield (%)	(%)
1000	82.4	74.1	8.3	84.7	79.2	5.5	80.6	71.5	9.1
	83.3	71.7	11.6	80.9	76.3	4.6	78.2	68.9	9.3
	81.7	69.8	11.9	79.2	72.7	6.5	77.5	67.3	10.2
5000	83.6	73.1	10.5	85.8	81.6	4.2	81.8	72.3	8.7
	80.2	72.3	7.9	81.9	77.8	4.1	78.2	70.1	8.9
	79.8	70.8	9	80.7	74.4	6.3	78.2	68.6	9.6
10000	81,7	69.9	11.8	83.6	79.7	3.9	80.2	66.1	14.1
	79.6	67.1	12.5	80.3	74.4	6.1	78.1	62.6	15.3
	78.1	65.9	12.2	81.9	71.8	10.1	76.8	60.1	16.7

due to lock up (non oscillation) of the VCO but, due to either an "ugly" (i.e., fluctuates outside the tolerated region) or delayed oscillation.

The Relative Error (RE) between our proposed approach and the MC technique (Columns 4, 7 and 10) becomes more pronounced when the number of Monte Carlo trials is increased due to the high MC sampling variance.

5   Conclusion

This paper presents a novel methodology for modeling and verification of nonlinear hybrid systems by computing reachable sets of possible state-space trajectories in the presence of uncertainties. In contrast to methods that use solely forward reachability, the refinement of the reachable state space is carried out in an intertwined forward/backward manner. The resulting set, which contains all periodic and aperiodic time bounded behaviors of the system under parameter variation and initial condition disturbance, can be used to verify critical properties such as bounds on voltages, currents, and cycle time (frequency) of embedded designs. Statistical verification based on hypothesis testing is then conducted on the resultant corrected reachable sets for an accurate parametric system failure estimation. Experimental results show that our intertwined forward/backward reachability analysis can succeed in accurately estimating the system failure rate (a.k.a yield) by reducing the highly over-approximation of the forward scheme in the presence of noise and process variations. Experimental results of a second order PLL application, our algorithm outperforms existing methods by providing up to 17% more reliable yield estimation of the locking time property. However, the computational cost of the proposed methodology highly increases with the number of process parameters and system properties to be verified. In our future research, we will further investigate the possibility of adopting efficient heuristics and parallelization techniques that may address the computational time issue. We plan to verify complex systems in presence of transient faults uncertainty [22] and that involve multiple performance metrics.

References

1. Lin, H., Antsaklis, P.J., et al.: Hybrid dynamical systems: an introduction to control and verification. Found. Trends Syst. Control **1**(1), 1–172 (2014)
2. Wolf, M.: High-performance embedded computing: applications in cyber-physical systems and mobile computing (2014)
3. da Silva Azevedo, L., Parker, D., Walker, M., Papadopoulos, Y., Araujo, R.E.: Assisted assignment of automotive safety requirements. IEEE Softw. J. **31**(1), 62–68 (2014)
4. Bouissou, M., Elmqvist, H., Otter, M., Benveniste, A.: Efficient Monte Carlo simulation of stochastic hybrid systems. (96), pp. 715–725 (2014)
5. Fränzle, M., Hermanns, H., Teige, T.: Stochastic satisfiability modulo theory: a novel technique for the analysis of probabilistic hybrid systems. In: International Workshop on Hybrid Systems: Computation and Control, pp. 172–186 (2008)
6. Fulton, N., Mitsch, S., Quesel, J.-D., Völp, M., Platzer, A., KeYmaera, X.: An axiomatic tactical theorem prover for hybrid systems. In: International Conference on Automated Deduction, pp. 527–538 (2015)
7. Adimoolam, A.S., Dang, T.: Template complex zonotopes: a new set representation for verification of hybrid systems. In: International Workshop on Symbolic and Numerical Methods for Reachability Analysis, pp. 1–2 (2016)
8. Milstein, G.N.: Numerical integration of stochastic differential equations, vol. 313 (1994)
9. Al-Sammane, G.: Simulation symbolique des circuits décrits au niveau algorithmique. Ph.D. thesis, Université Joseph-Fourier-Grenoble I, France (2005)
10. Kumar, P.R., Varaiya, P.: Stochastic systems: Estimation, identification, and adaptive control (2015)
11. Ikeda, N., Watanabe, S.: Stochastic differential equations and diffusion processes, vol. 24 (2014)
12. Revuz, D., Yor, M.: Continuous martingales and Brownian motion, vol. 293 (2013)
13. Milstein, G.N., Tretyakov, M.V.: Stochastic numerics for mathematical physics (2013)
14. Han, Y., Chung, C.Y., Wong, K.P., Lee, H.W., Zhang, J.H.: Probabilistic load flow evaluation with hybrid latin hypercube sampling and cholesky decomposition. IEEE Trans. Power Syst. **24**(2), 661–667 (2009)
15. Burrage, K., Burrage, P., Donovan, D., Thompson, B.: Populations of models, experimental designs and coverage of parameter space by Latin hypercube and orthogonal sampling. Procedia Comput. Sci. **51**, 1762–1771 (2015)
16. Martinez, W.L., Martinez, A.R.: Computational Statistics Handbook with MATLAB. CRC Press, Boca Raton (2007)
17. Seghaier, I., Tahar, S.: Intertwined global optimization based reachability analysis of analog and mixed signal designs; Technical report, Department of Electrical and Computer Engineering, Concordia University, June 2017. http://hvg.ece.concordia.ca/Publications/TECH_REP/IGO_TR17.pdf
18. Bonarini, A., Bontempi, G.: A qualitative simulation approach for fuzzy dynamical models. ACM Trans. Modeling Comput. Simul. **4**(4), 285–313 (1994)
19. Coleman, T., Branch, M.A., Grace, A.: Optimization toolbox. For Use with MATLAB. Users Guide for MATLAB 5, Version 2, Release II (1999)
20. Seghaier, I., Aridhi, H., Zaki, M.H., Tahar, S.: A qualitative simulation approach for verifying PLL locking property. In: Great Lakes Symposium on VLSI, pp. 317–322 (2014)

21. Seghaier, I., Zaki, M.H., Tahar, S.: Statistically validating the impact of process variations on analog and mixed signal designs, pp. 99–102 (2015)
22. Hamad, G.B., Kazma, G., Mohamed, O.A., Savaria, Y.: Efficient and accurate analysis of single event transients propagation using SMT-based techniques. In: International Conference on Computer-Aided Design, pp. 1–7 (2016)

Analyzing Distributed Pi-Calculus Systems by Using the Rewriting Engine Maude

Bogdan Aman[1,2] and Gabriel Ciobanu[1,2(✉)]

[1] Romanian Academy, Institute of Computer Science,
Blvd. Carol I No.8, 700505 Iași, Romania
bogdan.aman@gmail.com
[2] Faculty of Computer Science, "A.I.Cuza" University,
Blvd. Carol I No.11, 700506 Iași, Romania
gabriel@info.uaic.ro

Abstract. Distributed systems with explicit locations and process mobility are described in terms of the distributed π-calculus. The systems described in distributed π-calculus are translated into a rewriting logic which is executable on the Maude software platform. We prove an operational correspondence allowing to verify properly the properties of the distributed systems. The approach is illustrated by examples of distributed systems analyzed by using the powerful Maude platform. We verify whether some systems are behaviourally equivalent by involving the metalevels of Maude.

1 Introduction

Process calculi are developed and studied with the aim of modelling concurrent processes. The π-calculus [14] works with communicating mobile processes, where the mobility is expressed by sending certain channel names as messages to other processes. Other formalisms involving mobility are $D\pi$-calculus [11], ambient calculus [7] and mobile membranes in bio-inspired computing [2].

In this paper we consider distributed systems with an explicit notion of location (it is not possible to model locations faithfully only by using the channels of π-calculus), and an explicit migration of processes between different locations. In order to describe systems with explicit locations, explicit migration, replication and local communication among processes, we use the distributed π-calculus [11].

On the other hand, rewriting logic and rewrite theory [13] has been used for more than two decades as a computational framework able to express several paradigms. Computationally, rewriting logic is a semantic framework in which several models of concurrency and programming languages can be naturally expressed, analyzed, and executed as rewrite theories. Rewriting logic is a framework within which different logics can be represented. The Maude system is an implementation of the rewriting logic using powerful metaprogramming based on reflection [10]. There exist various Maude specifications for Petri nets [18], CCS [20], concurrent objects [8], membrane systems [1,3,4], Klaim [21], and

© Springer International Publishing AG 2017
K. Barkaoui et al. (Eds.): VECoS 2017, LNCS 10466, pp. 155–170, 2017.
DOI: 10.1007/978-3-319-66176-6_11

adaptive systems [6]. A more comprehensive list of calculi, programming paradigms, tools and applications implemented in Maude is presented in [13].

In this article we present an implementation in Maude of the distributed π-calculus based on a correspondence between the operational semantics of distributed π-calculus and its rewriting logic implementation. This allows the translation of distributed π-calculus systems into Maude, followed by their execution and then by verification of properties as searching if a given located process is reachable, returning all reachable or final states, or even obtaining the entire search graph. We insist on these properties because reachability is a fundamental problem to which several quantitative and qualitative aspects can be reduced.

We also implement new behavioural equivalences between distributed systems; this is done by involving the Maude metalevels by using the `metaXapply` operation to collect all rewriting results of a given system. Two systems are considered to be equivalent if they match each other's nature of the applied rules (e.g., if one system can perform a 'move', then the other can also do a 'move', but possibly at a different location). An advantage of this equivalence is that it is possible to obtain an interesting relationship between processes that otherwise would not be equivalent (by using the existing strong behavioural equivalences where the order of compared actions has to be exactly the same). We are able to give a coarser comparison of systems by looking either at the performed actions or involved locations, or both. We provide examples to illustrate the implementation, and show how the distributed systems can be analyzed in Maude.

Structure of the paper. In Sect. 2 we present the syntax and semantics of the distributed π-calculus, while rewriting logic is presented in the first part of Section 3. The rewriting specification of the distributed π-calculus processes is also presented in Sect. 3. It is proved a correspondence between the operational semantics of distributed π-calculus and its rewriting implementation. In Sect. 4 we analyze the distributed systems by using their rewriting implementation in Maude, including the behavioural equivalences of some systems. Conclusion and related work end the paper.

2   Distributed Pi-Calculus

In distributed π-calculus (shortly $D\pi$), the processes can migrate between locations of a distributed environment consisting of a number of explicit and distinct names for these locations. Two processes may interact (communicate) only if they are present at the same location.

Syntax. We use a variant of the distributed π-calculus which was then extended with timers to become the timed distributed π-calculus [9]. The syntax is given in Table 1, where we assume a set Loc of locations and a set $Chan$ of communication channels. Thus $a \in Chan$ is a communication channel, $l \in Loc$ is a location or a location variable, $e \in Chan \cup Loc$ is either a location or a channel name, X is a variable, V is an expression built from values, variables and operations. Tuples of variables or values are usually used in the distributed π-calculus defined in [11]; for simplicity, we consider only single variables or values.

Table 1. Syntax of distributed π-calculus used in this paper

Processes $P, Q, R ::=$	$a!\langle V \rangle.Q$	(output)
	$a?(X).Q$	(input)
	$goto\ l.Q$	(move)
	$!P$	(replication)
	$(\nu e)P$	(restriction)
	if $v_1 = v_2$ then Q else R	(matching)
	$P \mid Q$	(parallel)
	$stop$	(termination)
Systems $N, M ::=$	$l[[P]]$	(located processes)
	$N \parallel M$	(composition)
	$(\nu_k e)N$	(restriction)
	$void$	(empty)

The process $a!\langle V \rangle.Q$ represents the transmission of value V along the channel a followed by the execution of Q. The input from a channel a is expressed by $a?(X).Q$; such a process $a?(X).Q$ awaits for a value V along the channel a, and then executes $Q\{V/X\}$. $Q\{V/X\}$ denotes a process Q in which all free occurrences of the variable X are replaced by V, eventually after alpha-converting the bound variables in Q in order to avoid name clashes. The substitution $Q\{V/X\}$ may not take place if the value V and variable X do not match; therefore, the input action can be applied only when the received term is well-formed with respect to the expected format.

Migration is provided by a process $goto\ l.P$ which describes the migration from the current location to the location indicated by l, where it behaves as P. Since l can be a variable, and so its value is assigned dynamically through communication with other processes, this form of migration supports a flexible scheme for the movement of processes from one location to another. Thus, the behaviour can adapt to various changes of the distributed environment.

The replication $!P$ provides the necessary (potentially infinite) number of copies of P. $(\nu e)P$ is a scoping mechanism for names; for example, in the process $Q \mid (\nu e)P$ the name e is known to P, but not to Q. Names and values are transmitted from a process to another, and so in the course of a computation e may become known by P as the result of a local communication. The process if $v_1 = v_2$ then Q else R is a test for the identity of simple values v_1 and v_2; if the equality is true then Q is executed, otherwise R is executed. The parallel composition $P \mid Q$ is used to denote two processes running in parallel. The process $stop$ represents a process finishing an execution.

A located process $l[[P]]$ specifies a process P running at location l, and a system is built from parallel located processes. $(\nu_k @e)N$ is a scoping mechanism for names that restricts the use of name e from location k. $void$ represents an empty system.

The only binding constructors are $a?(X).P$ and $(\nu e)P$ which bind the variable X and name e within P. $fn(P)$ and $bn(P)$ are used to denote the free and bound names of a process P, respectively. Similarly, $fn(N)$ and $bn(N)$ denote the free and bound names for a system N.

A problem that might appear is that some processes can be infinitely branching; for instance, the term $!P$ can create an unbounded number of copies of process P. To overcome this problem, we consider a bounded replication construct of the form $!(m)P$ in which we specify the maximum number of P's (namely m) which can be created during computation.

Operational Semantics. The structural equivalence $\equiv$ is the smallest congruence such that the equalities in Table 2 hold. Essentially, the role of $\equiv$ is to rearrange a system in order to apply the rules of the operational semantics (given in Table 3). The rule (NNEW) is used to move the scope of a restricted name from inside a location l to outside this location, while the rule (NEXTR) is known as scope extrusion axiom. This axiom is central, since it describes how a bound name e may be extruded, causing the scope of e to be extended. When $e \in fn(M)$, the alpha-conversion may be used to allow the scope extension.

Table 2. Structural congruence

(PNULL)	$P \mid stop \equiv P$
(NNULL)	$N \parallel void \equiv N$
(NCOMM)	$N \parallel N' \equiv N' \parallel N$
(NASSOC)	$(N \parallel N') \parallel N'' \equiv N \parallel (N' \parallel N'')$
(NNEW)	$l[[(\nu e)P]] \equiv (\nu_l e)l[[P]]$ if $e \neq l$
(NEXTR)	$M \parallel (\nu_l e)N \equiv (\nu_l e)(M \parallel N)$ if $e \notin fn(M)$

The operational semantics rules of distributed π-calculus is presented in Table 3.

We use a labelled transition system in which the name of the applied rule is placed on transitions whenever the rules (COM), (MOVE), (REP), (EQTRUE), (EQFALSE) and (SPLIT) are used. The rules (PAR1), (PAR2) and (STRUCT) collect all the applied rules in one step. In rule (COM), a process $a!\langle V \rangle.P$ located at location k succeeds in sending a value V over channel a to the process $a?(X).Q$, also located at k. Both processes continue to execute at location k, the first one as P and the second one as $Q\{V/X\}$. In rule (MOVE), the process $goto\ l.P$ define a migration from location k to location l, followed by an execution as process P. Rule (REP) describes the evolution of a replicating process. The rules (EQTRUE) and (EQFALSE) test for equality between values; depending on the equality tests, the process if $v_1 = v_2$ then P else Q continues either as process P or as process Q. Using the (SPLIT) rule, a given distributed system N can always be transformed into a finite parallel composition of located processes of the form $l_1[[P_1]] \parallel \ldots \parallel l_n[[P_n]]$ such that no process P_i has the parallel composition operator at its topmost level. Each located process $l_i[[P_i]]$ is called

Table 3. Operational semantics of distributed π-calculus

(COM)	$k[[a!\langle V\rangle.P]] \parallel k[[a?(X).Q]] \xrightarrow{com} k[[P]] \parallel k[[Q\{V/X\}]]$
(MOVE)	$k[[goto\ l.P]] \xrightarrow{move} l[[P]]$
(REP)	$k[[!P]] \xrightarrow{rep} k[[P \mid !P]]$
(EQTRUE)	$k[[\text{if } v = v \text{ then } P \text{ else } Q]] \xrightarrow{eqtrue} k[[P]]$
(EQFALSE)	$k[[\text{if } v_1 = v_2 \text{ then } P \text{ else } Q]] \xrightarrow{eqfalse} k[[Q]] \text{ if } v_1 \neq v_2$
(SPLIT)	$k[[P \mid Q]] \xrightarrow{split} k[[P]] \parallel k[[Q]]$
(PAR1)	if $M \xrightarrow{\lambda_1} M'$ and $N \xrightarrow{\lambda_2} N'$ then $M \parallel N \xrightarrow{\lambda_1 \cup \lambda_2} M' \parallel N'$
(PAR2)	if $M \xrightarrow{\lambda} M'$ then $M \parallel N \xrightarrow{\lambda} M' \parallel N$
(STRUCT)	if $M \equiv N$ and $M \xrightarrow{\lambda} M'$ and $M' \equiv N'$ then $N \xrightarrow{\lambda} N'$

a component of N, and the whole expression $l_1[[P_1]] \parallel \ldots \parallel l_n[[P_n]]$ is called a *component decomposition* of the system N. This is done in order to be able to apply communication rules requiring that the two communicating processes are located processes residing at the same location. Rules (PAR1) and (PAR2) are used to obtain larger systems from smaller ones by putting them in parallel. The rule (STRUCT) is used to rearrange a system by bringing its components side by side in order to apply a rule.

Example 1. Let us consider a system $Travel$ consisting of the following agents:

- *Promoter* is located at location *agency*; in order to promote his *agency*, he moves to location *home* where a client is available; then returns to his *agency*.
- *Agent* is located at location *agency*, waiting to offer a destination to some potential clients, and then taking money for this service and going to *bank* to deposit the received cash.
- *Client* is located at location *home*; after talking with a promoter, he goes to the agency to check for vacation destinations and acquires an *offer* for which he pays 100, and then goes on vacation. If this is not working, namely there is no offer from the *Agent*, the *Client* returns *home*.

By using the syntax of Table 1, these agents are described as follows:

$Travel = Promoter \parallel Agent \parallel Client$

$Promoter = agency[[goto\ home.talk!\langle agency\rangle.\ goto\ agency.stop]]$

$Agent = agency[[offer!\langle dest\rangle.pay?(price).goto\ bank.stop]]$

$Client = home[[talk?(X).Client1]]$

$Client1 = goto\ X.\text{if } X = agency \text{ then } Client2 \text{ else } Client3$

$Client2 = offer?(Y).pay!\langle 100\rangle.goto\ Y.stop$

$Client3 = goto\ home.stop$.

A possible evolution of the system $Travel$ is presented below:

$Travel = \textbf{Promoter} \parallel Agent; \parallel; Client$

$\xrightarrow{move} home[[talk!\langle agency\rangle.goto\ agency.stop]] \parallel Agent \parallel \textbf{Client}$

$\xrightarrow{comm} home[[goto\ agency.stop]] \parallel home[[\textbf{Client1}\{\textbf{agency/X}\}]] \parallel Agent$

$\qquad \text{then } Client2 \text{ else } Client3]] \parallel Agent$

$\xrightarrow{move \ move}$ $agency[[stop]] \ || \ agency[[if \ agency = agency \ \text{then} \ Client2$
    $\text{else} \ Client3]] \ || \ Agent$

$\xrightarrow{eqtrue}$ $agency[[stop]] \ || \ agency[[Client2]] \ || \ Agent$

$\xrightarrow{comm}$ $agency[[stop]] \ || \ agency[[(pay!\langle 100 \rangle.goto \ Y.stop) \ \{dest/Y\}]]$
    $|| \ agency[[pay?(price).goto \ bank.stop]]$

$\xrightarrow{comm}$ $agency[[stop]] \ || \ agency[[goto \ \textbf{dest}.stop]] \ || \ agency[[goto \ \textbf{bank}.stop]]$

$\xrightarrow{move \ move}$ $agency[[stop] \ || \ dest[[stop]] \ || \ bank[[stop]]] \ .$

It should be noticed that at the end of this evolution, a *Client* ends its execution at location *dest*, the *Promoter* at location *home*, while the *Agent* ends at location *bank*. This is due to the fact that we use a simple syntax for these agents, enough to illustrate how the rules of Table 3 work. In this scenario it is possible to consider multiple processes having the same definition by using the replication operator. For instance, a process !*Client* defines several clients; in such a situation, there exist various possible behaviours of the system *Travel*.

2.1 Bisimulations for Distributed Systems with Migration

Bisimulation is a new and important notion related to the behaviours of concurrent and distributed systems [16]. In addition to the classical definition of bisimulation in which two systems are equivalent if they match each other's actions one by one, in this paper we consider a more relaxed notion such that two systems are equivalent if they match each other's nature of the applied rules (e.g., if one system can perform a (MOVE) rule then the other can also perform a (MOVE), but not necessarily involving the same locations). An advantage of the equivalences defined in this way is that we can get a correspondence between processes which otherwise would not be equivalent (by using the existing equivalences where the order of compared actions has to be exactly the same). Two processes are said to be equivalent if they are able to "simulate" each others' applied rules, step by step, and continue to be equivalent after each such step [14]. After formally defining such an equivalence, we describe certain simple scenarios illustrating the difference from the classical behaviour equivalence.

When choosing which equivalence relation to adopt for a given system, one needs to decide what properties should be preserved by the equivalence relation. In what follows, we denote by $M \xrightarrow{label} M'$ the fact that the system M evolves to the system M' by applying a rule with name (LABEL).

Definition 1. *A* **behavioural equivalence** *$\mathcal{R}$ over systems described in distributed π-calculus by using the rules from the set Labels $= \{Com, \ Move, \ Rep, \ EqTrue, \ EqFalse, \ Split\}$ is a symmetric binary relation such that:*

- *for all $(M, N) \in \mathcal{R}$, if $M \xrightarrow{label} M'$ for label $\in$ Labels, then $N \xrightarrow{label} N'$ and $(M', N') \in \mathcal{R}$ for some N'.*

Two distributed π-calculus systems M and N are **behavioural equivalent** *(denoted $M \sim N$) if and only if there is a behavioural equivalence containing them.*

This reasoning is based on the assumption that only the nature of the performed reduction can be observed. This means that the following four systems are equivalent according to Definition 1 as they all can perform one move.

```
eq P1 = k[[(goto 1) . stop]] .
eq P2 = m[[(goto 1) . stop]] .
eq P3 = m[[(goto s) . stop]] .
eq P4 = k[[(goto 1) . stop]] || m[[(offer ! < Y >) . stop]] .
```

It is assumed that an observer can distinguish between the performed actions and involved locations as in [5], in the sense that when a system performs an action, the observer knows the performed action and which location is responsible for it. If one looks only at the performed actions, the processes $P1$, $P2$ and $P4$ are still equivalent as they can perform the same action goto 1, while $P3$ is different as it moves to a different location s. By considering also that the locations are observable, then only $P1$ and $P4$ turn out to be equivalent. Therefore, it is easy to see that the locations are also important when comparing the behaviours of some distributed systems.

3   Translating Distributed Pi-Calculus into Maude

Rewriting logic is a computational logic which combines term rewriting with equational logic. A *rewrite theory* [10] is a triple $\mathcal{R} = (\Sigma, E, R)$ where Σ is a signature of function symbols, E is a set of (possibly conditional) Σ-equations, and R is a set of (possibly conditional) Σ-rewrite rules. Both equations and rewrite rules can be used as conditions for a rewrite rule. The pair (Σ, E) is an order-sorted equational logic which has sorts, subsort inclusions and kinds (connected components of sorts) [12]. If $T_\Sigma(X)_k$ denotes the set of Σ-terms of kind k over the variables in X and s is a sort in the kind k, then $T_\Sigma(X)_s \subset T_\Sigma(X)_k$. The sentences which $\mathcal{R}$ proves are of form $(\forall X)t \rightarrow t'$, with $t, t' \in T_\Sigma(X)_k$ for some kind k. These sentences are obtained from the inference rules described below, where the notation $\mathcal{R} \vdash t \rightarrow t'$ is used to express that $t \rightarrow t'$ is provable in the theory $\mathcal{R}$.

reflexivity For each $t \in T_\Sigma(X)$, $\dfrac{}{\mathcal{R} \vdash t \rightarrow t}$

equality $\dfrac{(\forall X)u \rightarrow v, E \vdash u = u', E \vdash v = v'}{(\forall X)u' \rightarrow v'}$

congruence For each $f \in \Sigma_{s_1 \ldots s_n, s}$, $t_i \in T_\Sigma(X)_{s_i}$

$\dfrac{(\forall X)t_j \rightarrow t'_j, j \in J \subseteq [n]}{(\forall X)f(t_1, \ldots, t_n) \rightarrow f(t'_1, \ldots, t'_n)}$, where $t'_i := t_i$ whenever $i \notin J$;

replacement For each $\theta : X \rightarrow T_\Sigma(Y)$ and for each rule in $\mathcal{R}$ of the form

$$(\forall X)t \rightarrow t' \text{ if } (\bigwedge_i u_i = u'_i) \wedge (\bigwedge w_j \rightarrow w'_j), \text{ we have}$$

$$\dfrac{\bigwedge_x (\forall Y)\theta(x) \rightarrow \theta'(x)) \wedge (\bigwedge_i (\forall Y)\theta(u_i) = \theta(u'_i)) \wedge (\bigwedge_j (\forall Y)\theta(w_j) \rightarrow \theta(w'_j))}{(\forall Y)\theta(x) \rightarrow \theta(x')}$$

where θ' is the substitution obtained from θ by some rewritings $\theta(x) \rightarrow \theta'(x)$ for each $x \in X$;

transitivity $\dfrac{(\forall X)t_1 \to t_2, (\forall X)t_2 \to t_3}{(\forall X)t_1 \to t_3}$

In what follows we use the rewriting engine Maude to describe a rewrite theory corresponding to the semantics presented in the previous section[1]. It is worth noting that the replication operator cannot be translated into Maude since it does not support infinite computations. To overcome this problem, we consider a bounded replication construct of the form $!(m)P$ in which we specify the maximum number m of P's which can be created during computation. This means that we need to replace the rule $k[[!P]] \xrightarrow{rep} k[[P \mid !P]]$ of Table 3 by the following two rules:

-    $k[[!(m)P]] \xrightarrow{rep} k[[P \mid !(m-1)P]]$;
-    $k[[!(1)P]] \xrightarrow{rep} k[[P]]$.

To translate the syntax of Table 1, we use sorts with easy-to-understand names: e.g., `Channel` is used to represent channel names of the set *Chan*. A new aspect comes from the sort `Guard` which is used to denote parts of the processes of the form $a!\langle V \rangle$, $a?(X)$ and *goto l*. These parts are used to construct certain sequential processes. Between the given sorts there exist some subsorting relations from which we mention `subsorts Var < Location Channel Value` illustrating the fact that the variables can be replaced by location names, channel names or values. The sort `MValue` is used when counting the names appearing in the system, while `RValue` is used to stand for restricted values, namely the values used in the scope operators.

```
sorts Channel Location Var Value RValue MValue Process Guard
      System MSystem .
subsorts Var < Location Channel Value < MValue .
subsorts Value < Location .
subsorts Location Channel < RValue .
subsort System < MSystem .
```

To represent the processes and distributed systems of Table 1, we use the following constructors which are inspired by the syntax of distributed π-calculus. For instance, the parallel operators | and || are described by using associative and commutative constructors. We use a precedence relation between constructors by providing a certain precedence value to each constructor.

```
op  _ ! < _ >  :  Channel Value -> Guard [prec 10 ctor] .
op  _ ? ( _ ) : Channel Var -> Guard [prec 10 ctor] .
op  goto _ : Location -> Guard [prec 10 ctor] .
op  _ . _ : Guard Process -> Process [prec 5 ctor] .
op  if _ = _ then _ else _ fi  :  Value Value Process Process
                         -> Process [prec 5 ctor] .
op  _ | _  :  Process Process -> Process [assoc comm prec 20 ctor] .
op  (new _ ) _ : RValue Process -> Process [prec 10 ctor] .
op  !( _ ) _ : Nat Process -> Process [prec 5 ctor] .
op stop : -> Process [ctor] .
op  [[ _ ]] : Location Process -> System [prec 15 ctor].
op  _ || _  :  System System -> System [assoc comm prec 30 ctor] .
op (new _ @ _ ) _ : RValue Location System -> System [prec 15 ctor] .
op void : -> System [ctor] .
```

[1] The full specification is available at iit.iit.tuiasi.ro/∼ baman/Maude/DpiSpec.maude.

To represent substitution as a result of communication between processes according to rule (COM)), we use a specific constructor (for explicit substitutions). The main idea in such a substitution is to preserve the bound names inside their binders, and to replace all the free occurrences.

```
eq ((c ! < X >) . P) {V / X} = (c ! < V >) . (P {V / X}) .
 ceq ((c ! < W >) . P) {V / X} = (c ! < W >) . (P {V / X}) if V =/= W .
eq ((c ? ( X )) . P) {V / X} = (c ? ( X )) . P .
ceq ((c ? ( Y )) . P) {V / X} = (c ? ( Y )) . (P {V / X}) if X =/= Y .
eq ((goto X) . P) {V / X} = (goto V) . (P {V / X}) .
ceq ((goto l) . P) {V / X} = (goto l) . (P {V / X}) if X =/= l .
eq (if X = X then P else Q fi) {V / X}
   = (if V = V then (P{V / X}) else (Q{V / X}) fi) .
ceq (if X = v1 then P else Q fi) {V / X}
   = (if V = v1 then (P{V / X}) else (Q{V / X}) fi) if v1 =/= X .
ceq (if v1 = X then P else Q {V / X} fi)
   = (if v1 = V then (P{V / X}) else (Q{V / X}) fi) if v1 =/= X .
ceq (if v1 = v2 then P else Q fi) {V / X}
   = (if v1 = v2 then (P{V / X}) else (Q{V / X}) fi)
                  if v1 =/= X /\ v2 =/= X .
eq (P | Q) {V / X} = (P {V / X}) | (Q {V / X}) .
eq stop {V / X} = stop .
eq (!(a) P) {V / X} = !(a) (P {V / X}) .
```

However, using only the above substitution it is possible for a process $P = (a(b).goto\ X.stop)$ to get the process $P\{b/X\} = a(b).goto\ b.stop$ by considering the substitution $\{b/X\}$, just because there is no alpha-conversion needed to avoid name clashes. More exactly, the bound name b in the input prefix should be alpha-converted to avoid the clash with the name b substituting X. To avoid name capturing during alpha-conversion, we consider that some fresh names are given as terms of the form $[X]$.

```
op [_] : Var -> System [ctor] .
```

These fresh names are placed in parallel with the system using the parallel operator $\|$. We consider fresh names as systems because we use them in the conditional rules presented below, and these rewrite rules work only with systems (namely, they transform systems into systems). We could consider initially a set of fresh variables as a single system, but using the [Split] rule from the set of rewriting rules presented below, we would eventually reach the situation in which each fresh variable is treated as a separate system.

The renaming appearing before substitution is defined using the operator presented below (we mention only the equations in which the renaming differs from the substitution, as the other equations are similar):

```
op _ (_ / _) : Process Value Var -> Process [prec 40] .
eq ((c ? ( X )) . P) (V / X) = (c ? ( V )) . (P (V / X)) .
```

The rules of Table 3 are simulated as conditional rewrite rules having a similar form as the simulated ones in which the premises appear as conditions of the rules. The inference rules (PAR1), (PAR2) and (STRUCT) are not directly implemented as rewrite rules, but are translated into the matching mechanism of Maude (congruence rewriting and associativity and commutativity of the parallel operator $\|$). Since rewrites do not use labels as in the rules of Table 3, we include the labels as part of the rules by identifying the name of the conditional rule with the corresponding label.

```
crl [Comm] : (k[[(c ! < V >) . P ]]) || (k[[(c ? ( X )) . Q ]])
    => ([X]) || (k [[ P ]]) || (k [[ Q {V / X} ]]) if notin(V , bnP(Q)) .
crl [Comm] : (([Z]) || (k[[(c ! < V >) . P ]])) || (k[[(c ? ( X )) . Q ]])
    => (([X]) || (k [[ P ]])) || (k [[ (Q (Z / V)) { V / X} ]])
                   if in(V , bnP(Q))  /\ (notin(Z , bnP(Q))) .
crl [Rep] : k[[(!(a) P]] => k[[P | (!( sd(a , 1)) P)]] if a > 1 .
rl [Rep] : k[[!(1) P]] => k[[P]] .
rl [EqTrue] : k[[if V = V then P else Q fi]] => k[[P]] .
crl [EqFalse] : k[[if v1 = v2 then P else Q fi]] => k[[Q]] if v1 =/= v2 .
rl [Move] : k[[(goto l) . P]] => l[[P]] .
rl [Split] : k[[P | Q]] => (k[[P]]) || (k[[Q]]) .
```

It should be noticed that there are two instances for each of the rules [Comm] and [Rep]. In the case of the [Comm] rule, the need for two rules is due to the fact that in some cases we need to do renaming of bound names to avoid accidental captures (when in(V, bnP(Q))), while in other we do not (when notin(V, bnP(Q)). In the case when one needs to rename bound names, we check if there exists a free variable (denoted by $[Z]$) which does not appear in the bound names of Q (denoted by notin(Z, bnP(Q))). The functions in and notin are used to test membership of the first parameter into the second one.

Maude's metalevel is required to select a particular rule and apply it to a system in order to get the derived system. A predefined module called *META-LEVEL* contains operators over the representation of terms and modules of sorts Term and Module, and allows reduction of metalevel computations to object-level ones. The constructor metaXapply returns a tuple of information about the next state of the evolution from which we can get the meta-representation of the reduced term by using the operation getTerm. Finally, the function downTerm takes a meta-representation of a term and returns the term. In order to use the obtained term in the equiv constructor, we declare Term as a subsort of System.

The behavioural equivalence over two systems in distributed π-calculus is verified by using the commutative constructor equivSS which returns a value of sort Bool indicating if the two compared systems are equivalent.

```
ceq equivSS(M', N', M, N, depth) = true if
    equivMM(M, N, nextSystemsComm(M, depth),
    nextSystemsComm(N, depth), depth) == true and
    ...
```

The first two systems M' and N' of the equivSS operator are used to keep track of the systems from which the compared systems (M and N, respectively) were obtained. When we go to the next reductions for comparing the systems obtained from M and N, these M' and N' will be updated to the M and N. Keeping track of the initial systems is useful when computing the consumed channel or location in order to have a more strict equivalence.

Since there could be more than one system in nextSystemsComm(M, depth) to which a given system M can reduce, we need additional constructors equivMM (comparing a multiset of systems with another multiset of systems) and equivSM (comparing a system with a multiset of systems) to check the equivalence.

The construct equivMM takes all the possible systems obtained after a reduction of a system, and compares it with all the other systems obtained after a reduction of the other system; if it finds that the two systems can mimic each other behaviour, than it will return true.

```
ceq equivMM(M', N', M |+| MM, MN, depth) = true
    if equivSM(M', N', M, MN, depth) == true
        and equivMM(M', N', MM, MN, depth) == true
        and M =/= void and MM =/= eM and MN =/= eM .
    ...
```

The construct `equivSM` takes one system from all possible obtained systems from `nextSystemsComm(M, depth)`, and compares it with the multiset of system `nextSystemsComm(N, depth)` obtained from N; if it finds one that mimics its behaviour, than it will return `true`. To be able to observe also the consumed action and locations, we use two additional constructors `consumed` and `locatedAt`.

```
ceq equivSM(M', N', M, N, depth) = equivSS(M', N', M, N, depth)
    if consumed(M', M) == consumed(N', N)
        and locatedAt(M', M) == locatedAt(N', N) .
    ...
```

As for each system there are several possible evolutions, in order to check the equivalence there are required various constructors to see what are the obtained reductions after each step. Checking what are the obtained systems after performing a `Move` rule, we need a recursive construction which stops when the application of the `metaXapply` constructor does return `failure`:

```
eq nextSystemsMove(M, depth) =
    if metaXapply(upModule('SIMPLE-COM,false), upTerm(M), 'Move, none,
        0, unbounded, depth) == failure then eM
    else downTerm(getTerm(metaXapply(upModule('SIMPLE-COM,false),
        upTerm(M), 'Move,  none, 0, unbounded, depth)), eM) |+|
    nextSystemsMove(M,  depth + 1) fi .
```

The correspondence between the operational semantics given by the transition system of the distributed π-calculus on one hand, and the rewrite theory on the other hand, is given by a mapping $\psi : D\pi \rightarrow$ System defined inductively by

$$\psi(M) = \begin{cases} l[[\varphi(P]] & \text{if } M = l[[P]] \\ \psi(N_1)||\psi(N_2) & \text{if } M = N_1||N_2 \\ (new\ e@l)\psi(N) & \text{if } M = (\nu_l e)N \\ void & \text{if } M = void \end{cases} ;$$

$$\varphi(P) = \begin{cases} a!\langle\ V\ \rangle\ .\ \varphi(Q) & \text{if } P = a!\langle V\rangle.Q \\ a?(X)\ .\ \varphi(Q) & \text{if } P = a?(X).Q \\ (goto\ l)\ .\ \varphi(Q) & \text{if } P = goto\ l.Q \\ stop & \text{if } P = stop \\ !\ Q & \text{if } P =!Q \\ (new\ e)\psi(Q) & \text{if } P = (\nu e)Q \\ \varphi(Q)\ |\ \varphi(R) & \text{if } P = Q\ |\ R \\ \text{if v1 = v2 then Q else R fi} & \text{if } P = \text{if } v_1 = v_2 \text{ then } Q \text{ else } R \end{cases}$$

By $\mathcal{R}_D$ we denote the rewrite theory defined by the rewrite rules [Comm], [Move], [Rep], [EqTrue], [EqFalse] and [Split] together with the operators and equations defining them. The next theorem emphasizes the correspondence between the dynamics of the distributed π-calculus systems and the rewrite theory.

Theorem 1. $M \xrightarrow{label} N$ *iff* $\mathcal{R}_D \vdash \psi(M) \Rightarrow \psi(N)$.

The next result emphasizes the connection between the equivalence relations defined in distributed π-calculus and in rewrite theory. In should be noticed that only one-step rewrites are considered as rewriting logic deductions.

Theorem 2. $M \sim N$ *implies* $\mathcal{R}_D \vdash equivSS(\psi(M), \psi(N))$.

These theorems ensure that our encoding is faithful and behaves as expected when studying the systems described in distributed π-calculus.

4   Analyzing Distributed Systems by Using Maude

We provide some examples of distributed systems described in terms of $D\pi$, and then analyze their behaviours by using Maude. In this way we can check that the rules are applied properly, and verify that the results are the desired ones.

Since we know how to translate $D\pi$ syntax into Maude rewriting system, the *Travel* system of Example 1 can be described now in Maude. However, in $D\pi$ the alpha-conversion is implicit, while in Maude we need to consider explicitly the fresh names; thus, we add to this encoding two fresh names $[X1]\|[X2]$ which are enough to avoid name capturing in our examples.

As an example, *Client*1 syntax in Maude is:

```
eq Client1 = (goto X) . (if X = agency then Client2 else Client3 fi) .
```

When using the rewrite command **rew Travel**, Maude executes the **Travel** specification by applying the previously presented rules and equations, and finally returns the following output:

```
rewrite in SIMPLE-COM : Travel .
rewrites: 66 in 0ms cpu (0ms real) (~rewrites/second)
result System: [X1] || [X2] || bank[[stop]]
        || dest[[stop]] || agency[[stop]]
```

It is possible to use the **frew** command in order to rewrite a system by using a depth-first position-fair strategy which makes possible for some rules to be applied even when they are not applied by using the **rew** command. For our example, there is no difference when these two commands are used.

We use Maude to check if certain configurations of a system can be reached.

```
search in SIMPLE-COM : Travel =>* bank[[stop]]
            || dest[[stop]] || agency[[stop]] .
No solution.
states: 18  rewrites: 131 in 0ms cpu (0ms real) (~ rewrites/second)
```

We use the **search** command to answer the following question: starting from the initial system **Travel**, can we get an empty location named **dest** meaning that a client went on vacation at this promoted destination? This is done by searching for states which match a corresponding pattern. In this example, we use the **=>!** symbol, meaning that we are searching for states which cannot be further rewritten. If one is interested in a bounded number of reachable final states, the command **search [n]** can be used to obtain systems reachable in n steps:

```
search in SIMPLE-COM : Travel =>! X:System || dest[[stop]] .
Solution 1 (state 17)
states: 18  rewrites: 131 in 0ms cpu (0ms real) (~ rewrites/second)
X:System --> [X1] || [X2] || bank[[stop]] || agency[[stop]]
No more solutions.
states: 18  rewrites: 131 in 0ms cpu (0ms real) (~ rewrites/second)
```

Since there are no more solutions, the desired state is numbered 18. The sequence of rewrites allowing to reach this state can be obtained by typing **show path 18**. However, since the number of states is rather large to be presented here, we ask only the first two reachable states, and present the second reached one:

```
show path 2 .
state 0, System: [X1] || [X2] || home[[(talk ?(X)) . (goto X) .
  if X = agency then (offer ?(Y)) . (pay ! < 100 >) . (goto Y) .
  stop else (goto home) . stop fi]]
  || agency[[(goto home) . (talk ! < agency >) .
  (goto agency) . stop]] || agency[[(offer ! < dest >) .
  (pay ?(price)) . (goto bank) . stop]]
...
===> state 2, System: [X1] || [X2] || home[[(goto agency) . stop]]
  || home[[(goto agency) . if agency = agency then (offer ?(Y)) .
  (pay ! < 100 >) . (goto Y) . stop else (goto home) . stop fi]]
  || agency[[(offer ! < dest >) . (pay ?(price)) . (goto bank) . stop]]
```

It is possible to get just the sequence of labels of applied rules up to the state 17 by using a **show** command. It can be noticed that the order of the applied rules is exactly as in Example 1.

```
show path labels 17 .
Move   Comm   Move   Move   EqTrue   Comm   Comm   Move   Move
```

It is also possible to obtain the search graph for the above rewriting by using the command **show search graph**. As this graph is rather large, we do not display here the result of this command.

To display all the reachable states (not only of the graph obtained using the previous search commands), we can use the command **search Travel =>* X:System**. To display the system configurations reachable only after one step, one can use the following command.

```
search in SIMPLE-COM : Travel =>1 X:System .
Solution 1 (state 1)
states: 2  rewrites: 8 in 0ms cpu (0ms real) (~ rewrites/second)
X:System -->  [X1] || [X2]
       || home[[(talk ! < agency >) . (goto agency) . stop]]
       || home[[(talk ? (X)) . (goto X) . if X = agency
         then (offer ? (Y)) . (pay ! < 100 >) . (goto Y) . stop
         else (goto home) . stop fi]] || agency[[(offer ! < dest >) .
         (pay ? (price)) . (goto bank) . stop]]
No more solutions.
states: 2  rewrites: 8 in 0ms cpu (0ms real) (~ rewrites/second)
```

Regarding the behavioural equivalence, in order to check if the behavioural equivalences work properly, we consider four very simple systems and check whether some of them are equivalent or not.

```
eq P1 = k[[(goto l) . stop]] .
eq P2 = m[[(goto l) . stop]] .
eq P3 = m[[(goto s) . stop]] .
eq P4 = k[[(goto l) . stop]] || m[[(offer ! < Y >) . stop]] .
eq E1 = s[[!(3) ((goto m) . stop)]] .
eq E2 = k[[!(3) ((goto n) . stop)]] .
```

We illustrate the equivalence checking when both the performed actions and locations are observed as in [16], namely we test if the systems are equivalent using the classical notion of equivalence. Additionally, we can also check other equivalences, for instance when only one of either the performed actions or locations are observed.

```
reduce in SIMPLE-COM : equivSS(P1, P2, P1, P2, 0) .
rewrites: 363 in 28ms cpu (26ms real) (12964 rewrites/second)
result Bool: false
==========================================
reduce in SIMPLE-COM : equivSS(P1, P3, P1, P3, 0) .
rewrites: 335 in 8ms cpu (8ms real) (41875 rewrites/second)
result Bool: false
==========================================
reduce in SIMPLE-COM : equivSS(P1, P4, P1, P4, 0) .
rewrites: 517 in 16ms cpu (15ms real) (32312 rewrites/second)
result Bool: true
==========================================
reduce in SIMPLE-COM : equivSS(E1, E2, E1, E2, 0) .
rewrites: 1670693 in 23000ms cpu (22999ms real) (72638 rewrites/second)
result Bool: false
```

As expected, the above verification return *false* when comparing $P1$ and $P2$ because they perform the same action *goto l*, but from different locations (k and m, respectively). Both pairs $P1$ with $P3$ and $E1$ with $E2$ are not equivalent because they perform different moving actions from different locations. Even they have different definitions, the only systems that are equivalent are $P1$ and $P4$, because they perform the same mobility action *goto l* from the same location k.

5   Conclusion and Related Work

Maude is a rewriting engine able to implement different kinds of semantics for process calculi in order to obtain quickly certain prototypes available for software experiments and for checking/proving properties. An implementation in Maude via explicit substitutions for the labelled semantics of asynchronous π-calculus was proposed in [19]. Also, in [15] was defined an implementation in Maude for mobile ambients, a calculus able to encode the asynchronous π-calculus.

Our approach is different. We use the distributed π-calculus, a synchronous calculus with distributed locations. One of the main differences consists in the fact that our way of modelling explicit substitutions is different from [15,19] in which the authors use an existing implementation of explicit substitutions in

Maude called CINNI [17]. In these approaches the authors use indexed names and variables, a fact which implies also defining functions to manage them. We took a more natural and easier to understand approach by using a set of fresh names placed near the system. The minimum size of this set represents work in progress; now we know that one needs to use at least the same number of fresh names as all appearances of the bound names in the system.

In this paper we provided an implementation and software analysis of high-level processes described in distributed π-calculus by using the rewriting engine Maude. The features of distributed π-calculus include the possibility to create a number of copies of certain processes and local communications between processes. Since Maude does not support infinite computations, we consider only bounded replications. In order to have correct communications between processes, we need to consider renaming of bound names with some fresh names in order to avoid accidental captures.

We started by presenting shortly the distributed π-calculus, and continued by defining the rewrite theory of the distributed π-calculus processes. We present the correspondence between the operational semantics of distributed π-calculus and its Maude implementation. In this way, any distributed system M described in $D\pi$ is implemented correctly in Maude, and so we can analyzed the high-level description of the distributed systems by using the rewriting engine Maude. We verified that for the initial system M the rules are applied properly, and the results are the desired ones. When using the rewrite command `rew M`, Maude executes the specification of M by applying the rules and equations of the Maude encoding, and finally returns an output system. By using the specific `search` command, Maude returns an answer to the following question: starting from the initial system M, can we reach a certain given output system? Maude can also displays all the reachable systems starting from a given one, and also to return the search graph.

We defined the behavioural equivalence between distributed systems based on the nature of the applied rules, the performed actions and the involved locations. We used the metalevels of Maude to collect all the results for a given system; in this way we checked whether some systems are equivalent according to some bisimulations. This verification emphasized an advantage of using Maude, namely its tower of metalevels allowing convenient operations which permit to control the execution of sets of rewrite rules, and to play with the inner structure of the Maude encoding.

References

1. Agrigoroaiei, O., Ciobanu, G.: Rewriting logic specification of membrane systems with promoters and inhibitors. Electron. Notes Theoret. Comput. Sci. **238**, 5–22 (2009)
2. Aman, B., Ciobanu, G.: Mobility in Process Calculi and Natural Computing. Natural Computing Series. Springer, New York (2011)

3. Andrei, O., Ciobanu, G., Lucanu, D.: Executable specifications of P systems. In: Mauri, G., Păun, G., Pérez-Jiménez, M.J., Rozenberg, G., Salomaa, A. (eds.) WMC 2004. LNCS, vol. 3365, pp. 126–145. Springer, Heidelberg (2005). doi:10.1007/978-3-540-31837-8_7

4. Andrei, O., Ciobanu, G., Lucanu, D.: A rewriting logic framework for operational semantics of membrane systems. Theoret. Comput. Sci. **373**, 163–181 (2007)

5. Boudol, G., Castellani, I., Hennessy, M., Kiehn, A.: Observing localities. Theoret. Comput. Sci. **114**(1), 31–61 (1993)

6. Bruni, R., Corradini, A., Gadducci, F., Lluch-Lafuente, A., Vandin, A.: Modelling and analyzing adaptive self-assembly strategies with maude. Sci. Comput. Program. **99**, 75–94 (2015)

7. Cardelli, L., Gordon, A.D.: Mobile ambients. Theoret. Comput. Sci. **240**, 177–213 (2000)

8. Ciobanu, G., Lucanu, D.: Communicating concurrent objects in HiddenCCS. Electron. Notes Theoret. Comput. Sci. **117**, 353–373 (2005)

9. Ciobanu, G., Prisacariu, C.: Timers for distributed systems. Electron. Notes Theoret. Comput. Sci. **164**, 81–99 (2006)

10. Clavel, M., Durán, F., Eker, S., Lincoln, P., Martí-Oliet, N., Meseguer, J., Talcott, C.: All About Maude - A High-Performance Logical Framework. LNCS, vol. 4350. Springer, Heidelberg (2007)

11. Hennessy, M.: A Distributed π-Calculus. Cambridge University Press, Cambridge (2007)

12. Meseguer, J.: Membership algebra as a logical framework for equational specification. In: Presicce, F.P. (ed.) WADT 1997. LNCS, vol. 1376, pp. 18–61. Springer, Heidelberg (1998). doi:10.1007/3-540-64299-4_26

13. Meseguer, J.: Twenty years of rewriting logic. J. Logic Algebraic Program. **81**(7–8), 721–781 (2012)

14. Milner, R.: Communicating and Mobile Systems: the π-calculus. Cambridge University Press, Cambridge (1999)

15. Rosa-Velardo, F., Segura, C., Verdejo, A.: Typed mobile ambients in maude. Electron. Notes Theoret. Comput. Sci. **147**(1), 135–161 (2006)

16. Sangiorgi, D.: Introduction to Bisimulation and Coinduction. Cambridge University Press, New York (2011)

17. Stehr, M.-O.: CINNI: a generic calculus of explicit substitutions and its application to λ-, ς- and π-calculi. Electron. Notes Theoret. Comput. Sci. **36**, 70–92 (2000)

18. Stehr, M.-O., Meseguer, J., Ölveczky, P.C.: Rewriting logic as a unifying framework for petri nets. In: Ehrig, H., Padberg, J., Juhás, G., Rozenberg, G. (eds.) Unifying Petri Nets. LNCS, vol. 2128, pp. 250–303. Springer, Heidelberg (2001). doi:10.1007/3-540-45541-8_9

19. Thati, P., Sen, K., Martí-Oliet, N.: An executable specification of asynchronous Pi-Calculus semantics and may testing in maude 2.0. Electron. Notes Theoret. Comput. Sci. **71**, 261–281 (2002)

20. Verdejo, A., Martí-Oliet, N.: Executable structural operational semantics in maude. J. Logic Algebraic Program. **67**(1–2), 226–293 (2006)

21. Wirsing, M., Eckhardt, J., Mühlbauer, T., Meseguer, J.: Design and analysis of cloud-based architectures with KLAIM and maude. In: Durán, F. (ed.) WRLA 2012. LNCS, vol. 7571, pp. 54–82. Springer, Heidelberg (2012). doi:10.1007/978-3-642-34005-5_4

TT-BIP: Using Correct-by-Design BIP Approach for Modelling Real-Time System with Time-Triggered Paradigm

Hela Guesmi[1]([⊠]), Belgacem Ben Hedia[1]([⊠]), Simon Bliudze[2],
Saddek Bensalem[3], and Briag Le Nabec[1]

[1] CEA-LIST, PC 172, 91191 Gif-sur-Yvette, France
{hela.guesmi,belgacem.benhedia,briag.lenabec}@cea.fr
[2] EPFL IC IIF RiSD, 1015 Lausanne, Switzerland
simon.bliudze@epfl.ch
[3] Verimag, 38610 Gieres, France
saddek.bensalem@imag.fr

Abstract. In order to combine advantages of Real-Time Operating Systems (RTOS) implementing the Time-Triggered (TT) execution model and model-based design frameworks, we aim at proposing a correct-by-design methodology that derives correct TT implementations from high-level models. This methodology consists of two main steps; (1) transforming the high-level model into an intermediate which respects the TT communication principles and where all communication between components are simple send/receive interactions, and (2) transforming the obtained intermediate model into the programming language of the target platform.

In this paper, we focus on the presentation of the methodology of the first step of the design flow. This methodology produces a correct-by-construction TT model by starting from a high-level model of the application software in Behaviour, Interaction, Priority (BIP).

Keywords: Component-based design · Time-triggered paradigm · Model to model transformation · Correct-by-design transformation · Formal methods

1 Introduction

The Time-Triggered (TT) paradigm for the design of real-time systems was introduced by Kopetz [14]. TT systems are based on a periodic clock synchronization in order to enable a TT communication and computation. Each subsystem of a TT architecture is isolated by a so-called *temporal firewall*. It consists of a shared memory element for unidirectional exchange of information between sender and receiver task components. It is the responsibility of the *TT communication system* to transport, by relying on the common global time the information from the

© Springer International Publishing AG 2017
K. Barkaoui et al. (Eds.): VECoS 2017, LNCS 10466, pp. 171–188, 2017.
DOI: 10.1007/978-3-319-66176-6_12

sender firewall to the receiver firewall. The strong isolation provided by the temporal firewall is key to ensuring the determinism of task execution and, thereby, allowing the implementation of efficient scheduling policies.

Developing embedded real-time systems based on the TT paradigm is a challenging task due to the increasing complexity of such systems and the necessity to manage, already in the programming model, the fine-grained temporal constraints and the low-level communication primitives imposed by the temporal firewall abstraction. Several Real-Time Operating Systems (RTOS) implement the TT execution model, such as PharOS [4] and PikeOS [13]. However, they do not provide high-level programming models that would allow the developers to think on a higher level of abstraction and to tackle the complexity of large safety-critical real-time systems. Model-based design frameworks, such as BIP [1] and SCADE [7], allow the specification, design and simulation of real-time systems. In particular, BIP—a component-based framework for the design of real-time systems—allows verification of behavioural properties, such as deadlock-freedom, and lends itself well to model transformations.

To the best of our knowledge, few connections exist between high-level component-based design frameworks, allowing reasoning about application models and verification of their functional behaviour and TT execution platforms, which guarantee temporal determinism of the system.

In this work, we propose a framework that performs the first step to perform link between the model-based design framework BIP and TT execution platforms. This first step transforms a generic BIP model into a restricted model—called TT-BIP model, which lends itself well to an implementation based on TT communication primitives. We have outlined this transformation in a previous publication [11]. In this paper, we present new substantial results about this step, identify the key difficulties in defining this transformation, propose exhaustive solutions to address these difficulties and prove that this transformation is semantics-preserving.

The rest of this paper is structured as follows. Section 2 presents the BIP framework. In Sect. 3, we discuss challenges of the transformation and explain approach allowing to address them as well as choices leading to the definition of the structure of the target TT-BIP model. In Sect. 4, we formally define the transformation of a high-level BIP model into a TT-BIP model. Section 5 presents the application of the proposed approach on an industrial use case. Due to lack of space the correctness proofs of the proposed transformation are not included to the paper but may be provided by e-mail by one of the authors.

2   The BIP Framework

BIP is a component framework for constructing systems by superposing three layers of modelling: Behaviour, Interaction, and Priority. The Behaviour layer consists of a set of *components* defined by timed automata [3] extended with data and C functions. Transition labels of a component automaton are called *ports*. *Interactions* are sets of ports used for synchronization. Thus, the Interaction layer describes all possible synchronisations among components as a set of interactions. The third layer defines priorities among interactions, providing a mechanism for conflict resolution. In this paper, we do not consider priorities. Thus, we only consider BIP models obtained by composing components with interactions. Before formally defining BIP components and their semantics, we introduce some notations. For a variable x, denote $D(x)$ its domain (i.e. the set of all values possibly taken by x). A valuation on a set of variables X is a function $v : X \to \bigcup_{x \in X} D(x)$, such that $v(x) \in D(x)$, for all $x \in X$. We denote by $\mathcal{V}(X)$ (resp. $G_X = \mathbb{B}^{\mathcal{V}(X)}$) the set of all possible valuations (resp. *Boolean guards*) on X.

Definition 1 (Clock constraints). *Let C be a set of clocks. The associated set G_C of clock constraints CC is defined by the following grammar:*
$CC := True \mid False \mid c \sim a \mid CC \wedge CC$, *with $c \in C$, $\sim \in \{\leq, =, \geq\}$ and $a \in \mathbb{Z}_+$. Notice that any guard CC can be written as:*

$$CC := \bigwedge_{c \in C} l_c \leq c \leq u_c, \text{ where } \forall c \in C,\, l_c, u_c \in \mathbb{Z}_+ \cup \{+\infty\}. \tag{1}$$

Definition 2. *A component is a tuple $B = (L, P, X, C, T, tpc)$, where L is a finite set of locations; P is a finite set of ports; X is a finite set of local variables; C is a finite set of clocks; $T \subseteq L \times (P \times G_X \times G_C \times 2^C \times \mathcal{V}(X)^{\mathcal{V}(X)}) \times L$ is a finite set of transitions, each labelled with a port, two Boolean guards (on variables and on clocks), a set of clocks to be reset and a function updating a subset of variables of X; the function $tpc : L \to G_C$ assigns a time progress condition to each location, such that, for any $l \in L$, the constraint $tpc(l)$ is a conjunction of constraints of the form $c \leq u_c$.*

Definition 3 (Semantics of a component). *The semantics of a component $B = (L, P, X, C, T, tpc)$ is defined as a Labelled Transition System (LTS) $(Q, P, \to)$, where $Q = L \times \mathcal{V}(X) \times \mathcal{V}(C)$ denotes the set of states of B and $\to \subseteq Q \times (P \cup \mathbb{R}_{\geq 0}) \times Q$ is the set of transitions defined as follows. Let (l, v_x, v_c) and (l', v'_x, v'_c) be two states, $p \in P$ and $\delta \in \mathbb{R}_{\geq 0}$.*

- ***Jump transitions:** We have $(l, v_x, v_c) \xrightarrow{p} (l', v'_x, v'_c)$ iff there exists a transition $\tau = (l, p, g_X, g_C, R, f, l') \in T$, such that $g_C(v_c) = g_X(v_x) = True$, $v'_x = f(v_x)$ and*

$$v'_c(c) = \begin{cases} 0, & \text{for all } c \in R, \\ v_c(c) & \text{for all } c \in C \setminus R. \end{cases}$$

- ***Delay transitions:** We have $(l, v_x, v_c) \xrightarrow{\delta} (l, v_x, v_c + \delta)$ iff $\forall \delta' \in [0, \delta]$, $tpc(l)(v_c + \delta') = True$, where $(v_c + \delta)(c) \stackrel{def}{=} v_c(c) + \delta$, for all $c \in C$.*

A component B can execute a transition $\tau = (l, p, g_X, g_C, R, f_\tau, l')$ from a state (l, v_x, v_c) if its timing constraint is met by the valuation v_c. The execution of τ corresponds to moving from control location l to l', updating variables and resetting clocks of R. Alternatively, it can wait for a duration $\delta > 0$, if the time progress condition $tpc(l)$ stays *True*. This increases all the clock values by δ. Notice that execution of jump transitions is instantaneous; control location cannot change while time elapses.

Components communicate by means of interactions. An interaction is a synchronization between transitions of a fixed subset of components. It is possible only if all the participating components can execute the corresponding transitions. A formal definition can be found in [1], we omit it here for the sake of conciseness.

3   Problem Statement and the Proposed Solution

Transforming a user-defined task mapping and a high-level BIP model based on multi-party interaction model into an equivalent model where interactions comply with the TT communication pattern, is a challenging task. From one hand, introducing TT settings consists in (1) modelling the TT communication system by introducing dedicated atomic components and (2) restricting the synchronous multiparty inter-task interactions to simple unidirectional communications with the introduced communication components. From the other hand, the derived model is required to be observationally equivalent to the original BIP model.

In order to respect TT communication settings, the derived model should handle each inter-task communication through a dedicated BIP component which stands for the TT communication system. This latter can communicate with tasks only through message-passing. The challenge here is to switch from the high-level BIP model, where multi-party interactions provide component synchronization on top of data transfer, to asynchronous message-passing communications while preserving the models equivalence.

This issue is addressed by breaking the atomicity of execution of interactions. A task can execute unobservable actions to notify the communication component about their states. If all participating components are ready, the communication component can execute the corresponding interaction.

The execution of interactions sometimes generates conflicts that need to be resolved. In high-level BIP model, such conflicts are resolved by the single engine. TT communication components in the derived model must ensure that execution of conflicting interactions is mutually exclusive.

In order to tackle this challenge, we use the solution proposed in [12,15,16], which consists in instantiating a BIP component that implements the algorithm proposed in [5]. The latter uses message counts to ensure synchronization and reduces the conflict resolution problem to dining or drinking philosophers [9].

The target TT-BIP model
The target TT-BIP model—that satisfies the TT settings and addresses the previously cited challenges—is structured following a three-layer architecture called TT-BIP architecture:

The Task Components Layer consists of a transformation of atomic components corresponding to the behavior layer of the initial model. This layer depends also on a user-defined task mapping. A task component can interfere even in an internal computation, intra-task interaction (i.e. communication between components of the same task) or inter-task interaction (i.e. communication with other tasks). Components within a task that are concerned by the inter-task interaction or participating in an intra-task interaction that is conflicting with an inter-task interaction, operate in partial-state semantics.

The communication Layer aims at modelling the TT communication system by hosting inter-task interactions and allowing to resolve their potential conflicts by soliciting the third layer. This layer contains TT communication component (TTCC) hosting each an inter-task interaction of the original model. We have essentially two conflict cases involving inter-task interactions; conflict between only inter-task interactions and conflict between inter-task interactions and intra-task interactions or internal computations. By dedicating a third layer for resolving conflicts, the first case of conflicts, if existing, can be directly resolved. Resolving the second conflict case, can not be resolved locally since a task has a partial observability of the system. This needs however, to host the conflicting intra-task interaction or internal computation in the communication layer in order to be resolved by requesting the third layer. Thus, this layer consists of components hosting each either an inter-task interaction or an interaction that is either *directly* or *indirectly* conflicting with another inter-task interaction. For simplifying the notation, all constituent components of the communication layer are denoted by TTCC components.

The Conflict Resolution Protocol (CRP) Layer resolves the conflicts requested by the communication layer. In the original model, these conflicts are resolved by the BIP engine. In order to guarantee conflicts resolution in the derived model, we reuse the same solution proposed in [12,15,16] which consists in dedicating a third layer to implement the fully centralized committee coordination algorithm presented in [5].

Cross-layer interactions are send/receive interactions, i.e. providing a unidirectional data transfer from one sender component to one or more receiver(s).

A BIP model complies with the TT-BIP architecture if it consists of three layers: Tasks layer, TTCC layer and CRP layer, organized by the following abstract grammar:

$$TT\text{-}BIP\text{-}Model ::= Task^+ \ . \ TTCC^+ \ . \ CRP \ . \ S/R\text{-}connector^+$$
$$Task \qquad\qquad ::= atomic\text{-}component^+ \ . \ atomic\text{-}talking\text{-}component^+ \ . \ connectors^+$$
$$TTCC \qquad\qquad ::= TTCC^{NC} \mid TTCC^C$$

The TT-BIP model consists of a set of Tasks, TTCC and CRP components. A task component is a composite component consisting of one or more atomic components. Atomic components within a task which interfere in inter-task interactions (via the task interface) are called *atomic-talking-components* (ATC). These latter can only communicate with a TTCC component or a component within the same task. The behavior of a TTCC component depends on whether the interaction it is hosting is conflicting or not. If the interaction is conflicting, the TTCC component is denoted by $TTCC^C$ and needs to communicate with

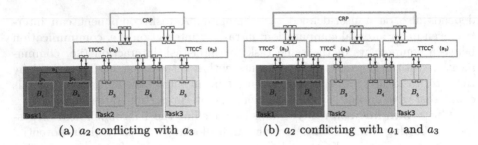

(a) a_2 conflicting with a_3 (b) a_2 conflicting with a_1 and a_3

Fig. 1. Overview of a TT-BIP model

the CRP component. Otherwise, it is denoted by $TTCC^{NC}$. Conflicts between different $TTCC^C$ components, are resolved through CRP component.

Task components (resp. TTCC components) and TTCCs (resp. CRP components) communicate with each other through message-passing, i.e. send/receive interactions. Such interaction is a set of one send port and one or more receive ports. Communications between components inside a task are classic multi-party BIP interactions. Notice that in Fig. 1a, we assume that the interaction a_2 is conflicting only with the interaction a_3, while in Fig. 1b a_2 is conflicting with both a_1 and a_3.

Formally, we define a TT-BIP model as follows:

Definition 4. *We say that $B^{TT} = \gamma^{TT}(B_1^{TT}, ..., B_n^{TT})$ is a TT-BIP model iff we can partition the set of its ports into three sets P_u, P_s and P_r that are respectively the set of unary ports, send ports and receive ports, such that:*

- *Each interaction $\alpha \in \gamma^{TT}$ is either a send/receive interaction with $P_\alpha = s, r_1, ..., r_k$, $s \in P_s$, $r_1, ..., r_k \in P_r$, $G_\alpha = True$ and F_α copies variables exported by port s to variables associated with ports $r_1, ..., r_k$, or a unary interaction—called also external interaction—where $P_\alpha = p_\alpha$ with $p_\alpha \in P_u$, $G_\alpha = True$ and F_α is the identity function.*
- *Interactions that are relating components of the same task are classic multi-party interactions—called internal interaction—.*
- *If s is a port in P_s, then there exists one and only one send/receive interaction $\alpha \in \gamma^{TT}$ with $P_\alpha = (s, r_1, ..., r_k)$ and all ports $r_1, ..., r_k$ are receive ports. We say that $r_1, ..., r_k$ are receive ports of s,*
- *If $\alpha \in \gamma^{TT}$ is a send/receive interaction such that $P_\alpha = (s, r_1, ..., r_k)$ and s is enabled at some global state of B^{TT}, then all its receive ports $r_1, ..., r_k$ are also enabled at that state.*

The proposed solution, leads out to a 3-layer architecture structuring the target model of the transformation. Although our work doesn't have the same goal as transformational approaches proposed in [12,15,16], but there is some intersection between both target models' architectures. Aiming at deriving distributed implementations from high-level BIP model, these cited approaches propose an intermediate model called send/receive model. This latter is a 3-layer model consisting of atomic components layer, schedulers layer and CRP layer.

We reuse the third layer of the send/receive model (i.e. the CRP layer) since it is, so far, the unique solution to guarantee the conflicts resolution without requesting the BIP engine. The difference between the send/receive and the TT-BIP architectures, lies in the task notion introduced in the TT-BIP architecture. Thus, we build the task layer depending on a user-defined task mapping, and we construct communication components in order to handle inter-task interactions and other conflicting interactions. In the second layer of send/receive models, are introduced schedulers allowing to handle interactions between all atomic components. Also, we introduce one component per external interaction, while a scheduler of send/receive model can handle more than one interaction.

4   Transformation of a BIP Model into a TT-BIP Model

In our work we assume that the input model is flat, i.e. it consists only of atomic components and flat connectors. This restriction is obtained by using the flattening tool from previous research work [8,12]. This tool replaces all hierarchical connectors and composite components of a BIP model by an equivalent set of flat connectors and atomic components.

In this section, we describe in details our technique for transforming a BIP model $B \stackrel{def}{=} \gamma(B_1, ..., B_n)$ into a TT-BIP model $B^{TT} = \gamma^{TT}(B_1^{TT}, ..., B_n^{TT}, TTCC_1, ..., TTCC_m, CRP)$.

One parameter to this transformation is the user-defined task mapping which consists in associating to each task T_k a group of atomic components of the model B. We denote by $\mathcal{B}$ the set of atomic components of model B. The task mapping is formally defined as follows:

Definition 5 (Task mapping). *We assume, we have $K \leq n$ tasks and we denote by $\mathcal{T} = \{T_k\}_{k \in K}$ the task set, such that $\mathcal{T}$ is a partition of $\mathcal{B}$: where for all $j, k \in K$ and $j \neq k, T_j \cap T_k = \emptyset$. For all $k \in K$ we have $T_k = \{B_i\}_{i \in I_k}, I_k \subseteq K$ such that $\bigcup_{k \in K} I_k = K$.*

The transformation process is performed in two steps. First, depending on the given task mapping, the original model is analysed in order to define the set of components and connectors to be transformed. Then, the BIP model is transformed into a TT-BIP model where only inter-task interactions and other related conflicting interactions are replaced by TTCC components. Non conflicting intra-task interactions remain intact. Components mapped to the same task are gathered in a composite task component.

We first present details about the analysis phase in Subsect. 4.1. Then, we explain how concerned atomic components are transformed and how task components are instantiated in Subsect. 4.2. Then we show how TTCC components are built in order to coordinate task components in Subsect. 4.4. Behavior of the CRP component is detailed in Subsect. 4.5. Finally, we define the cross-layer connections in Subsect. 4.6.

4.1   Analysis Phase

We have first to identify internal and external interactions as well as ATC components denoted respectively A_E, A_I and $\mathcal{B}^{ATC}$. These obtained sets are inputs for the transformation of components and connectors of B into B^{TT}.

External interactions

In order to be able to define the set A_E, we need first to define the set of inter-task interactions denoted A_{IT}. An interaction $a \in \gamma$ is an inter-task interaction iff at least two of its participant components belong to two different tasks. Formally, $A_{IT} = \{\alpha \in \gamma \,|\, \exists B_1, B_2 \in comp(\alpha), T_1, T_2 \in \mathcal{T} : B_1 \in T_1, B_2 \in T_2,\}$ $T_1 \neq T_2$. We denote intra-task interactions that are either *directly* or *indirectly* conflicting with inter-task ones by $A_{IT}^{\#}$ defined as follows:

$$A_{IT}^{\#} = \{a \in \gamma \,|\, a \notin A_{IT}, \exists \alpha \in A_{IT} : a\#\alpha\}$$
$$\cup \{a \in \gamma \,|\, a \notin A_{IT}, \exists b \notin A_{inter}, \exists \alpha \in A_{inter} : a \neq b, a\#b, b\#\alpha\}.$$

And we denote the set of transitions labelled by internal ports and conflicting with interactions of $A_{IT}^{\#} \cap A_{IT}$ by A_{IT}^{p}. It is sefined as follows:

$$A_{IT}^{p} = \{p \,|\, \forall a \in \gamma, p \notin P_a, \exists \alpha \in A_{IT} \cup A_{IT}^{\#}, q \in P_\alpha, \exists \in [1, n], \exists \in L_i : l \xrightarrow{p}, l \xrightarrow{q}\}.$$

As explained in Definition 4, A_E consists of inter-task interactions A_{IT}, intra-task interactions $A_{IT}^{\#}$ and internal transitions A_{IT}^{p} that are either *directly* or *indirectly* conflicting with inter-task ones. Thus, we have: $A_E = A_{IT} \cup A_{IT}^{\#} \cup A_{IT}^{p}$

Internal interactions

A_I set in defined as the set of intra-task interactions (i.e. participating components are belonging to the same task) which are neither *directly* nor *indirectly* conflicting with inter-task components: $A_I = \gamma \setminus A_E$.

Atomic talking components

$\mathcal{B}^{ATC}$ set is the set of atomic components in $\mathcal{B}$ that are concerned by external interactions A_E. We define: $\mathcal{B}^{ATC} = \{B \in \mathcal{B} \,|\, A_E \cap P_B \neq \emptyset\}$, where P_B is the port set of the component B.

4.2   Transformation of Task Components

We transform each ATC atomic component $B_i \in \mathcal{B} \cap \mathcal{B}^{ATC}$ of a BIP model into a TT ATC component B_i^{TT} that is capable of communicating with $TTCC$ component(s). This transformation consists mainly in decomposing each "atomic" inter-task synchronization into send and receive actions. The synchronization between the ATC component (via the task interface) and the TTCC layer is implemented as a two-phase protocol.

First, B_i^{TT} sends communication *offers* through dedicated send ports. Then, in the second step, it waits for a notification coming from the TTCC component via a receive port. The communication *offer* contains information about the enabledness of the interaction. Each offer is associated to one of the enabled ports of B_i through which the component is ready to interact. An offer consists of a set of variables related to the corresponding enabled port. Let p be such port enabled from a location l (i.e. $l \xrightarrow{p}$). The set of variables of the corresponding offer includes variables initially exported by p since they may be read and written by the interaction. It includes also variables tc_p and tpc_l storing respectively timing constraint of transition labelled by p and enabled from l and the time progress condition of the location l. Another variable g_p is dedicated to store the evaluation of the Boolean guard of the transition labelled by p and enabled from l. The offer contains also a variable f_i storing the update function of the transition labelled by the port p. In order to be able to resolve conflicts, each offer contains the *participation count* variable nb of the component B_i^{TT}. This variable counts the number of interactions B_i^{TT} has participated in.

The notification —received after sending offers—allows the ATC component to execute the transition triggered by the enabled receive port marking the end of the interaction.

Notice that each offer —sent by a component—contains information about only one enabled interaction among the enabled interaction set. Therefore, if in the original model B, more than one interaction involving B_i are enabled, then B_i^{TT} has to send first successive offers before waiting for notification from the TTCC component executing the interaction selected after conflict resolution.

Let a location l, in B_i, from which $p_1, ..., p_n$ are enabled such that at least one of the n ports interferes in an inter-task interaction. In B_i^{TT}, we split such a location l into $n+1$ locations, namely l itself and locations $\{\bot_{p_i}^l\}_{i \in [1,n]}$ from which corresponding offers are sent.

Consider the case when, in the original model B_i, time is allowed to progress from location l, i.e. before executing the interaction. In order to enforce correctness of the target model, time should be able to progress until the interaction is actually executed. Thus we associate to locations $\bot_{p_i}^l$ the time progress condition of location l originally defined in the atomic component B_i.

4.3 Expressing Timing Constraints and Time Progress Conditions over a Common Global Clock

In BIP framework, each atomic component can define its own local set of clocks. These clocks can be reset at any time and are used in definitions of timing constraints and time progress conditions.

In order to execute an external interaction $a = p_i, i \in I$, a TTCC component needs to evaluate the timing constraint of the interaction, i.e. the conjunction of timing constraints of transitions labelled by ports p_i involved in the interaction in the original model. These respective timing constraints are sent by respective ATC components to the TTCC layer within offers. In order to allow the TTCC to compute interactions between tasks components and schedule them correctly, we need to reduce the effort of keeping track of different clocks of participating components. This can be resolved by expressing timing constraints in terms of a single time scale, that is, a single global clock. Moreover, the global time scale is a key feature of the TT paradigm targeted by the transformation.

For these two reasons, we need to translate all timing constraints and express them over the global clock.
We denote by c^g, the global clock which is initialized to 0 and measures the absolute time elapsed since the system started executing, i.e. c^g is never reset.

We follow a similar approach as in [2] in order to translate selected timing constraints. Here are the different translation steps: (1) for each component $B_i \in \mathcal{B}$ and for each clock $c \in C$, we introduce a variable w_c that stores the absolute time of the last reset of c. The variable w_c is initialized to zero and updated to the absolute time (i.e. the valuation of the global clock c^g) whenever the component executes a transition resetting clock c. (2) Each atomic expressions $lb \leqslant c \leqslant ub$ involved in a timing constraint tc, is rewritten by using the global clock c^g and the variable w_c. Mainly, we have to add to the initial lower and upper bounds the last reset value w_c of the local clock c as follows: $lb \leqslant c \leqslant ub \equiv lb + w_c \leqslant c^g \leqslant ub + w_c$. (3) Similarly, we rewrite each atomic expressions $c \leqslant ub$ of time progress conditions tpc —defined on all locations from which an external interaction can be enabled—as follows: $c \leqslant ub \equiv c^g \leqslant ub + w_c$.

Notice that the value of each local clock c can be computed from the current value of the global clock c^g and the variable w_c by using the equality $c = c^g - w_c$. This allows to entirely remove clocks of components B_i, keeping only the clock c^g and variables w_c; $c \in C$.

After applying the described rules, we can formally define the obtained component in function of the original one.

Definition 6. *Formally, B_i^{TT} is obtained from B_i as follows:*

- $L_i^{TT} = L_i \cup L_\perp$, where $L_\perp = \{\perp_p^l \mid \exists l \in L_i, \exists \tau = (l, p, g, tc, r, f, l') \in T_i, p \in P_i \cap A_E\}$,
- $P_i^{TT} = P_i \cup P_o$, where $P_o = \{o_p \mid p \in P_i \cap A_E\}$. *Each port o_p exports the set of variables $X_{o_p}^{TT} = X_p \cup \{tpc, tc_p, g_p, f_p, nb\}$. For all ports in $p \in P_i \cap A_E$, we have $X_p^{TT} = X_p$. For all ports $p \in P_i \setminus A_I$, we have $X_p^{TT} = X_p$.*,
- $X_i^{TT} = X_i \cup \{tpc\} \cup \{tc_p, g_p, f_p\}_{p \in P_i \cap A_E} \cup \{w_c\}_{c \in C_i} \cup \{nb\}$,
- $C_i^{TT} = \{c^g\}$,
- $T_i^{TT} = \{\tau_{o_p}\}_{p \in P_i \cap A_E} \cup \{\tau_p'\}_{p \in P_i}$. *Such that for each $\tau_p = (l, p, g_{\tau_p}, tc_{\tau_p}, r_{\tau_p}, f_{\tau_p}, l') \in T_i$ we have: $\tau_{o_p} = (\perp_{o_p}^l, o_p, True, True, \emptyset, Id, \perp_{o_p}^{l'})$ if $p \in P_i \cap A_E$ and $\tau_p' = (l, p, True, True, r_{\tau_p}, f_{\tau_p'}, l')$, where $\perp_{o_p}^{l'}$ is l or $\perp_{o_q}^{l}$ if $l \xrightarrow{q}$. If $p \in P_i \cap A_E$, the update function $f_{\tau_p'}$ (1) updates the clock reset variables: $\forall c \in r_{\tau_{p_j}}$, $w_c = v_c(c^g)$, where v_c is the clock valuation function, (2) increments the participation count variable nb and (3) updates variables of offers sent from next reached state. If $p \in P_i \setminus A_E$, $f_{\tau_p'}$ (1) applies the original update function f_{τ_p}, (2) updates the clock reset variables: $\forall c \in r_{\tau_{p_j}}$, $w_c = v_c(c^g)$, where v_c is the clock valuation function, (3) increments the participation count variable nb and (4) updates variables of offers sent from next reached state.*
- *For places of $L_\perp$, the time progress condition $tpc^{TT}(\perp_{o_p}^l) = tpc(l)$.*

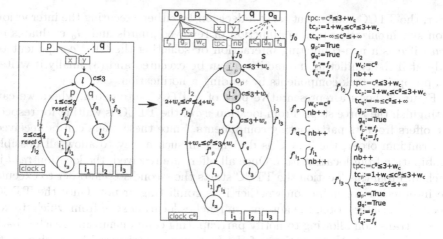

Fig. 2. Example of transformation of an ATC component

Example 1. Figure 2 illustrates transformation of an ATC component into its corresponding ATC TT component. In this example we consider that ports p and q are participating in external interactions.

Once all ATC components are transformed, we instantiate the composite component of each task, which corresponds to gathering all components mapped to that task and exporting send and receive ports of ATC components.

4.4   Building TTCC Components

As explained before, a TTCC component layer is introduced initially in order to handle intertask interactions and thus model the TT communication system. By considering the need for operational equivalence, and in order to be able to resolve all conflicts of the target model interactions, the TTCC layer handles, on top of intertask interactions, other interactions that are conflicting *directly or indirectly* with these latter. Recall that all interactions of the original model, that are handled in the TTCC layer are called external interactions.

Initially, all components are doing their initial computations and the TTCC layer does not know their state or their enabled communication ports until they send offers. Handling only one external interaction, a TTCC can execute this latter only when all participating tasks' components have sent their offers and are ready to execute the interaction.

When the interaction is conflicting with another external interaction, the TTCC has to communicate, after checking the enabledness of the interaction, with the CRP in order to get the permission or not to execute. We call this communication a reservation mechanism.

To summarize, the behavior of a TTCC component handling an interaction $a = (a, G_a, F_a) \in \gamma$ is made of three steps: (1) it waits for offers from its participating task components, (2) once all offers are received —regardless their order, the TTCC component takes a decision by either executing the interaction upon synchronization (i.e., conjunction of revevied guards and G_a evaluates to *True*) if a is a non-conflicting interaction or soliciting the CRP component to find out if the conflicting interaction a can be executed and (3) finally it writes on appropriate task components by sending a notification.

Figure 3 shows a representative part of a TTCC automaton, where we can distinguish the three steps. From location *wait*, the TTCC is waiting for respective offers from its participating components. Since these offers can be received in a random order, the TTCC is designed in such a way to allow all possible combination from location *wait*. Once all offers are received, the location *read* is reached. From this location the TTCC starts the second step in order to execute the interaction depending on whether it is conflicting or not. Once the TTCC executes the interaction, the automaton reaches location *send* from which it executes a transition allowing to notify participating components and reaches back the location *wait*. All transitions of the first step are triggered by receive ports corresponding to respective offers. Transition of the third step is triggered by a send port. Behaviour and ports triggering transitions of the second step are detailed later.

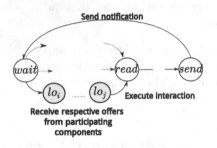

Fig. 3. Skeleton of a TTCC automaton

Let a TTCC component handling an external interaction $\alpha = (P_\alpha, G_\alpha, F_\alpha) \in \gamma \cap A_E$. We denote by n the number of components related to TTCC, i.e. the number of participating components of α.

In the case when α is a non conflicting interaction, the execution of this latter is performed without requesting the CRP component. As shown in Fig. 4a, the TTCC executes a transition from location *read* to *send* labelled by a unary port denoted p_α. Its update function executes the update function F_α of the interaction α, and then respective update functions that are received in offers. The transition p_α is guarded by the conjunction of the guard G_α and respective guards and timing constraints received in offers. If the conjunction of these guards evaluates to *True*, the interaction is executed and the TTCC sends notification to participating components.

In the case when α is conflicting with another interaction, the TTCC goes through a reservation mechanism (cf. Fig. 4b). If the interaction is enabled, i.e. the conjunction of the guard G_α and respective guards and timing constraints received in offers evaluates to *True*, the TTCC executes transition rsv_α from location *read*. This transition reaches location *try*. By the execution of rsv_α, a reservation request is sent to the CRP component. This reservation contains different values of participation count variables of α participating components. Based on these participation counters, the CRP decides whether to allow or disallow the interaction execution. It notifies the TTCC component either through

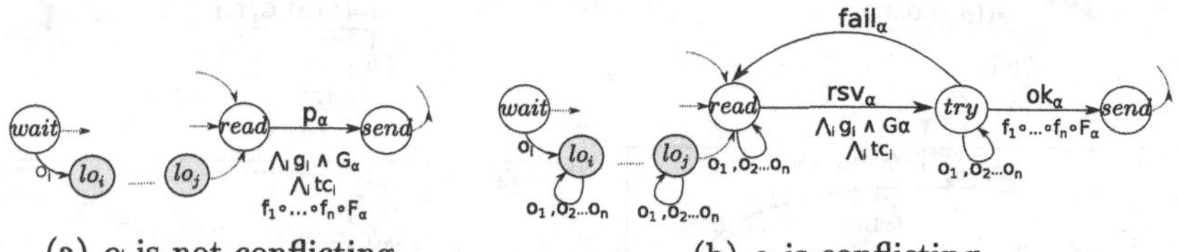

Fig. 4. Mechanisms for execution of interaction $\alpha = (P_\alpha, G_\alpha, F_\alpha)$

port ok_α in case when the reservation succeeds or through port $fail_\alpha$ if the reservation can not be made. While waiting for CRP notification, the TTCC occupies the location try. If the port ok_α is enabled, then it executes the transition reaching location $send$ from which notification to components are ready to be sent. Note that update function F_α composed with those of received offers is associated with the transition labelled by the ok_α port. If the port $fail_\alpha$ is enabled, the TTCC reaches back the location $read$ in order to proceed again for the reservation.

When an ATC component is participating in two conflicting interactions α_1 and α_2, it sends successively offers to each of the corresponding TTCC components $TTCC_{\alpha_1}$ and $TTCC_{\alpha_2}$ and waits from a notification from one of them. After resolving the conflict by requesting the CRP, suppose $TTCC_{\alpha_1}$ will notify the component after successfully executing the interaction α_1, while $TTCC_{\alpha_2}$ reaches back its location $read$ in order to proceed to a new reservation attempt. The component is able to continue execution of its next transitions. And it may reach again the location allowing to send again offers to $TTCC_{\alpha_1}$ and $TTCC_{\alpha_2}$. Both TTCC components should be ready to receive the offers. For that, we add loop transitions in TTCC automata labelled by offers receive ports over locations $read$ and try. Furthermore, such an ATC component may need to resend an offer to a TTCC even before this latter receives other offers from the rest of its participating components. This is resolved by adding loop transitions labelled by offer receive ports over locations that are placed between location $wait$ and $read$ (cf. Fig. 4b). These added loop transitions allow to respect the last point of Definition 4 stating that whenever a send port is activated, all its receive ports are enabled as well.

Example 2. In Fig. 5a (resp. Fig. 5b), we illustrate transformation of a conflicting (resp. non conflicting) external interactions α into its corresponding TTCC component. In these examples we consider that ports p and q of the interaction α are exporting respectively variables x_p and x_q.

4.5   Conflict Resolution Protocol Component

The conflict resolution protocol (CRP) that we use in our work is the same CRP used in [12, 15, 16]. It is, so far, the unique solution to guarantee the resolution

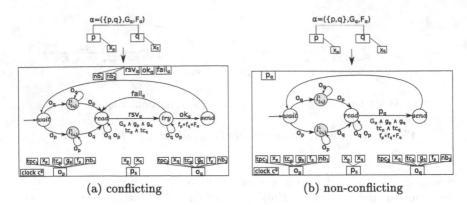

Fig. 5. Example of transformation of a external interaction into a TTCC component

of conflicts without requesting the BIP execution engine. In order to simplify the presentation of the behavior of the CRP component, authors of [12] opted for the Petri Net formalism. They choose in particular to use 1-safe Petri Nets. The CRP accommodates the algorithm proposed in [5]. It uses message counts to ensure synchronization and reduces the conflict resolution problem to dining or drinking philosophers [9]. Its main role is to check the freshness of requests received for an interaction, that is, to check that no conflicting interactions has been already executed using the same request. In each request, an interaction sends the participation numbers of its components, i.e. number of interactions each ATC component has participated in. This ensures that two conflicting interactions cannot execute with the same request. Mutual exclusion is ensured using participation numbers. To this end, the conflict resolution protocol keeps the last participation number NB_i of each component B_i and compares it with the participation number nb_i provided along with the reservation request from TTCC components. If each participation number from the request is greater than the one recorded by the conflict resolution protocol ($nb_i > NB_i$), the interaction is then granted to execute and NB_i is updated to nb_i. Otherwise, the interaction execution is disallowed.

4.6   Cross-Layer Interactions

Tasks and TTCC components exchange offers and notifications. Communication between TTCC components and the CRP component involves transmission of messages corresponding to rsv, ok and $fail$. For each task component $B_{T_j}^{TT}$ participating originally in interaction α, we include in γ^{TT} the offer interaction based on ports ($B_{T_j}^{TT}.o_p$, $TTCC_\alpha.o_p$). For each TTCC component $TTCC_\alpha$ and its participating components $\{B_{T_j}^{TT}\}_{j \in J}$, we include the notification interaction based on ports ($TTCC_\alpha.p_s$, $\{B_{T_j}^{TT}.p_j\}_{j \in J}$), where for all $j \in J$, $p_j \in \alpha$. Its guard is set to *True*. And its update function copies variables associated with $TTCC_\alpha.p_s$ to those of the receive ports $B_{T_j}^{TT}.p_j$. If $\alpha \in \gamma$ that is not conflicting, we include the unary interaction having as unique port $(TTCC_\alpha.p_\alpha)$, where $TTCC_\alpha$ is the TTCC component handling the interaction α. Its guard is set to *True*. And its update function is the identity function. If $\alpha \in \gamma$ that is conflicting, we include a triplet of interactions having respectively the following sets of ports: $(TTCC_\alpha.rsv_\alpha, CRP.rsv_\alpha)$, $(CRP.ok_\alpha, TTCC_\alpha.ok_\alpha)$ and $(CRP.fail_\alpha, TTCC_\alpha.fail_\alpha)$. All their guards are set to *True*. The update function of the former interaction copies variables of ports $TTCC_\alpha.rsv_\alpha$ to port $CRP.rsv_\alpha$. Since ports $CRP.ok_\alpha$ and $CRP.fail_\alpha$ do not have any associated variables, the update function of the last two interactions is the identity function.

Due to lack of space the formal definition of all transformation rules are not included to the paper but may be provided by e-mail by one of the authors.

5 Implemantation and Use Case

The transformation is implemanted into BIP toolset as a eclipse plugins called BIP2TT-BIP. The approach is validate on the Flight Similator use case.

The Flight Simulator (FS) application [6] dedicated to the navigation of DIY radio controlled planes. The original application is written in Modelica [10]. This application provides a simulation of the physics of a plane and an automatic pilot who tries to reach given way-points on a map. The simulation of the Modelica model gives a display of the road followed by the plane (specifically the trajectories of left and right wingtips).

The Modelica model consists of a set of six communicating sub-models (cf. Fig. 6b): autopilot, fly-by-wire, route planner, servo (i.e. the actuator), simulator and sensor. The autopilot models the pilot commands in function of the flight state. It has four main functionalities: flight state reception from sensor component, execution of the route planner, execution of fly-by-wire and sending command to servo component. The software architecture of the original Modelica model is shown in Fig. 6a.

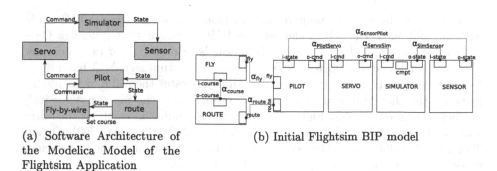

(a) Software Architecture of the Modelica Model of the Flightsim Application

(b) Initial Flightsim BIP model

Fig. 6. Overview of the Flightsim Appilication

We have first modelled the FS application in BIP language. This latter — coupled with different task mapping strategies—is the input of transformation tools. We also simulate the initial BIP model, the TT-BIP model (the output of the BIP2TT-BIP tool) in order to compare their respective behavior.

Each sub-model of the modelica model is modelled as a BIP component, communication between different components is modeled using BIP connectors. In Fig. 6b, the overall architecture of the BIP model is displayed. The bihavior of each component is modeled with a timed automata. We apply the transformation of the BIP2TT-BIP tool in order to derive the TT-BIP model following different task mapping strategies. In this paper we consider the task mapping strategy $TM1 : T_1 = \{FLY\}, T_2 = \{ROUTE\}, T_3 = \{PILOT\}, T_4 = \{SERVO\}, T_5 = \{SIMULATOR\}, T_6 = \{SENSOR\}$.

Figure 7a, shows the obtained model for the task mapping $TM1$. For clarity reason, behaviours of TTCC and CRP components are not displayed. Nonetheless, since all TTCC components are connecting exactly two tasks, their automata are strictly similar to those of Fig. 5a and b.

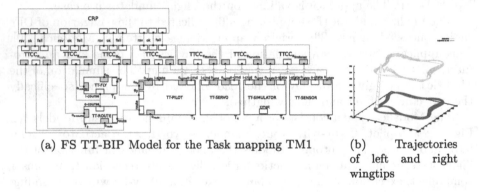

(a) FS TT-BIP Model for the Task mapping TM1   (b)   Trajectories of left and right wingtips

Fig. 7. Overview of TT-BIP transformation of the Flightsim Appilication

In order to be able to compare the functionality of the original BIP model with the obtained TT-BIP model, we use BIP simulator that generates C++ code from the original and the TT-BIP models. Simulation of two generated C++ codes allowed us to visualize and compare the output signals. A band shows the trajectories of left and right wingtips and illustrates the roll movement that precedes the change in course at each waypoint, while the plane progressively reaches its desired altitude. Figure 7b presents the simulation results of the initial and the derived models, for the waypoints (300, 0, 300), (300, 300, 300), (0, 300, 300) and (0, 0, 300). Visual inspection reveals that the output of the transformed model is strictly similar to that of the original model.

6   Conclusion

In this paper, we have presented a model to model transformational method allowing to explicit TT communication settings in the obtained model. The obtained model is structured following the TT-BIP architecture. It consists of tasks layer, communication layer and the conflict resolution layer. The first layer is obtained after transforming components participating in external interactions depending on a user-defined task mapping. Each TTCC component of the second layer is dedicated to handle one external interaction and communicate with tasks of the layer underneath in two steps; it receives offers and sends notification after executing the interaction. The third layer is responsible of resolving conflicts between different interactions handled by the second layer.

The obtained model is based on one global clock, implements multiparty interactions through dedicated communication media (i.e. TTCC components) and ensures communication between different layers by using message passing interactions (i.e. Send/receive interactions). Even though the obtained model satisfies the TT settings described in the opening of Sect. 3, it is yet still far from being intuitively translatable to the programming language of a target platform which is based on the TT execution model.

In an ongoing work, we present a method for generating TT implementation from the obtained TT-BIP model.

References

1. Abdellatif, T.: Rigourous Implementation of real-time Systems. Ph.D. thesis, UJF (2012)
2. Abdellatif, T., Combaz, J., Sifakis, J.: Model-based implementation of real-time applications, pp. 229–238, May 2010
3. Alur, R., Dill, D.L.: A theory of timed automata. Theoret. Comput. Sci. **126**(2), 183–235 (1994)
4. Aussagues, C., Chabrol, D., David, V., Roux, D., Willey, N., Tournadre, A., Graniou, M.: Pharos, a multicore os ready for safety-related automotive systems: results and future prospects. In: Proceedings of the Embedded Real-Time Software and Systems (ERTS2) (2010)
5. Bagrodia, R.: Process synchronization: design and performance evaluation of distributed algorithms. IEEE Trans. Softw. Eng. **15**(9), 1053–1065 (1989)
6. Hedia, B.B., Hamelin, E.: Projet openprod rapport r4.28: Model to embedded real-time transformation. Technical report (2012)
7. Boulanger, J.-L., Fornari, F.-X., Camus, J.-L., Dion, B.: Language and applications. Scade: Language and applications (2015)
8. Bozga, M., Jaber, M., Sifakis, J.: Source-to-source architecture transformation for performance optimization in BIP. IEEE Trans. Industr. Inf. **6**(4), 708–718 (2010)
9. Chandy, K.M., Misra, J.: The drinking philosophers problem. ACM Trans. Program. Lang. Syst. (TOPLAS) **6**(4), 632–646 (1984)
10. Elmqvist, H., Mattsson, S.E.: An introduction to the physical modeling language modelica. In: Proceedings of the 9th European Simulation Symposium, ESS, vol. 97, pp. 19–23. Citeseer (1997)
11. Guesmi, H., Hedia, B.B., Bliudze, S., Bensalem, S., Combaz, J.: Towards time-triggered component-based system models. In: ICSEA 2015, Barcelone, Spain, ThinkMind, pp. 157–169, November 2015

12. Jaber, M.: Centralized and Distributed Implementations of Correct-by-construction Component-based Systems by using Source-to-source Transformations in BIP. Theses, Université Joseph-Fourier - Grenoble I, October 2010
13. Kaiser, R., Wagner, S.: Evolution of the pikeos microkernel. In: Proceedings of the 1st International Workshop on Microkernels for Embedded Systems, pp. 50–57 (2007)
14. Kopetz, H.: The time-triggered approach to real-time system design. In: Randell, B., et al. (eds.) Predictably Dependable Computing Systems. Springer, Luxembourg (1995)
15. Quilbeuf, J.: Distributed Implementations of Component-based Systems with Prioritized Multiparty Interactions. Application to the BIP Framework. Ph.D. thesis, Université de Grenoble (2013)
16. Triki, A.: Distributed Implementations of Timed Component-based Systems. Ph.D. thesis, Grenoble Alpes (2015)

Uppaal vs Event-B for Modelling Optimised Link State Routing

Mojgan Kamali[✉] and Luigia Petre

Åbo Akademi University, Turku, Finland
{mojgan.kamali,lpetre}@abo.fi

Abstract. In this paper we compare models developed in two formal frameworks, Uppaal and Event-B, for the Optimised Link State Routing (OLSR) protocol. OLSR is one of the proactive routing protocols used in Mobile Ad-hoc Networks (MANETs) and Wireless Mesh Networks (WMNs). We also describe different aspects of the Uppaal and Event-B formalisms. This leads to a more general comparison of both formalisms, considering the following criteria: their specification languages, their update of variables mechanism, their modularity methods, their verification strategies, their scalability potentials and their real-time modelling capabilities. Based on it, we provide several guidelines for when to use Uppaal or Event-B for formal modelling and analysis.

1 Introduction

Continuous connectivity is a defining feature of our current working routines as well as of our free-time ones. We expect to be able to access information at all times as well as be able to communicate to various entities at all times. Technically, this is ensured with myriads of interconnected networks that offer us coverage and route all our requests for information and communication in certain ways. Hence, routing is a fundamental stone of our lifestyles and as such, presents enormous interest for study. Routing is obviously not a new concept for the era of continuous connectivity; it has been around since the first networks were developed some decades ago. Along with network evolution, routing has however evolved as well, with numerous algorithms in use today.

Routing protocols are divided into two main categories: proactive and reactive. Proactive protocols select routes in advance, by having network nodes exchanging (control) messages about all the other network nodes. Consequently, an injected data packet can be delivered to the destination immediately. Examples of such protocols are Optimised Link State Routing (OLSR) protocol [10], Better Approach To Mobile Ad hoc Networking (BATMAN) routing protocol [22], etc. Reactive protocols search for routes to destination nodes on demand, whenever a data packet is injected into the network. Examples of reactive protocols are Ad hoc On-Demand Distance Vector (AODV) protocol [23], Dynamic Source Routing (DSR) protocol [14], etc.

In this paper we compare two models for the OLSR proactive protocol. This protocol is used for routing in Wireless Mesh Networks (WMNs). WMNs are

© Springer International Publishing AG 2017
K. Barkaoui et al. (Eds.): VECoS 2017, LNCS 10466, pp. 189–203, 2017.
DOI: 10.1007/978-3-319-66176-6_13

self-healing and self-organising wireless technologies supporting broadband communication without requiring any wired infrastructure. They are employed in a wide range of application areas such as emergency response networks, communication systems, video surveillance, etc. A central feature of a WMN is that its topology, in terms of active nodes and links, can vary quite much. OLSR is adapted to this feature by continuously updating the information that any node has about any other node, based on the most recent 'scanning' of the network. It thus finds good-enough routes to all destinations.

Previously, our goal was to model OLSR and analyse its properties [15,17,18]. There are numerous frameworks and techniques, formal and less formal, that one can choose for modelling purposes. Since we are interested in analysis, formal methods with their underlying mathematical foundations are best suited. However, the question is which formal method to choose. In this paper we resume our experiences with two formal methods, the Uppaal model checker and the Event-B theorem prover.

In Uppaal [7], safety and liveness properties are expressed using Computation Tree Logic (CTL). Constants, data structures and procedures are defined in a C-like language and modularity is addressed via components, represented as timed automata, that communicate with each other via channels. Uppaal has a model checking tool[1], that supports the basic computational model and checks whether properties hold for a model or not, in the latter case providing a counterexample. In Event-B [2], safety properties are expressed in first-order logic, while constants, data structures, variables and their updates are modelled in a guarded command language. Event-B has a theorem prover tool, the Eclipse-based Rodin platform[2], that supports the basic modelling and analysis, based on generating and discharging proof obligations. Modularity is addressed via refinement: a model is initially abstract and details are added to it in proof-safe manner. Liveness properties are modelled logically or with specific update types.

Contributions. After modelling and analysing OLSR with both Uppaal and Event-B, we found that both formal methods are useful, but at different scales and for emphasising different aspects of modelling and analysis. In this paper, our contribution is to provide a comparison of our respective models as well as of these formal methods, with suggestions for modellers as to when to use one or another. We take into account four main criteria w.r.t. our models (Uppaal and Event-B models) comparison: parts of the protocols that have been modelled, particular properties that have been verified, networks topologies that have been modelled and data structures that have been used when modelling. To overview the applicability of Uppaal and Event-B, we provide a comparison between them by focusing on their specification languages, their mechanism for variable updating, their modularity methods, their verification strategies, their scalability potentials and their real-time modelling capabilities. Based on our

---

[1] http://uppaal.org/.
[2] http://www.event-b.org/.

considerations, we provide several guidelines for when to use Uppaal or Event-B for formal modelling and analysis.

Outline. We proceed as follows.[3] In Sect. 2 we describe in some detail the formal tools employed in the paper, namely Uppaal and Event-B. In Sect. 3 we overview the OLSR protocol and in Sect. 4 we summarise our modelling of OLSR in Uppaal and Event-B, respectively. In Sect. 5 we compare our Uppaal and Event-B models as well as the frameworks themselves. We draw some usage guidelines of these formal tools in practical situations in Sect. 6.

2 Formal Methods, Model Checking, and Theorem Proving

A formal method usually refers to a framework allowing one to model, analyse, verify, and animate a system. A formal methods has a formal semantics based on mathematics, and can thus provide precise answers to questions about systems properties. A formal method includes a specification (or modelling) language, analysis methods, various modularity mechanisms addressing the scale of a system; nowadays, successful formal methods also have tools associated to them, including editors, analysers, animators, and more.

When modelling the dynamic behaviour of a system with a formal method, each execution step in the model follows from a semantical rule of inference and hence can be checked by a mechanical process. The advantage of formal methods is that they provide valuable means to symbolically examine the entire state space of a system model and establish a correctness or safety property that is true for all possible inputs. These methods have a great potential on improving the correctness and precision of design and development, as they produce reliable results. However, this is rarely done in practice today, except for safety critical systems. In the rather recent past, one of the reasons was the lack of user friendly and scaling tools, combined with the enormous complexity of real systems. Nowadays however, we have good tools for several formal methods, so one of the questions remaining for the adoption of formal methods in industry remains: which tool is more suitable for a certain (type of) system?

In this paper we set out to examine two different tools associated to two formal methods, namely model checking and theorem proving.

2.1 Model Checking–Uppaal's Timed Automata

Model checking (e.g. [9]) is an algorithmic and automatic approach used to validate and verify key correctness properties in finite representations of a formal system model. By modelling the behaviour of a system in mathematical language, model checking exhaustively and automatically checks whether the model meets

---

[3] The detailed descriptions of our models appear in [16] for the Uppaal model and in [19] for the Event-B model.

a given specification. In model checking, Temporal Logic (TL) is used to specify and check the correct behaviour of a system. One of the most used model checking tools nowadays is the Uppaal model checker.

Uppaal [7,20] is an integrated model checker for modelling, simulating (validating) and verifying real-time systems. It is appropriate for systems that can be modelled as networks of timed automata extended with bounded integer variables, structured data types, functions and synchronisation channels. A timed-automata is a finite-state machine with clock variables that measure time progression. Each automaton can be represented as a graph consists of locations (optionally also consisting invariants) and edges between those locations having guards, synchronisation channels, and updates of some variables. A state of a system is defined by automata's locations, value of clocks, and the value of all local and global variables. An edge can be fired in an automaton which leads to a new state. This edge can be fired separately in the automaton or between different automata used for synchronisation.

Uppaal's verifier uses Computation Tree Logic (CTL) (e.g. [11]) to express system requirements (properties) offering two types of formulas: state formulas and path formulas. State formulas describe individual states of the model, whereas path formulas quantify over paths in the model.

2.2 Theorem Proving–Event-B

Event-B [2] is a formal technique based on the B-Method [1] and on the Action Systems [5] framework, provides means to model and analyse parallel, reactive and distributed systems. Rodin Platform [3] provides automated support for modelling and verifying such systems. Event-B uses two modules for defining system specifications and for expressing system properties, namely **context** and **machine**. A context consists of carrier sets and constants, and their properties are defined as axioms of the model. So, a context deals with the static part of the system whereas a machine contains the dynamic part of the system. A machine can access the contents of a context which is defined by the keyword **Sees** determining the relationship between the machine and the context.

A machine expresses the model state using **variables** that are updated by **events**. Events can have **guards** that need to evaluate to **true**, allowing the event to be executed. When having several events enabled simultaneously, one event is selected non-deterministically. A machine may also contain **invariants**, i.e., properties which must hold for any reachable state in the model. In other words, invariants must be satisfied before and after the occurrence of all events.

The **refinement** is the main developing strategy in Event-B where a machine, let's say machine A, is refined by another machine, let's say machine B, i.e., A ⊑ B. This happens when A's behaviour is not altered by B in any way and more new variables are added in B as well as new events to update the new variables. This type of refinement employed for our modelling is called **superposition** refinement. In order to prove that machine B is the refinement of machine A, a set of so-called **proof obligations** is generated by the Rodin platform. Some of these proof obligations are discharged automatically by Rodin and some require interactive discharging with the help of the modeller.

3   An Overview of Optimised Link State Routing

The Optimised Link State Routing (OLSR) is a proactive routing protocol developed for Mobile Ad-hoc Networks (MANETs) and Wireless Mesh Networks (WMNs). OLSR operates as a routing table-driven protocol; each node keeps information about all the other nodes of the network in order to transfer data packets from a source node to a destination node. Examples of information stored in the routing table of a node a are: to get to node b (from a) the next node to take is node c; or, to get to node b from a takes n hops, where a, b, c are nodes in the network and n is a natural number. Keeping the information in the routing table up-to-date is realised by nodes periodically exchanging specific *control* messages. OLSR is an optimisation over other link state protocols, since it decreases the network traffic by restricting the broadcasting of control messages to only specific nodes.

OLSR works in a completely distributed manner and does not require any central entity for coordination. Each node selects a set of one-hop neighbour nodes that have links to the two-hop neighbours of that selector node. The selected nodes are called MultiPoint Relays (MPRs) and are allowed to transmit control messages intended for diffusion into the entire network. There are two types of control messages, namely HELLO and TC (Topology Control) messages.

HELLO messages are broadcast every 2 s and are used to determine one-hop and two-hop neighbours of each node as well as to select MPR nodes. These messages are only broadcast on single hops (to one-hop neighbours) and are not forwarded. TC messages are broadcast every 5 s for building and refreshing topological information in the routing tables. These messages are broadcast on single hops and can be forwarded through the network via MPR nodes. Upon receipt of HELLO or TC messages, the receiving node updates its routing table based on the information in the received control message. Therefore, the topological information is always kept up-to-date in the routing tables in order to deliver data packets to arbitrary destination nodes.

4   Formal Modelling of the OLSR

We now present the overview of our OLSR models, i.e., Uppaal and Event-B models of the OLSR protocol. Both formal models are described in detail in our technical reports [16, 19].

4.1   Uppaal Model of the OLSR

In [15], we modelled OLSR in Uppaal as a parallel composition of identical processes, each indicating the behaviour of each node of the network. Every

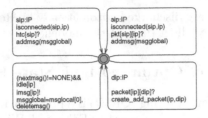

Fig. 1. Overview of model development

process is itself a parallel composition of two timed-automata, i.e., OLSR and Queue. The OLSR automaton is modelling the complete behaviour of the routing protocol [10] and Queue automaton (depicted in Fig. 1) is chosen to model the input buffer of every node in the network.

Nodes are able to broadcast and handle different types of messages (HELLO, TC and PACKET) in the network (modelled by OLSR) and the connected neighbour nodes can receive the incoming messages and store these messages in their input buffer (modelled by Queue). Whenever the OLSR is ready to handle a message (is not busy) and there are messages stored in the Queue, the OLSR and the Queue synchronise together on the imsg channel, moving a message from the Queue to the OLSR for processing.

The OLSR models the routing table of a node using a local data structure. Routing tables provide all the necessary information to route data packets to different destination nodes. Connectivity between two nodes is modelled by the predicate isconnected[i][j], denoting a node-to-node communication. If two nodes are in transmission range of each other, they can communicate with each other via channels. In order to model rigorous timing behaviour, we defined several clocks for each OLSR to model on-time broadcasting control messages, to consider time spent to send every message, and to update and refresh the information in the routing tables.

Based on [10], each node in the network broadcasts a HELLO message every 2 s containing the information about the originator of the message and the one-hop neighbours of the HELLO message originator. Upon receipt of a HELLO, the receiving node updates its routing table for the HELLO message originator and its two-hop neighbours (one-hop neighbours of the HELLO message originator). The receiving node also selects its MPR nodes which are able to broadcast TC messages through the network. Such nodes (MPRs) then broadcast TC messages every 5 s through the network. TC messages contain the information about the originator of the TC messages, MPR nodes of the message originator, etc. When a node receives a TC message, it first checks if the message is considered for processing following some conditions. If so, then the receiving node updates its routing table for the TC message originator and the MPR nodes of the TC originator. Afterwards, if the receiving node is an MPR and the TC message is considered for forwarding, the TC is forwarded to the next nodes.

The `Queue` (Fig. 1) models storing incoming messages from other nodes (directly connected neighbour nodes) of the network. The incoming messages are buffered and in turn are sent to the `OLSR` for further processing. Messages can be received only if the receiving node is connected to the sender of the message. In this case, the `Queue` of the receiving nodes stores the messages to its local data queue.

4.2   Event-B Model of the OLSR

In [18], we developed a formal model of the OLSR protocol at five different levels of abstraction (depicted in Fig. 2) using Event-B (Rodin platform). We have defined two contexts containing constants and carrier sets, whose properties are expressed as a list of axioms for the model. These contexts contain the static part of the system. The dynamic part of our system is modelled using five machines that describe the state of the model with their variables which are updated by events. These five machines are related to the contexts and can access them using the keyword sees as shown in Fig. 2. Also, the more abstract machines and contexts are refined into more concrete machines and contexts using keywords 'refines' and 'extends', respectively.

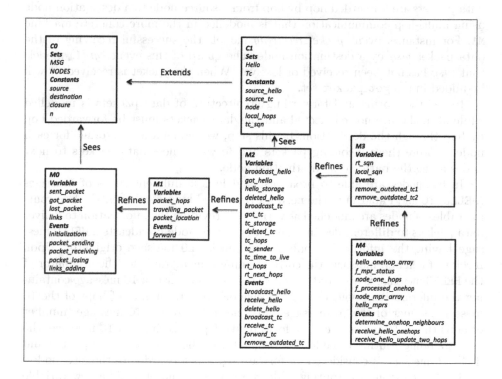

Fig. 2. Overview of model development

Our initial model M0 deals with basic protocol behaviour, i.e., sending, receiving, and losing data packets as well as an abstraction of proactive routing behaviour (adding links between nodes). First refinement M1 models a storing and forwarding architecture when data packets are transferred hop by hop from a source node to a destination node. Second refinement M2 models the basic behaviour of the route discovery protocol, describing the OLSR behaviour when sending and receiving control messages as well as updating routing tables. Third refinement M3 models how the protocol decides to process only new control messages and how to avoid processing control messages with old information. Fourth refinement M4 models the selection of MPR nodes, helping to decrease the traffic in the network.

$$
\begin{aligned}
&\textbf{Event} \quad packet\_receiving \ \widehat{=} \\
&\textbf{any} \\
&\quad msg \\
&\textbf{where} \\
&\quad \textbf{grd1} \ : msg \in sent\_packet \setminus (got\_packet \cup lost\_packet) \\
&\textbf{then} \\
&\quad \textbf{act1} \ : got\_packet := got\_packet \cup \{msg\} \\
&\textbf{end}
\end{aligned}
$$

In M0, data packets are received from a source node to a destination node in an atomic step which is of course not the case in reality. In real protocols, data packets are forwarded hop by hop from a source node to a destination node using multi-hop communication that is modelled in the more concrete machine M1. For instance, event *packet_receiving* models the successful receiving of the data packet *msg* by a destination node. The guard of this event (*grd1*) models that *msg* has not been received or lost yet. When the packet is received, it will be added in the got_packet set.

In M1, the storing and forwarding architecture of data packets is modelled while all nodes are not connected and the data packets must be forwarded hop by hop through the destination. In this step, we model a local storage for each node to store these incoming packets and forward these data packets to next nodes along the path to the destination node.

In M2, nodes are able to broadcast and handle different types of messages (HELLO, TC and PACKET) in the network (modelled by several events). Also routing tables of nodes are modelled as variables, providing the information to deliver data packets to different destination nodes. Every node broadcasts a HELLO message having the information only about the HELLO message originator. Upon receipt of a HELLO message, the corresponding routing table for the originator of the HELLO message is updated. Also, each node broadcasts a TC message containing the information about the TC message originator, number of hops of the TC message, sender of the TC message and time to live of the TC message (number of hops that a TC message can be forwarded). Upon receipt of a TC message, the corresponding routing table for the originator of the TC message is updated and if the TC message is considered for forwarding, it is forwarded to the next nodes.

In M3, we extend the routing table of every node and also add a new variable in the TC message in order to model sequence numbers. Sequence numbers are embedded in TC messages to avoid processing messages with old information.

Also, we defined several events to update the local sequence number of each node and to remove out-dated messages from the network.

In M4, we restrict the broadcasting of TC messages to only specific nodes, namely MPRs, and not all nodes broadcast TC messages through the network. We added one-hop neighbours of the HELLO message originator in the HELLO messages so that upon receipt of a HELLO message, the two-hop neighbours of the receiving nodes can be also updated. In this case, nodes can determine their MPR nodes and also nodes are able to recognise whether or not they are MPR nodes of some other nodes in the network. If some nodes are selected to be MPRs, then they can broadcast/forward TC messages through the network.

5   Comparison

In this section, we compare our OLSR models, the Uppaal model [15] and the Event-B model [18] as well as the modelling tools Uppaal [7] and Event-B [2].

5.1   Uppaal Model vs Event-B Model

Table 1 depicts an overview of our comparison. We take into the account four main criteria: what parts of the protocol we've modelled, what properties we've verified for our models, for what types of network topologies we modelled the protocol and what data structures we've used.

Table 1. Overview of our models comparison

	Uppaal model	Event-B model
Protocol	Core functionality	Core functionality with timing abstraction
Properties	Route establishment packet delivery non-optimal route finding recovery time	Route establishment packet delivery non-optimal route finding
Topologies	All topologies up to 5 nodes	All topologies with n nodes
Data Structures	Queues	Relations, functions

Protocol. We were able to model the core functionality of the OLSR protocol [10] in both Uppaal and Event-B. This functionality refers to the behaviour that is always required for the protocol to perform. The only feature that we abstracted away in our Event-B model was the timing of messages. In the OLSR protocol [10], HELLO and TC messages are sent periodically. We have abstracted away the treatment of time in Event-B as this is still incipient, involving a rather different perspective of treating variables as continuous functions of time [4,6].

Table 2. Overview of Uppaal and Event-B comparison

	Uppaal	Event-B
Specification Language	Timed automata, C-like language	Set theory, guarded commands language
Variables Update	Transition: selection guard update	Event: parameter guard action
Modularity	Divided into several automata at the same level of abstraction	Divided into several machines at different levels of abstraction
Verification	CTL automatically providing counterexamples	First-order logic automatically and interactively no counterexamples
Scalability	Small-scale systems (finite)	Large-scale systems (infinite)
Real Time	Precisely models timing variables	Partially models timing variables

Properties. We verified our OLSR model in Uppaal for the following properties: route establishment, packet delivery, optimal route finding, and recovery time. We were able to verify that all nodes in the network can establish routes to different destination nodes as well as deliver data packets to these destinations. We proved by finding a counterexample that OLSR is not always able to find optimal routes to all the destinations as well as showed that OLSR needs a relatively long time to recover after a link breakage in the network [15]. In our Event-B model, we verified our OLSR model for the following properties: route establishment, packet delivery and optimal route finding. We came to the same conclusions as for our Uppaal model. Routes are established to all destinations and data packets are delivered to these destinations; however, these routes may be non-optimal w.r.t. the hop counts. Since we abstracted away from timing properties, we did not investigate the recovery time of OLSR in Event-B.

Topologies. We verified our Uppaal model of OLSR for all network topologies up to 5 nodes. Since the model checking technique suffers from the state space explosion problem, we were not able to extend our analysis for more realistic networks. However, when modelling in Event-B, we were not restricted by the number of nodes in the network and we could verify the protocol for arbitrary networks with n number of nodes.

Data Structures. We modelled the OLSR protocol in Uppaal and Event-B with different data structures. In our Uppaal model, we have defined the `Queue` timed automata to store different types of incoming messages to a node. In Event-B, we modelled the storing architecture using relations between nodes and messages. We defined a specific data structure in Uppaal to model the routing tables, whereas in Event-B we defined different variables to model routing tables. The types of nodes in the network were defined by integers in Uppaal, while in Event-B we introduced a carrier set to model the network nodes. We defined a common data structure for all types of messages in Uppaal; in Event-B, we introduced different carrier sets for each type of message. We note here that we can have the same data structure (modelling all types of messages, i.e., data packets and control messages) also in Event-B, and this is part of some future generalisation that we plan for modelling various network protocols in Event-B.

5.2 Uppaal vs Event-B

Table 2 depicts an overview of the comparison between Uppaal and Event-B. We detail this table below, namely we compare the specification languages, the variable updating mechanisms, the modularity methods, the verification strategies, the scalability potential, and the real-time modelling capabilities.

Specification Language. The Uppaal model checker uses *timed-automata* as the specification language whereas Event-B is based on *set theory*. In Uppaal, constants, data structures and procedures are defined in a C-like language. In Event-B, constants, data structures, variables and their updates are modelled in a guarded command language.

Variable Updating Mechanism. In Uppaal *transitions* are used to update the variables while in Event-B *events* accomplish the same thing. In both formal methods, the state of the model is determined by the values of the variables. We show the similarities between transitions in Uppaal and events in Event-B by sketching an example based on our models when a node receives a message as depicted in Fig. 3. By this, we also demonstrate how our models in Uppaal and Event-B are equivalent. These similarities are as following:

– *Selection of Parameters.* In Uppaal, the `select` label of a transition consists of a list of `name:type` expressions, where `name` is the variable's name and `type` is its type. As depicted in Fig. 3 (Transition), `IP` is the type of variable `ip`, i.e., an integer in our model. This variable is only accessible for the respective

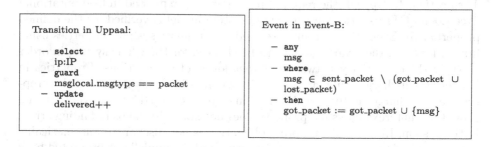

Fig. 3. Transition and event in Uppaal and Event-B.

transition and it takes a non-deterministic value in the range of its respective types (integer type in our model). In Event-B (Event), the **any** clause of an event lists the parameters (or local variables) of the event, i.e., msg in Fig. 3; the types of these parameters are usually specified in the guards of the events.

- *Guards.* In Uppaal, the **guard** label refers to logical expressions that determine if the respective transitions are enabled (when guards hold). In Fig. 3 (Transition), msglocal.msgtype == packet is the guard of the transition and shows if the received message is a new packet. In Event-B, the **where** clause contains the guards of the events, i.e., the logical conditions for the event to be enabled (when guards hold). The guard of the (Event) in Fig. 3 is shown as msg ∈ sent_packet \ (got_packet ∪ lost_packet).

- *Updates and Actions.* In Uppaal, the **update** label of a transition contains a list of expressions that update the values of variables. In Fig. 3 (Transition), delivered++ is the update that increases the value of integer variable delivered showing that the packet has been received. In Event-B, the **then** clause lists the actions of the event that modify some variables of the model. In Fig. 3 (Event), got_packet := got_packet ∪ {msg} is the action that adds the receiving packet to the received messages set. In both frameworks, the variable updating mechanism takes place only if the guards of transitions or events respectively hold.

Modularity. In order to model the whole system's behaviour in Uppaal, several automata are introduced, each modelling different parts of the system. These automata need to synchronise with each other, to keep the consistency and relevance between different parts of the system model. However, it is not always possible to split the system into different automata and thus a system model may remain too complex to understand, having too numerous transitions. In Event-B, different machines are introduced to fully model the behaviour of the system at different levels of abstraction, starting from a very simple and abstract level. This abstract model is stepwise developed using refinement methods to finally model the complete behaviour of the entire system. Consistency between the different levels of refinements is verified by discharging proof obligations. The stepwise development allows to split the complexity of the system into different levels and makes it easier to understand the model and discharge the proof obligations.

Verification. In Uppaal, the required properties are expressed in Computational Tree Logic (CTL) syntax and the whole system model is verified for the defined properties. In Event-B, invariants are used to formulate system properties using first-order logic; the invariants have to be checked for the whole system in order to show the consistency between different levels of abstractions. Properties in Uppaal are discharged fully automatically whereas in Event-B some of the properties are discharged automatically and some are discharged interactively. Uppaal provides counterexamples if a property does not hold; this helps in finding errors in the system. In Event-B, if a proof obligation is not discharged automatically, this typically signals some modelling problem and the modeller is prompted back to remodel certain aspects.

Scalability. Uppaal, like all model checking tools, suffers from the state space explosion problem, hence it is not able to verify very large and complex systems. Event-B allows to verify even large and complex systems. Event-B checks the general validity of a property for *all* models (i.e., also for infinite models) whereas Uppaal is dedicated to small-scale, finite systems.

Real-Time. Uppaal provides clock variables to model timing behaviour of real-time systems whereas for Event-B modelling timing behaviour is still incipient. In Uppaal, clock variables model discrete timing behaviour. In Event-B, advances are made to model hybrid behaviour including discrete and continuous time modelling [4,6], but these are not implemented in the Rodin platform yet. In Event-B, the time can be defined as a function that can be mapped to an integer variable increasing by the events.

6   Conclusions and Usage Guidelines

To resume our experiences of modelling OLSR with Uppaal and Event-B, we essentially found that the two formalisms require different approaches to modelling. In Uppaal, the modeller attempts to capture the whole system, in all its complexity, from the beginning, aided in this task by the modularity technique of splitting the model into communicating time automata. In Event-B, the modeller gets to understand the system's complexity by modelling it in increasingly more detailed levels of abstraction. When we have a conceptually complex system (behaviour of routing protocols), choosing Uppaal or Event-B for modelling it and analysing it is ultimately a matter depending on the modeller's experience.

One can specify properties to prove in both formalisms, but the verification of these properties differs in the two frameworks. In Uppaal, the verification depends on the size of the model and may be unsuccessful if the size is bigger (networks of realistic size) than some arbitrary and typically small value. This is because model checking enforces a brute force verification of properties in all possible states of the system, thus leading relatively fast to overflow. Approaches are taken to overcome this problem, such as partial order reduction techniques [21] and statistical model checking. The former assumes that not all states are worth verifying, and thus defines a priority-based order relation that imposes the verification of the most important states only. The latter employs probabilities and gives results such as the property holds with a 0.99 probability; these probabilities are calculated based on many random walks through the state space (simulations of) the system. In Event-B, the verification of properties is based on logic and proof engines that are built to work for any defined mathematical concepts, including infinite-sized models. When properties are not verified automatically, Uppaal provides counterexamples exposing the offending state: this can be quite useful for correcting errors. In the same situation, the Rodin platform shows the unsatisfied proof obligation and thus the modeller gets some feedback on what does not work. We note here that, if there are flaws in the system, often they are exposed even for small-scale models, see [12,15].

Both Uppaal and Event-B are supported by performant software platforms for modelling and proving; depending on how advanced these platforms are, some aspects can be modelled or not, such as real-time properties. Uppaal was designed to include clock variables and time modelling, while Event-B was designed as a general refinement-based framework. We can precisely model real-time properties of communication protocols in Uppaal, e.g., broadcasting a control message at a certain time. Recently, several approaches were proposed on how to add real-time modelling in Event-B in a conservative manner, e.g. Hybrid Event-B [6] or [4]. This would imply that all variables except clocks are functions of time, so a slight change of perspective is needed here. Real-time properties are typically closely related to implementation details, for instance, to various network parameters; hence, even if we can model timing, when translating the final model into a software product, we might need to alter various properties and parameters anyway.

For modelling and verifying routing protocols, Uppaal remains very useful, as it provides synchronisation mechanisms used in wireless networks: broadcast and binary synchronisation. This allows to closely understand the communication between network nodes. Besides these clear differences, we found that modelling in either framework is quite natural and rewarding and, once the modeller is experienced enough with the framework, quite efficient as well.

To the best of our knowledge, this is the first paper comparing Uppaal and Event-B with respect to what each can model and prove. Relations between model checking and theorem proving in general have been studied before, e.g. [13], where for solving a (rather simple) puzzle, arguments are given for using model checking instead of theorem proving. We note that real systems are very complex nowadays and thus, proving properties for the system, independently of its size, is quite important. Another interesting observation made in [13] is that theorem proving helps in constructing the model, while model checking can be used when we already understand the model quite well. Other approaches connecting model checking and theorem proving are [8], where the idea is to combine the two methods and more recently [24], where refinement is studied in the context of both Uppaal and Event-B.

References

1. Abrial, J.R.: The B-book: Assigning Programs to Meanings. Cambridge University Press, New York (1996)
2. Abrial, J.R.: Modeling in Event-B - System and Software Engineering. Cambridge University Press, New York (2010)
3. Abrial, J.R., Butler, M., Hallerstede, S., Hoang, T.S., Mehta, F., Voisin, L.: Rodin: an open toolset for modelling and reasoning in Event-B. STTT **12**(6), 447–466 (2010)
4. Abrial, J.-R., Su, W., Zhu, H.: Formalizing hybrid systems with Event-B. In: Derrick, J., Fitzgerald, J., Gnesi, S., Khurshid, S., Leuschel, M., Reeves, S., Riccobene, E. (eds.) ABZ 2012. LNCS, vol. 7316, pp. 178–193. Springer, Heidelberg (2012). doi:10.1007/978-3-642-30885-7_13

5. Back, R.J.R., Sere, K.: From action systems to modular systems. In: Naftalin, M., Denvir, T., Bertran, M. (eds.) FME 1994. LNCS, vol. 873, pp. 1–25. Springer, Heidelberg (1994). doi:10.1007/3-540-58555-9_83
6. Banach, R., Butler, M., Qin, S., Verma, N., Zhu, H.: Core hybrid Event-B I: single hybrid Event-B machines. Sci. Comput. Program. **105**, 92–123 (2015)
7. Behrmann, G., David, A., Larsen, K.G.: A tutorial on UPPAAL. In: Bernardo, M., Corradini, F. (eds.) SFM-RT 2004. LNCS, vol. 3185, pp. 200–236. Springer, Heidelberg (2004). doi:10.1007/978-3-540-30080-9_7
8. Berezin, S.: Model checking and theorem proving: a unified framework. Ph.D. thesis, Carnegie Mellon University (2002)
9. Clarke, E.M., Emerson, E.A., Sifakis, J.: Model checking: algorithmic verification and debugging. Commun. ACM **52**(11), 74–84 (2009)
10. Clausen, T., Jacquet, P.: Optimized link state routing protocol (OLSR). RFC 3626 (Experimental) (2003). http://www.ietf.org/rfc/rfc3626
11. Emerson, E.A.: Temporal and modal logic. In: Handbook of Theoretical Computer Science, vol. B. Formal Models and Semantics, pp. 995–1072. MIT (1995)
12. Fehnker, A., van Glabbeek, R., Höfner, P., McIver, A., Portmann, M., Tan, W.L.: Modelling and analysis of AODV in UPPAAL. In: 1st International Workshop on Rigorous Protocol Engineering, pp. 1–6 (2011)
13. Halpern, J., Vardi, M.: Model checking vs. theorem proving: a manifesto. In: Lifschitz, V. (ed.) Artificial Intelligence and Mathematical Theory of Computation, pp. 151–176. Academic Press Professional, Inc. (1991)
14. Johnson, D., Hu, Y., Maltz, D.: The Dynamic Source Routing Protocol (DSR). RFC 4728 (Experimental) (2007). http://www.ietf.org/rfc/rfc4728
15. Kamali, M., Höfner, P., Kamali, M., Petre, L.: Formal analysis of proactive, distributed routing. In: Calinescu, R., Rumpe, B. (eds.) SEFM 2015. LNCS, vol. 9276, pp. 175–189. Springer, Cham (2015). doi:10.1007/978-3-319-22969-0_13
16. Kamali, M., Kamali, M., Petre, L.: Formally analyzing proactive, distributed routing. Technical report 1125, TUCS - Turku Centre for Computer Science (2014)
17. Kamali, M., Petre, L.: Improved recovery for proactive, distributed routing. In: 20th International Conference on Engineering of Complex Computer Systems (ICECCS 2015), pp. 178–181. IEEE (2015)
18. Kamali, M., Petre, L.: Modelling link state routing in Event-B. In: 21st International Conference on Engineering of Complex Computer Systems, ICECCS 2016, pp. 207–210. IEEE (2016)
19. Kamali, M., Petre, L.: Modelling link state routing in Event-B. Technical report 1154, TUCS - Turku Centre for Computer Science (2016)
20. Larsen, K.G., Pettersson, P., Yi, W.: Uppaal in a nutshell. Int. J. Softw. Tools Technol. Transf. (STTT) **1**(1), 134–152 (1997)
21. Larsen, K.G., Larsson, F., Pettersson, P., Yi, W.: Compact data structures and state-space reduction for model-checking real-time systems. Real-Time Syst. **25**(2–3), 255–275 (2003)
22. Neumann, A., Aichele, C., Lindner, M.: Better Approach To Mobile Ad-hoc Networking Routing Protocol (B.A.T.M.A.N.). IETF Draft (2008). https://tools.ietf.org/id/draft-openmesh-b-a-t-m-a-n-00.txt
23. Perkins, C., Belding-Royer, E., Das, S.: Ad hoc On-Demand Distance Vector Routing Protocol (AODV). RFC 3561 (Experimental) (2003). http://www.ietf.org/rfc/rfc3561
24. Vain, J., Tsiopoulos, L., Bostrom, P.: Integrating refinement-based methods for developing timed systems. In: Petre, L., Sekerinski, E. (eds.) From Action Systems to Distributed Systems: The Refinement Approach, pp. 171–185. CRC Press (2016)

Author Index

Printed in the United States
By Bookmasters